OF GOOD COURAGE

The Incredible True Story of Lt. Merle D. Green
and the Green Hornets

JUSTIN R. BURKE

For Rose and Merle

CONTENTS

PREFACE

Merle Green, my grandfather, died six years before I was born. My grandmother, Rose, passed away when I was one following a tough, but courageously fought battle with cancer and as such, in a way I never really knew my grandparents. Nonetheless, their adventures and exploits were kept alive through a bountiful collection of government documents, military records, wartime letters, old photos, and a scattering of a few family stories. My mother had preserved dozens of her parents' letters, various keepsakes and military memorabilia; foresight and dedication that would not only prove invaluable in writing this book but an amazing record to be cherished by generations of family to come. One of those photographs in the collection has been imprinted on my mind since I was young; a crew picture taken before my grandfather and his team were sent to war. In the photo, Merle is standing in the back row and although he is surrounded by his band of smiling patriots, my grandfather's face is barely distinguishable, washed out due to the camera's exposure. For me, the photo was the perfect representation of my grandfather: on the surface, an American hero but once you look closely, he is a largely indistinguishable, enigmatic figure. Even as a young boy I had the impression that those grainy, black and white pictures and faded, time-worn letters were not only invaluable to the family, but they also were proof of an incredible, although unusual, adventure.

The stories that were told to me about Rose and Merle were limited to romanticized, albeit entertaining, tales that, to me, seemed almost to be taken out of a Hollywood movie: the striking brunette from the city falls for the humble farm boy who whisks the sharp-tongued belle off on adventures over the countryside in his father's airplane. The two fall in love and marry but just as the pieces of their young lives appear to be falling into place, war pulls them apart and for the next few years my grandfather trains for battle. He becomes a pilot in the Army Air Forces and is awarded command of his own crew before shipping off to England to wage war with and bomb the evil Nazis. But this is where the romanticized narrative ends. In actuality, instead of coming home the celebrated protagonist, he arrived heartbroken, haunted, damaged, and aged well beyond his 23 years. "He'd come home messed up from the War," I'd been told, and little more was said about it. For a time, the Greens settled into life without war and started a family but ultimately, his experiences in Europe in 1944 and 1945 contributed to a series of irreconcilable differences-ultimately the catalyst of the couple's separation. In turn, Rose was left to raise the kids on her own and endeavored to instill her deep-rooted, unbreakable Faith in her daughter and five sons. All the children would harbor varying degrees of animosity towards the estranged patriarch; feelings that were still present long after his death in 1976.

Early on I found I had a great interest in the world of flight; a trait inherited from my grandfather, no doubt. I loved to watch movies like *Tora Tora Tora, Top Gun, Flight of the Intruder, and Memphis Belle*; the latter film being based loosely on the true-to-life exploits of the so-named famous bomber and her crew during World War II. In my free time, I assembled model aircraft kits and deployed my fleet of airships in the space above my bed, hung there suspended by fishing line. I probably destroyed quite a few brain cells with model glue vapors and paint fumes in the process of producing the massive fleets; quantities of plastic aircraft that almost certainly rivaled that of Boeing. Some of the fondest memories of my youth are of attending air shows held at the local airparks around Phoenix, Arizona where I grew up, or nearby at Luke Air Force Base. We watched with excitement as the Blue Angels and Thunderbirds executed their skillful maneuvers overhead, toured the cockpits of the latest fighter jets, and inspected the arsenal of military helicopters all while a patriotic soundtrack blared over the loudspeakers. The machines were always of great interest to me, but I would inevitably find myself scanning the tarmac, anxiously searching for a sight of the "Flying Fortress" over the heads of the crowd.

In the 1990s, my father began to research my grandfather's time in the Army Air Forces and while Merle wasn't his father, he felt it important for his sons to know more about the man. With help from the 8th Air Force Historical Society, it was discovered that a few of the surviving members of Merle's crew were still alive. The men, now in their 70s, were phoned individually and, after introductions were made and pleasantries exchanged, the old airmen happily began sharing memories from the War. I found interest in the discussions but I, a teenager at the time, failed to recognize the invaluable opportunity before me. I do recall one conversation with my grandfather's ball turret gunner, a man by the name of James Gegenheimer, or "Geg" as he was affectionately known by our family. In his smooth Louisiana drawl, the man relayed some of his fondest memories of that incredible time, fifty years before. He spoke fondly and at length about both of my grandparents whom he had known since the crew was assembled in early 1944 and it was then that the Greens, along with Jim's girlfriend-later his wife, established a deep friendship, one that would continue after the War. Unfortunately, by the time Merle and Rose parted ways in the late 1960s, Geg had lost all contact with his friends. The loss had affected him tremendously but when my mother and father were able to reconnect with the aging gunner, the heartache was much lessened. From out of those invaluable interviews that followed with Geg and the others, an astonishing story began to emerge; one that would provide clarification, consolation, and further insight into an extraordinary series of events.

In December 2018, I discovered Donald Miller's, Masters of the Air: America's Bomber Boys Who Fought the Air War Against Nazi Germany. The renowned book is considered a must-have history of the American Eighth Air Force's origin and amazing exploits. Today, in the summer of 2022, Miller's work is being translated into the third installment in Steven Spielberg's WWII series, after Band of Brothers and The Pacific. I found 'Masters' very fascinating as it gave me a great insight into what my own grandfather may have experienced, at least to some degree, during his time in England and in the aerial battles over Europe. The book renewed my interest in my grandfather's story, one that was becoming slightly clearer but still was very fragmented and mysterious. I soon found another amazing story, this one by the author Steve Snyder. He tells of his father's remarkable journey in Shot Down: The True Story of Pilot Howard Snyder and the Crew of the Susan Ruth, a multi-award-winning work. Snyder's story was a personal tale, wonderfully told and a big inspiration for me to begin to author my own book.

I felt that if I was going to write about my grandfather, it could not be properly told without also including and elaborating on my grandmother's unique journey and struggles. She had, after all, been instrumental in holding the families together during the crew's deployment overseas, as well as providing a solid foundation for my grandfather upon his return. Additionally, in the midst of the War she suffered the loss of her mother during a period when her husband was otherwise engaged in Europe. Rose had also raised six rambunctious Green kids, mostly by herself; no easy feat, especially considering my mother and uncles. The task is appreciated so much more as I watch my wife raise our own boys with amazing strength, self-sacrifice, dedication, and unconditional love. While not deployed on the battlefield on the other side of the ocean, Rose performed her role with honor, dignity, faith, and bravery. She is the inspiration for the title of this book.

During my research I was fortunate to be able to make contact with historians and researchers across the US, as well as others in England and Germany, and, thanks to the internet, exchange information with ease. Many of these amazing individuals provided me with incredible never before seen photos and remarkable eyewitness accounts of previously unknown events directly related to my grandfather's journey. Perhaps the most significant find during the project was connecting with my grandfather's sibling's family who provided countless extraordinary recollections, mementos, and oral histories, many of which I have been fortunate to include in this book. When I visited the family in January of 2022, they happily chauffeured me around to my grandfather's old stomping grounds, identified the location of the family's farm, and shared memories and food at the Green's priceless, handcrafted, century old kitchen table. I cannot express the emotions that I had when, to my astonishment, I was presented my grandfather's pocket Bible and silver pilot wings; items kept preserved by Merle's sister, Zenobia, and her amazing family for decades in a home not 10 miles from where my mother's house was located.

Some of the information that I have uncovered, whether through official records, witnesses' interviews, or personal family stories is, at times, uncomfortable to address. War, after all, is far too often tragic and the wounds remain long after the bullets stop flying. I hope this book does justice to the stories of all involved but above all else, I hope that by telling this story, all of the families can find some degree of solace or healing and pride in what their loved one did and sacrificed. Mysteries do remain, but I can now say that Merle Green is no longer that hazy figure standing in the back row of that old photograph.

In the days following my 18th birthday I received a card from Mr. Gegenheimer and his wife, Mary Lee. The gesture, like the man, was truly considerate, amazing, and influential beyond his words. It has left a lasting impression on me, as I am sure he has for countless others, and I have kept the card among my most prized possessions. The note, in part, reads as follows:

> *Congratulations. I am interested in hearing what is going on in your life at 18. May I comment that 15 days after my 18th birthday I entered the Army Air Corp[s] and 6 days before I was 19 I was a P.O.W. I pray that your 18th and 19th years will be so much happier. Your grandfather and his crew, as well as millions of others like us, suffered much to save this country when the whole free world was in peril. We hope and pray that you will have a good year.*
>
> *Jim G.*

1
THE BLACKBIRD

Perhaps the boy sensed an instinctual connection between himself and the avian kind- some visceral fellowship that stirred within him, instilled from the very beginning, ever summoning him to break free of his earthly bonds. Even his name held an affiliation with the world of flight. The word was derived from "merula", meaning "blackbird", a creature that held enigmatic and mystic qualities for many cultures. Ancient Celtic lore, like those observed by his family's Gaelic and Anglian ancestors, had embraced the "black druid" bird as a symbol of rebirth and transformation. It had also been revered by the tribes of the American Plains who had formerly cultivated the strata of earth upon which now sat the family's farmstead. For the Native Americans, the appearance of the thrush was believed to bestow a blessing on the maize crop and its musical refrain, said to summon the rains, always a welcomed circumstance for planters in central Illinois. While considered a good omen by some, the "merula" was also alleged to possess far darker talents. Due to its mystical abilities, it was supposed to serve as an intermediary between the worlds and help to navigate lost souls through purgatory. Others cautioned that the bird was cursed, forever damned to a life of torment and limbo. Ultimately, the reasoning behind bestowing the title on the boy with was far less menacing. Each Spring, the indigenous population of blackbird return to the Midwest and as luck would have it, the flock's reappearance in March of 1921 coincided with the arrival of Hattie and Otto Green's firstborn son.

It was on Otto's tenant farm, situated just south of the village of Mount Pulaski, Illinois that the story of Merle Dean Green began.

Hattie, Merle, and Otto Green

Little had changed since multitudes of bold American pioneers, just generations before, had braved their way into the vast stretch of rolling grasslands and sweeping plain of the then-named "Northwest Territory", where depending on the season and God's plan, they both cursed and praised the flow of the Illinois and Sangamon Rivers. After clearing off the timber and fighting away the wolves, they found the land a virtual "garden of Eden"; a bounty of resources lying among the immense emptiness of steppe and prairie savannah. It was said that Pulaski was a "city set upon a hill, whose light cannot be hid". And shine it did as, for a brief spell, Mt. Pulaski even served as the county seat, but the town's beacon-like lure would last for decades to come.

During the "Age of Prohibition", enticed travelers were drawn to the area where underground booze markets, rumored to be aided by local high school boys who help load the large wooden vinegar barrels containing the priceless hooch onto the railcars, anticipated the call "All off for Vinegar Hill": the town's fitting, albeit spirited nickname. But in Pulaski Township, it was not alcohol that ultimately reigned, but coal and corn. One amongst those who scratched a living out of the clay and silt was Otto Green. Green managed to weather the economic swells and troughs of the period by tending crops and rearing an assortment of livestock, all while raising his clan. He and Hattie Boggs had wed in 1916. The following year, their first child, Zenobia, was born, arriving during a winter so frigid that when hot water was fetched from the nearest neighbor's lot, it arrived at the

Green farm a solid block of ice.

On the tail of Merle's entrance four years later in 1921, the prosperities seen in the "Golden Age of Agriculture"; the profitable period following the agrarian production boom generated by the "Great War", dried up, leaving many growers to find themselves out of luck, out of cash, and out a farm. In response to the waning market, Otto sold his stock of horses, mules, "milch" cows, and oxen, packed up his family, and relocated to a little community just west of Springfield where he had secured more favorable arrangements. Left behind in Mt. Pulaski, but not forgotten, were much of Merle's kin, including a deceased infant sister. In 1918, the "Spanish Flu" had broken out in Logan County. The sickness struck the community without mercy, as witnessed by the local doctor who, upon keeping occupied with making house calls throughout the township to check on his plagued neighbors,

Merle (Front row middle) and Hattie (Back row center), Schwanke Collection

noted, "…most or all of the family would be sick in bed, with the dead children on the kitchen floor." Whether influenza-related or not, within only a few months of coming into the world, the Green's baby girl, Margaret, fell ill and died.

Having earned a reputation as a resilient, honest worker, Merle's father was brought on as a co-operative for a sprawling 225-acre farm, situated eleven miles outside of the capital city along the pike leading to the village of Pleasant Plains. The property, known as the "Red Top Farm", had two large barns, a milk house, one garage, a corn crib, and a two-story, seven-room, brick farmhouse, where the Greens settled in and called it home. Although the house was later outfitted with at least one essential luxury for the day: electricity, heating was provided by a coal-burning stove. Thinking back on Hattie and Otto, one friend of the Greens remembers that they "worked, worked, worked…and like many local farmers, they worked hard to do

3

their part for the country." A few years after assuming the property, the farm was touted as "one of the finest, black, level improved farms

in the state." Not surprisingly, the Greens swiftly established a strong bond with their new tight-knit community and for the next two decades, there they could be found, religiously attending to their crops, minding their animals, and improving the land. Though times were tough and funds were tight, fortunes were proving better for the family.

The hardships of raising crops and livestock, coupled with the onset of the Great Depression in 1929, postponed the addition of the Green's last child, a son named Robert, until 1931. It wasn't long after they began to waddle after their parents that the youngsters had a hand in the family business. At first, the little ones tagged along with Hattie, helping with chores, washing clothes, tending to the garden, and

Merle, Zenobia and Rover, Schwanke Collection

tossing feed. As time went by, however, the children began to shadow Otto out into the fields where they would scrape and pick at the earth, working the soil, nursing their tract, and toiling for long hours, earning their sinewy frames, calloused hands, and sturdy backs. When not busied in the fields, all hands were required to mind the dairy cows and help coordinate the family's grade-A milk operation. This proved to be no easy task as the herd required two-a-day milkings, the first of which was collected, bottled, and set out for the milkman for delivery to Springfield patrons every morning.

As kids, they witnessed the cycle of life firsthand, being closely interwoven in the experiences of both the birth and death of the creatures of their herds. They learned to be mindful of the land, to respect nature, and appreciate even the simplest of God's blessings, and when the day's work was done, they were rewarded with humble returns. When the light of each day slipped beyond the western horizon, the family gathered at their kitchen table. There they gave thanks and shared in their meager fare; a simple meal that they had produced, trapped, fished, or hunted themselves at the cost of their own blood, sweat, energy, time, and tears, only to repeat the practice beginning in the pre-dawn hours the following morning. With the support of their kinfolk, neighbors, and the community, along with a steady flow of prayers, they endured drought and floods, wildfire and blizzards, death and disease.

Like most agrarian-rooted folks, the Green's livelihood was dictated by the season and the weather. In the Spring, with the frost having played out, the Greens turned the soil and fired the corn stalks left standing after the previous season's harvest. It was an endless, cyclical ritual that cleansed the acres of the past and cleared the tract for the future crop, all the while improving the health of the soil by returning nutrients to the clay. They fertilized the fields and, with the help of their horse and tractors, tilled the earth, preparing their parcels for seeding which was accomplished by walking the fields and introducing seed by hand. Wheat, soybeans, oats, and an assortment of garden vegetables were the most common crops harvested on the farm. As the fields were rotated by season, fallow plots were converted to clover fields to help supplement feed for the family's fifty heifers, two hundred hogs, and one dozen sheep. In the summer, the family followed the progress of their maturing plants, namely the "stretching" of the corn that hinted towards a decent harvest if the stalks stood at least "knee-high by the Fourth of July." They cut and stacked their yield of oat in anticipation of the threshing crews who worked their way through the community, farm by farm. The days spent running the oat through the machines that separated the grain from the stalks were long and hard, but they were also delightful experiences as the occurrence provided ample opportunity for families to eat, play, and socialize with their neighbors. At day's end, the men would retire to the farmhouse and a feast, which Hattie had somehow managed to produce in between her routine of continuous household responsibilities, obligations around the farm, and her work in the garden.

On occasion, the Greens would load into their Ford truck and make the commute into Pleasant Plains to hobnob with their neighbors or partake in community picnics and potlucks, many of which were organized in the meadows around the old Christian Church. Dances were held on Saturdays and Wednesday evenings, and during the summer, the community would host a series of outdoor films, free of charge, where families could lounge about in front of a large portable movie screen that had been arranged in the street in the center of town. To help ward off the muggy summer heat, ice cream cones were slung to movie patrons and folks meandering along the village sidewalks. After Sunday services, children sipped on glasses of tea and lemonade at church social functions while the ladies took to gossip, the men to heated debate and the older folk gathering on neighbor's porches to "spin a yarn". Radiating country kindness, with its telephone office, single grocery store, and lone petrol station, Pleasant Plains was the classic American "old country town".

In the fall, the entire family got down to "huskin' and cribbin'" the season's variety of corn- the predominant crop produced on the Green's property. When the foliage began to change hues and with the harvest complete, the children were free to return to their schooling. Early each day after completing their morning chores, the local children would descend upon the small, one-room schoolhouse known as Richland Grade School where the lone teacher would deliver lessons to the entire group; an assembly of no more than twenty students whose ages and academic aptitudes spanned eight grades. Most, like Zenobia and Merle, made the trek on foot, but a few sauntered in from the backcountry on horseback. Once free of the crops, Otto took to repairing the barns, pens, sheds, and farmhouse in preparation for the imminent harsh Illinois winter. Many chilly, snowy nights saw the family sitting sheltered in the warmth of their stove, listening to radio broadcasts emanating from the big metropolis of Chicago. To bolster his meager income and offset his losses, Merle's father managed to scratch together enough funds to purchase an old biplane and, in between working his fields, provided crop-dusting services to neighbors. In an era before Federal Aviation Administration regulations and long before the military's aerial arm neared its heyday, many civilian pilots, especially those in the risky arena of crop-dusting, considered flying more of an art than an actual science with much of the craft passed on between the generations of fliers. Some airfields offered flying classes, and while Otto's skills were more than likely acquired through impromptu opportunities from an aviator friend who required an extra pair of hands, his interest in flight, one that he would pass on to his oldest son, was fueled much earlier.

On September 29th, 1910, none other than Wilbur Wright of the famous flying brothers had passed through Mt. Pulaski on an exciting Chicago-to-Springfield "Bi-Plane-Train Race". Wright's boxy two-winged fabric and glue, wood-framed aeroplane lost a wheel upon approach to the village but managed to set down nearby in an

Wilbur Wright's 'Bi-Plane' landing in Mt Pulaski,
Mount Pulaski Township Historical Society Collection

improvised landing field. While the apparatus sat in a grassy meadow near the center of town to take on water and oil, the entire population of the village and surrounding countryside seemed to turn out to watch as the fascinating contraption was mended. Ironically, the celebrated inventor was not piloting the airship himself, which putted away to the southwest after departing at a frenzied pace of 33 miles per hour, but instead rode as an observer onboard the locomotive due to a busted leg. Nonetheless, his presence and $10,000 in prize money helped promote air travel in Illinois and lent inspiration to droves of aerial enthusiasts, including Otto Green.

Aerial application of insecticides and fungicides was an innovative idea that emerged in the American South during the 1920s. The demand for a good "duster" increased as growers looked for more efficient strategies to protect their leafy investments against pest invasions. Coordinating with a flagman on the ground, the pilot flew organized patterns over the fields, releasing loads of powdered lead arsenic, or "dust", over the crops and orchards. The key was to operate the aircraft low enough to prevent the chemical "drift" of the highly toxic product, thus cutting down on wastage and avoiding undesired contamination. Pilots were at the mercy of Mother Nature as they operated by "playing the winds"-flying with regard to the strength and direction of the seasonal breezes. Business flowed and ebbed not only with the weather but also in relation to any insect offensives. The birdman's reputation, and in turn, prosperity, not only rested on his ability to keep his plane airworthy and quickly accessible, but it also depended on the potency of his pesticide formula and ability to fly tight patterns. In addition to gaining the skills of a mechanic and weatherman, "dusters" consequently became amateur entomologists.

Lindbergh (second from right) at Springfield's Bosa Field for an airmail-practice flight,
Sangamon Valley Collection

Operating in the rural setting presented abundant threats for crop-dusting fliers. Characteristically, pilots worked mere feet above the ground, sailing low enough to clip their flagman with a tire or wing following a moment's loss of focus or a slight miscalculation. To avoid striking one of the countless obstacles or structures that surrounded the fields, at the end of each pass, the aviator had fractions of a second to complete a rapid climb or sharp turn before banking, realigning and, once again, gracefully swooping down to deliver another application.

'Spirit of St. Louis' at Lindbergh Field, 1927, Sangamon Valley Collection

More than one tail wheel, and the occasional flier, was lost to an irrigation standpipe, fence post, powerline, or water tower. To be a talented crop-duster, it was said, one had to possess nerves of steel, superb concentration, composure, quick reflexes, instinctual piloting skills, and a broad mechanical aptitude, not to mention plenty of daring that hinted on the verge of madness. The last quality, as the theory goes, was a consequence of working around their batches of poisonous pesticides for too long. Despite this, whenever a local "duster" took to the skies to distribute his powdered payload, it was inevitable that folks could be found gathering to sit and watch the acrobatics and bold performances on display.

The period after the "Great War" witnessed the rise of the "flying circus". It was the era of barnstormers where Army Air Service-trained aviators buzzed from town to town to show off their talents for the amusement of fascinated locals. After securing a temporary landing strip through negotiations with a farmer, the aviators, clad in their traditional regalia of riding pants, silk scarf, flying cap and goggles, drew large crowds of onlookers. After quickly shutting down the town for the thrilling event, townspeople eagerly converged on the makeshift airfield to watch the visitors perform stunts and other electrifying daredevilry. The low passes and barrel rolls were always a crowd-pleaser, but it was the candy-drop that was the favorite performance of the children. To earn an income, the airmen transported the bolder of souls up into the blue where, for a small fee or room and board for the night, they could experience the sensation of breaking free of their terrestrial restraints and soar above the heads of their envious neighbors.

Air traffic over Sangamon County, Illinois during the 1920s and 30s was composed of more than just the local fleet of "dusters" and gypsy fliers. By 1926, Contract Air Mail Route #2 was established to serve the communities along a track between St. Louis and Chicago; only the third officially authorized airmail route in the entire United States. Shoring up in the capital city, the mail carrier could exchange his canvas bags full of correspondence and take advantage of a short break to stretch his legs or shoot the breeze with residents while the company's scarlet red biplane was refueled. One pilot, nicknamed "Slim", would execute the route's first official flight on the 15th of April 1926; an event widely promoted in Springfield newspapers weeks in advance. When the day arrived, 5,000 locals descended on the William Bosa farm, four miles west of downtown where sixty flat, grassy acres had been obtained for a permanent airstrip. Thirteen months and five days later, that same pilot would appear in headlines

Amelia Earhart (center) at Springfield Airport, 1934, Sangamon Valley Collection

worldwide after completing the first-ever non-stop flight from New York to Paris. The plane that took the former mail carrier over the great expanse of the Atlantic was christened *Spirit of St. Louis* and the pilot's name was Charles Lindbergh. When the now world-famous adventurer returned to Springfield the following year, he steered his *Spirit* into the newly renamed "Lindbergh Field." Besieged by an army of his starstruck friends, the lanky 25-year-old flying pioneer was heard to remark, "It's like coming home, flying to Springfield." Just a few years later, Amelia Earhart landed at the city's second airstrip, a commercial airport located in the southern outskirts of town where the famous record-setting aviator, crisscrossing the US while on a lecture tour to buoy support for her soon-to-be tragic and puzzling endeavor to circumnavigate the globe, was presented as the special guest of honor for the dedication ceremony.

A short, two-mile jaunt from "Lindbergh Field", the Green farm sat just alongside the St. Louis-Peoria leg of the mail route. The buzz of mail carriers and the ever-increasing air traffic created a fascinating distraction for Merle; a boy who always seemed to have one eye to the sky. He, like most youngsters of the day, saw their

Merle (second from left back row), Pleasant Plains HS Basketball Squad, 1937, Prairie Skies Library Collection

imaginations filled with tales of airborne trailblazers, fighter aces, and racers like Eddie Rickenbacker, Frank Luke, and James "Jimmy" Doolittle. The latter flier nearly clipped the Illinois Statehouse in Springfield, the dome clearly visible from the Green's property, during a race in the 1930s. When the flying machines sank out of sight, young Merle was left to study the ravens and buzzards, watching as they, drifting and dancing overhead, rode the thermals, envious of their ability to have conquered the oppressive pull of gravity.

But the young Green boy was no stranger to flight, himself. In fact, Merle had motored into the heavens with his father on many occasions. Otto was known to boost the lad up into the open bucket seat of his small wood and fabric-covered biplane, plant the sprout on his lap, and bind themselves to the aircraft. Then, with his son donning a pair of large goggles and an oversized flying cap, they would set off, first motoring away from the barn, then bumping through the backyard and finally wheeling up onto his makeshift runway in the grass between the fields. It was in those early years that his passion for flight was realized and by the time he had turned ten, Merle had already acquired countless hours gliding over Midwestern terra firma. By his mid-teens, he was commonly found flying solo, piloting the aircraft with ease and the confidence of a skilled aviator. As his peers were just beginning to gain the freedom to borrow the family truck, Merle was operating as an expert "duster" with his father.

While afforded the rare experience of piloting an airplane during a time when commercial air travel was far from commonplace, Merle spent most of his boyhood exploring the countryside, known to locals as "the Plains", with his troop of companions. The time between chores and school granted the band of youngsters the opportunity to launch off on the exciting odysseys unique to rural boyhood in a simpler time. Raised along the same trails that a young Abraham Lincoln had ridden nearly ninety years before during his time covering the "Illinois circuit" as a lawyer, their unruly, tiny army was not

MERLE GREEN

Merle Green 4-H Club, Prairie Skies Library Collection

dissimilar to that of any other American youth of the period. Merle's gang was composed of the Lehmann brothers, the Boesdorfer boys, Eddie Fetzer, and Ray McMillan. Unknown to them, they had been destined to be born in the short span of years that would soon expose them to hardships and unspeakable horrors that would transform them, for better or worse, into men that would forever after be remembered as part of the "Greatest Generation". For now, their days would be spent running barefoot through grassy pastures, wrestling in the shade of the hickories, hunting for Indian arrowheads in freshly ploughed farmland, dodging slithering blue racers, gorging themselves on wild blackberries and floating in the creeks as their fishing lures drifted lazily along the cool waters.

At Pleasant Plains High School, clubs and organized sports provided exciting prospects for the teenagers. Grown tall, wiry, and athletic, Merle ran track and secured spots on both the school's basketball squad and baseball team. The affiliation allowed him to escape on a bus once a week with his pals and travel to one of the half-dozen little towns across central and western Illinois to challenge rival schools. Being from hearty farming stock, Merle and his best pal Eddie also attended meetings organized by the 4-H Club and Future Farmers of America. The two entered numerous competitions and consistently earned high marks for their Poland China pigs, although Fetzer's contestant always seemed to root out Merle's for first prize. While students attended a variety of subjects at the high school including shorthand, bookkeeping, and "orthology", academically Merle excelled in English, mathematics, science, and, not surprisingly, agricultural studies.

A few miles down the road from the Green farm, Springfield was an alluring venture for the youths. As their area of operation, and at times, misguided boldness, grew, conducting runs into the capital city became part of the boy's routine. With its soaring 15-story-tall skyscrapers, countless restaurants, large shopping district, mass transportation system, bustling public square, and close to 71,000 primarily Catholic, German, and Irish inhabitants, next to Pleasant Plains, Springfield was "the big city". It was a town where police "booze squads" still periodically scrapped with hooch-slinging gangsters, rumored to be linked

Merle Green, Schwanke Collection

to crime syndicates in the North. Still, the town was more well known for hosting the annual State Fair where the tractor exhibitions, livestock shows, and displays of the latest farm equipment drew throngs of country folk. In the summertime, the oppressive humidity and record heat waves of the 30s drove squads of local teens to the sandwich stands that stood, beacon-like, along the streets of midtown

13

where the kids could cool off with a chilled bottle of root beer. Grand parades rolled down Washington Street as children sat atop their parent's shoulders to watch the procession of beauty queens, greying Civil War soldiers, hollowed-eyed Great War vets, and mustachioed firefighters stroll along to the soundtrack provided by high school marching bands. Along the beaches of Lake Springfield, girls in bathing suits lounged in the sun while their counterparts, seeking the attention of the females, splashed and grappled with one another in the water, competing for the day's bragging rights. When the lake would freeze over during the winter months, residents went ice skating and then defrosted themselves next to one of the many large bonfires that glowed along the shoreline.

Downtown Springfield was home to a total of seven theaters, some also hosting vaudeville shows and jazz bands, but all offering a temporary distraction from the toll of the economic recession of the '30s. Of all the genres, musicals, westerns, and gangster shows were most popular. Some of the most significant and influential cinematic

Merle Green

pieces were projected onto picture screens during this period including *King Kong, The Adventures of Robin Hood, The Wizard of Oz,* and *Gone With the Wind.* Also to be found amongst the titles posted on local marquees was *Snow White and the Seven Dwarfs,* Walt Disney's first full-length animated feature, released in 1938. Before being entertained by Hollywood's leading men and entranced by beautiful starlets, moviegoers would be shown a newsreel depicting the latest national and world events. While the descriptions of the escalating happenings in Europe and the "Far East" were ominous, they were largely written off by the adolescents as an annoying interruption to be suffered before the lights dimmed and the show began.

At the beginning of the 1930s, Japanese Imperial Forces steamrolled over Chinese Manchuria, butchering the inhabitants in the process and eyeing even more territory in Burma, Hong Kong, and the Dutch East Indies. By the end of the decade, as Merle and twenty-two other students from his class of 1939 graduated, the National Socialist German Worker's Party, the "Nazis", were solidifying their occupation of Austria and occupying Prague. Americans were aware that Adolph Hitler, ironically Time Magazine's 1938 Man of the Year, was making the lives of the German Jewish community as difficult as possible with the goal of displacing them from the "Fatherland" completely. What was virtually unknown to most Americans, and much of the world at the time, was that the Nazis were in the process of implementing much more sinister plans. "Work camps" had been established inside Germany and the State was already "rehabilitating" traitors, troublemakers, social outcasts, and political rivals. As Hitler annexed the Sudetenland and finalized plans for his war apparatus to carry out a lightning-quick advance east to capture Poland, the world was suddenly thrust one step closer to a great global conflict and, quite possibly, Armageddon.

2
A DEVIL OF A TIME

There was no doubt that by the time Hitler set off to conquer Eastern Europe in September of 1939, Germany was fielding the best aerial force in the world. Although the "Luftwaffe"; the name given to the German Air Force, operated numerous models of single and twin-engine interceptors and attack aircraft, the backbone of their formidable airborne arm was the Messerschmitt Bf 109, later the Me 109, and Focke-Wulf 190, the Fw 190 "Butcher Bird". Both were agile fighters capable of reaching speeds between 350 to 425 miles per hour

Me 109, USAF

and each could climb to 36,000 feet-well above the loftiness American bombers would typically tread during the War. Supplementary to an array of machine guns, the Knights of Herman Goering's air force flew fighters equipped with 20 and 30mm cannon, which fired explosive projectiles. Upon contact, the shells packed a wallop more potent than that of a hand grenade.

It was 1940, just months after being drawn into a conflict with Germany, and the Royal Air Force (RAF) abandoned the notion of pushing their bombers into the hostile, Luftwaffe-dominated airspace over Axis-held territories at any time other than under the veil of darkness. As was expected, the Brits would ridicule those first American fliers who turned up two years later, in ever-increasing

16

numbers throughout Suffolk and Norfolk counties, expecting to muscle themselves into the European sky war through daylight penetration raids into occupied Netherlands, France and Northern Germany. The first US raid dispatched by the newly established VIII Bomber Command, headquartered just west of London and later redesignated and here forth referred to by the author as the 8th Army Air Forces (AAF), would be launched on August 17th, 1942. That day the force that assembled to hit marshaling yards in Nazi-controlled France numbered a dozen bombers; a mere whisper of the thousand-aircraft fleets that would be fielded on a daily basis during the final six months of the War.

With the coming of '43 and the ghost of four months of costly and unproven campaigns hovering over them, 8th AAF commanders would attend a gathering of leadership in Morocco. Known as the "Casablanca Conferences", the assembly, including Winston Churchill and President Roosevelt-Stalin was currently engaged with German advances driving deep into the Russian Motherland, would cover the logistics for the possibility of an Anglo-American invasion of the European continent, tentatively slated for the following year. Also on the agenda would be the hotly-contested debate concerning the seemingly haphazard and yet-to-be vindicated American daylight bombing strategy. Tremendously high casualty rates of US aircrews would regularly overshadow the rare operation that did produce

Fw 190, USAF

results. The numbers alone would be telling, and the entire bombing agenda would appear to be, not in the "pickle barrel", as United States Army Air Forces (USAAF) proponents had boasted about their capabilities long before any American bomber had even reached British soil, but on the chopping block. Despite nearly losing its autonomy to the RAF where the bombers would have also been committed to midnight strikes, determined leaders in US high command would manage to persuade Churchill and Roosevelt to allow them to carry on with their messy daytime business and ask them to trust in the process. So it was, as the English bombed in the black of night, the 8th would take the day shift.

From out of the conference would come the Combined Bomber Offensive: a united English-American aerial onslaught. The idea relied on round-the-clock bombing; unrelenting attacks directed on German fighter production plants and manufacturing infrastructure. U-boat pens would also be targeted, with ball-bearing manufacturing sites, oil and synthetic fuel production facilities, rubber production plants, and vehicle manufacturing targets being listed in order of priority. Whatever the target, destroying the German Air Force was paramount. Up to that point, Allied flyboys and bomber crews had been knocking down Goering's airmen at a respectable rate, but the German war industry would prove incredibly efficient. It was this productivity that permitted the Luftwaffe to offset their losses in aircraft and allowed new ranks of pilots, as well as those who survived being shot down over German-held territory, to continue to take to the sky, inevitably prolonging their domination in the air. Although they had convinced the Allies of the contrary before the start of the War, the German Air Force had become, undeniably, far more than a conglomeration of airborne hobbyists and glider clubs.

St. Paul's Cathedral during the 'Blitz', NARA

As the bloodletting continued for the 8th, their RAF brethren would embrace a new strategy. After stiffening against the Nazi "Blitz" for nearly three years where 40,000 were killed, more than 80,000 were injured, and 2 million homes were razed from the earth, the English would cut loose their bombers on non-military targets within Germany itself. The Germans would soon suffer British retaliation, having to shelter against explosives released from Lancaster, Halifax, Wellington, and Stirling bombers that now detonated among their own. The outcome of one such raid, the 1943 RAF attack on Hamburg, would sit uncomfortably with American bomber command, led by General Ira Eaker and operating under the Strategic Air Forces commander, General Carl Spaatz. It was not the extermination of Nazi disciples that would turn their stomachs, but the political fallout back in the States where public sentiment was fickle towards endangering women and children, even if they were the enemy. The fact that the German Air Force had ravaged the city center of Warsaw four years earlier, crushed the heart of Rotterdam in 1940, and wrecked both Stalingrad and Malta the year before, did little to lessen the angsts of not only 8th AAF Command but of American civilians who rested in relative peace and security far across the vast waters of the Atlantic. The Americans would never officially authorize the bombing of civilians, nor did it formally adopt the RAF's way of "carpet bombing", "area bombing", or "saturation bombing" but the 8th did fly missions to smash non-military targets. Most such raids would occur in late 1944, and many of those runs would see US bombers primed with a higher percentage of incendiary munitions, leading many historians to ponder if the intention, despite the proclamation of the contrary, was to cause deliberate destruction among light construction type buildings, more specifically, ordinary houses, and aid in the spread of fire. The Brits, on the other hand, would make no qualms about deliberately aiming to break the German's will to resist, killing civilians in the process of targeted missions, and would do little to disguise their "morale bombing" policy. It was, after all, cities and towns like London, Coventry, Birmingham, and Liverpool that were being hit by German Dornier bombers for the past four years and not New York City, Washington DC, Philadelphia, or Richmond.

Excluding their involvement in the Spanish Civil War in the late '30s and following four years of clashes with units of Polish, Soviet, French, British, Australian, South African, and American air forces, by 1943 to say that the Luftwaffe had perfected their craft would be an understatement. There had been losses, clearly, many at the cost of some of their most experienced and talented fliers, but the campaigns had won them countless victories, and with it, a reputation that commanded respect even before the call of "bandits" could be heard over the intercoms of Allied aircrews. But every German flier, whether a novice or "*experten*", would recognize that as they danced along the razor-thin line between victory and oblivion, closely intertwined with their romanticized work was the ever-present veil of death. Paradoxically, nearing the end of the War the fighter pilots, once so revered by their countrymen and women, would later become the scapegoat for the people's frustrations. With their cities laying in ruin, German citizens pinned the destruction on the aces as they were seen to have failed in their duty to stop the American "four motors".

On the hunt, German defense interceptor squadrons, "*staffels*", would organize their "*schwarms*" of fighters just beyond the range of the enemy bomber's heavy defensive guns and fly parallel with the bomber stream to organize for the attack. The sight would leave an impression that the assailants, in the words of one Luftwaffe assault survivor would put it, were "queuing up at feeding time!" After advancing ahead of the Allied formations, which the Germans called "herds", the fighters would then wheel directly into the intruder's path and attack head-on, spitting bullets and cannon shells at closing speeds of nearly 500 miles per hour. Taking advantage of the intense glare of the sun as it masked their approach, the frontal charge would be utilized by the Luftwaffe for quite some time and with outstanding

A smoking B-17 'Flying Fortress', NARA

success. However, this practice offered the predators only a fraction of a second to blast away at the bomber's vital and vulnerable organs- the cockpit, nose, fuel tanks and engines, before hurtling the bombers, swerving off, or inverting and plunging away only to reset for another blitz. Naturally, the conditions demanded that these encounters would be swift and vicious, and the Luftwaffe was always looking for ways to refine their techniques of slaughter.

Allied fighter coverage and the overlapping web of defensive firepower- the product of tight formation flying where vigilant gunners, armed with heavy guns that burped out a fusillade of twelve rounds per second, would become a justifiable deterrent, even for the most capable German aviator. As one Luftwaffe flier later explained, assaulting a Flying Fortress was equated to "trying to make love to a porcupine that was on fire". Nevertheless, the "*staffels*" would seem to be forever sizing up their prey, nipping at the pack as it slowly but steadily migrated across their hunting grounds and back again, ever attentive for an opportunity to dive in for the kill to weed out careless or damaged enemy bombers; the unskilled and sick members of the flock.

Beginning in the Fall of 1943, with October soon to prove the costliest month yet, the effectiveness and morale of US bomber units in England would plummet to an all-time low. Scores of American aircrews would find themselves afflicted with the "Messerschmitt twitch" and the "Focke-Wulf Jitters", a result of the bloody high-altitude brawls with their spirited and talented counterparts in the aerial arena above Europe. "Fighters hit us from every angle", wrote one B-17 tail gunner in his war diary. He elaborated further:

> *I saw Forts and fighters blowing up, Forts and fighters going down smoking and burning, wings coming off, tails coming off, the sky full of parachutes....One guy floated into a low Fort-he was churned up by the propellers and took the Fort with him. It just rolled over into a dive. The sky was so full of tracers, 20mm cannon shells exploding, and even rockets. Steel was ripping into our ship with sickening sounds. There were times when I was afraid to shoot for fear of hitting one of our own planes or some poor guy in a parachute.*

Just as the predicament couldn't seem to get any worse, German anti-aircraft defenses would also improve substantially and deal their deadly work upon aluminum, the psyche, and the flesh with significant effect. It would be no surprise that trips to Bremen, called "Flak City" or up the Ruhr Valley, known as "Flak Alley" due to the extensive cannon defenses of the area, elicited groans and muffled curses from the combat men at pre-mission briefings.

On top of the Hun's intimidating defense system, the job of an American bomber crewman was inherently hazardous. While the airmen were equipped with some of the most technologically advanced gear, equipment, and machines of the age, they wrestled with glitches, snafus, limitations, and other ergonomic dilemmas unique to their wildly-unproven occupation, not to mention the hostile and unforgiving environment. On every incursion over the continent, fliers faced being shredded by shrapnel, punctured by cannon shells, bored

B-17s push through anti-aircraft 'flak', NARA

to death, scared to delirium, electrocuted or seared by faulty heating gear, frozen by windblast and sub-zero temperatures, incinerated by gas and oxygen-fueled fires, obliterated to atoms in explosions, drowned by Channel waters, and crushed by centrifugal forces as their bombers tumbled out of the air. If they survived being shot down, they risked suffering the wrath of angry German civilians. Escaping death but not capture, fliers were intensely interrogated and, at times, threatened by their captors. Once resigned to the fact that an indefinite period of detainment now awaited them, they soon found themselves, while no longer starved of oxygen in the sky, starved of food in one of the Reich's hellacious prison camps.

But it was not just the airspace over the continent that would be risky and full of hazards. English skies would hold their own dangers. When one crew returned to their station and entered into their landing pattern after a mission in late 1944, they watched as a Fortress of their unit suddenly blew up just above the runway. Maneuvering overhead, the stupefied crew realized that the B-17 that had abruptly converted into a ball of fire and flame was that of their roommates; boys that they had shared a Nissen hut with for the better part of a year. The immense blast "blew it to dust," reported one airman watching from above. "There was nothing left...nothing left." Beginning with their training in the States, the men had grown accustomed to tragic accidents such as this, but the bonds forged in the experience of war would forever intimately endear the men and crews with one another. "We were very close to those guys, and to see them disappear like that was very, very, very hurtful." The flier, a seasoned officer of over a dozen electrifying combat forays to some of the worst targets in Europe, continued, "I think I almost had a breakdown. I felt like the world was coming to an end." In the days leading up to the raid, the bombardiers on the two crews, both friends and bunkmates, had secured a double date with a pair of smitten lasses in London and had scheduled the rendezvous for the day after their return. Needless to say, the date never happened. "It was a washout," recalled the luckier of the two bomb droppers.

Those who would be crewing the bombers learned quickly that whether in the sights of Axis guns over the continent or floating above the sanctity of their home airfields, death was an ever-present wingman. It would call on the fliers, most merely boys, at random but with unforgiving ferocity, and it would come to reap the brave, the bold, and the meek alike. The men who made it back to the aircraft dispersal pads and Nissen huts after each outing: true survivors of an incredible ordeal that was required to be replicated up to thirty-five times before they could go home, fared only slightly better than those lost over the continent. They would find little, if any, liberation from the horrors of their reality. Visions would flash into their head during the day and revisit them in equally terrifying dreams at night, interrupted only by a pat on the shoulder, a soft rousing from their slumber: the sign to rise and do it all again. To them, it would matter not that these manifestations were merely the reaction of their psyches desperately striving to process the surreal, indescribable, grotesque experiences that they would endure day after day. Those men who

23

would pull themselves up into the nose hatches and step through the aircraft access doors before each flight, particularly the ones who had witnessed the extermination of their friends and the slaying of the great machines, are, without a doubt, among the most outstanding examples of courage and bravery that have ever been borne to any battlefield in human history. With the casualty rates spiking to more than 38 percent, AAF losses would be the highest among all US military service branches, including front-line infantry and Marine units. The average age of a US bomber airman during the War was 22.

Back on the home front, in an effort to win the battle over the "hearts and minds" of the nation, the extraordinarily high losses suffered by the 8th would be widely hidden from the general public. This would include the ranks of idealistic and determined Army Air Forces enlistees who were desperately trying to avoid washing out of cadet training schools across the nation, determined to earn a coveted pair of silver airman wings. Little did the mothers and fathers of the bomber boys know that their sons flying in the "heavies" across the pond in late 1943 averaged surviving no more than six combat flights. The figures are sobering in of themselves, but the impact can easily be lost in the numbers. For instance, casualties sustained by the 8th after the Schweinfurt-Regensburg raid on October 14, 1943, where over 550 American boys were killed or captured at the conclusion of the attack, would be equivalent to wiping out the entire community of Pleasant Plains, Illinois, in less than eight hours. And that would be the price of just one day's labor. Beyond question, combat in the skies over Europe was, as one historian put it, "organized murder". This crushing truth would shock many of the freshly deployed, jittery crews recently arrived in the British Isles. Enlightened of the reality of their deadly business, completing the number of missions required of their tour became a seemingly inconsequential figure, leaving one man to joke that "to fly in the Eighth Air Force then was to hold a ticket to a funeral…your own."

In early January 1944, the 8th's command structure would receive an overhaul as General "Jimmy" Doolittle, leader of the famed retaliatory raid on Japan two years prior, assumed the reins. Upon being placed at the apex of the floundering 8th AAF, he would immediately set about expanding the size of his newly acquired colossal air weapon. Understanding that while high attrition rates would continue, a strategy that suggested of General Ulysses S. Grant's policy of standing toe-to-toe to deliver massive death blows that would eventually strangle and bleed the Confederacy dry during the American Civil War, Doolittle would predict that it would be through fielding greater numbers of fighting men and aircraft that would eventually prevail and lead to victory. The General would recognize that it was not simply a war between rival air forces but one between Junkers and Ford, Focke-Wulf and Lockheed, Bavarian Motor Works and Goodyear, Heinkel and Martin, Messerschmitt and Boeing.

As Doolittle concentrated on packing on more aerial muscle, the 8th USAAF would be complemented by an upgraded fighter force. With the introduction of the more efficient model of the P-51 Mustang which sported "drop tanks" that would extend their legs, bomber crews could expect to be accompanied by their "little friends" to targets deep into the heart of the Third Reich and back home again. As one airman soon explained, "Up to that point, we had a devil of a time getting to and from our targets." It would take some time before results would be realized, but the 8th had, in fact, found the means that would harvest the desired effect. From then forward, the kids in the big bombers "…could have a fighter escort for about a hundred percent of the missions. That took a big worry off our back."

With 1944 grinding on, the Anglo-American coalition would finally begin to detect a hint of success. This would not only be due to the efforts of their fliers, ground crews, and support staff, but also to the resiliency, patriotism, ingenuity, sacrifice, and determination of millions of hardworking Americans back home; a formula that would prove unbelievably influential in the outcome of the War. Each day, more "Jerry" fighters were being knocked out of the sky in dogfights with Allied aces and it would not be uncommon to see Mustangs, P-38 Lightnings, and P-47 Thunderbolts, pitched in battle, outnumbering the enemy thirty, forty, sometimes fifty-to-one. When one German soldier scanned the skies of Western Europe just after D-Day, he was said to remark, "if you see a silver plane, it is American. If you see a black plane, it is British and if you see no plane, it is German."

Flanked with fighter escort support and stacked in assemblies of more than a thousand bombers droning through the skies in streams 90 miles or more in length, the "Mighty Eighth," as it would one day be remembered, would no longer attempt to avoid the Luftwaffe. On the contrary, they would now be looking for a fight and Allied Command would use the Liberators and Fortresses as bait. So as bursts of sunlight flashed and glistened off the unpainted hulls of immeasurable numbers of American bombers in the skies above Western Europe, the message was clear; "Here we are. Come try and stop us."

3

"WHEN THE WHOLE FREE WORLD WAS IN PERIL"

Fall 1940
Pleasant Plains, Sangamon County, Illinois

With France succumbing to Hitler in June and in response to events escalating in Asia, the US instituted the first peace-time draft requiring men ages 21 to 36 years old to register for selective service. Tens of thousands of young menfolk from across the Country registered, but for Merle Green and his gang, the requisite did not yet apply. With graduation behind him, Merle went back to work for his father on the farm, pocketing a hard-earned $33.00 per month: just over a dollar a day. Having married, Zenobia had relocated to town, leaving Hattie heavily outnumbered by the Green boys. Merle also continued to assist

Merle Green's Senior Photo, Schwanke Collection

Otto with the crop-dusting business and while both Greens treasured the experience of flight, when it came to work, both took their craft very seriously. Not only was there the expense of fuel, maintenance,

Merle (left), and Otto (second from left)

pesticide, and time, but a spoiled reputation or one poor showing could prove just as costly to their business. As a result, above the meadows, woodlands, and pastures of rural Illinois, Merle refined his aerial skills, advanced his talents, and learned tricks of his trade that would become unbelievably valuable in the years to come. He navigated, or more appropriately "avigated", not by radar, radio, or map, but by landmarks such as roads, streams, rail lines; what old fliers referred to as the "iron compass", and by the names of the neighboring towns that were painted on water towers. Green learned how increased humidity tweaked the tautness of his plane's bracing wires; the cables that helped to secure the upper and lower wings. He could judge the speed of the aircraft by listening to the whistle of the wires as he cruised through the air, and he could calculate engine rpms simply by assessing the frequency and performance of the motor. Turbulence varied with elevation, and even with his eyes closed he could discern when he was crossing over a pond, lake, stream, or thicket as the aircraft's altitude would fluctuate ever so slightly due to the change of terrain. This was literally fly-by–the-seat-of-your-pants aviating: understanding the feel of the machine. Just as essential, Merle had learned to mitigate in-flight predicaments, including accommodating for sudden engine failure, executing "dead-stick" landings, troubleshooting aircraft malfunctions, eluding unexpected weather fronts, and identifying improvised landing strips, both near and on country lanes and on the rare occasion, side yards of rural homesteads, all at a moment's notice. The youthful aviator quickly came to appreciate the most vital rule of surviving precarious moments in the sky, a tenet that is just as true for modern-day pilots as it was for the first airborne pioneers: despite all the chaos and calamities that may occur, before fixing power loss or extinguishing engine fires or dealing with damage to the airframe, the first, most vital action that a pilot can take in the event of a mid-flight emergency is to continue to fly the plane. To survive the dangers in the sky, Merle understood that he had to first keep the plane in the air.

Merle (3rd from left), and Otto (far right)

"US IN WAR"; so read the headlines in Springfield newspapers on the morning of December 8th, 1941. The previous day, many "Plains" families, including the Greens, became aware of the strike via a more traditional method on that, most-infamous Sunday in American history. Such deplorable news would not wait, not even for the conclusion of church services where the Green's minister suddenly halted his sermon after being approached by a messenger and informed his stunned congregation of the dastardly attack. Sensing a wave of diverse emotions rippling through his unsettled assembly, the preacher embarked upon a new lesson about God and Country and led the group in a prayer for the injured, the fallen, and for the Nation. While the Green's sat in silent contemplation in a pew of the Pleasant

Plains Christian Church, others who resided in the countryside were made aware of the incident by radio broadcast or by neighbors "hollerin'" the tragic newsflash. Nationally, the raid struck hard at every American and inspired an immense patriotic wave that swept the Country. No longer would the US be a nation of "noninterventionists" as a unifying, nationalistic surge, never before seen and perhaps only equivalent to the response of the 9-11-2001 terrorist attacks, flooded into every community, heart, and home.

Rose Marie Denny

Among the first of the Irish to migrate to the Colonies, the Denny family would settle in the still-untamed frontier ancestral land of the Illini tribes just before the start of the "War Between the States". Like Otto Green, Howard Denny was also a planter, although his lot was situated along the Illinois River, west and south of the capital. Denny narrowly avoided the "Dust Bowl" of the '30s, where farmers and ranchers boarded up their homes and hunkered low in their cellars to escape the towering walls of topsoil that swept across their land while plague-like swarms of grasshoppers feasted upon their greenage. Instead, he sold off the homestead and moved his family to Springfield, gained employment as a telegraph operator and later worked with the railroad. Trading farming for a steady government paycheck, Springfield was also desirable to Denny and his wife Frances as it possessed a large Roman Catholic population, most of whom were Irish and German immigrants or second-generationers drawn to the region's coal mining industry. The move also offered the family the opportunity to see that their children, Mary, Margaret, Robert, Rose Marie, William, and later Helen, Joseph, John, and Frank, received a respectable, parochial education.

After promoting from Saint Patrick's School, Rose Marie enrolled in Sacred Heart Academy which possessed, arguably, one of the loveliest churches in town. The Franciscan Nuns who staffed the school provided a secular foundation and a well-rounded curriculum that expanded into commerce, economics, sociology, and, of course, Latin. In between instructions, Rose Marie cheered on teams from Sacred Heart's all-male partner school, Cathedral High. A charming socialite, she helped organize her class's raffles and parties, culminating with prom. However, the highlight of her junior year occurred when the young ladies of Sacred Heart presented the community with an original play, narrated by Rose. The Sisters instilled grace and discipline in their pupils and encouraged a sense of dedication to family, the parish, Faith, and the world. Unaware of it at the time, her developing convictions and sureness in God's design would serve her well in the years to follow and beyond as the depth and strength of her foundation would be tested. Upon graduation, Rose Marie departed as one of the Sister's favorites in the class, many of whom added endearing parting comments in her yearbook alongside a fan club of friends.

The alluring, blue-eyed Denny girl was no stranger to being the focus of attention, especially to those of the opposite sex. Rose Marie was a familiar face in the local beauty pageant scene. Known for her charm and poise, coupled with flowing chestnut locks, piercing sapphire eyes, and prominent cheekbones, she frequently earned awards and accolades, including placing within the top ten in the "Miss Central Illinois" pageant. As a young lady, her allure only became more mesmerizing to the ranks of would-be wooers clambering for her attention. Merle was one such admirer and quickly became completely enamored by the dark-haired beauty, but it was not just her good looks that had captured Green's attention. Rose was graced with a healthy intellect and could chat freely on a variety of topics ranging from her studies at Sacred Heart to the Scriptures, her family, and her passion to become a nurse. Adding to her desirability, Merle admired her devotion to God and commitment to her faith. She could be tenacious, even fiery at times, and didn't hide the fact that she was rather high maintenance, a fact that frequently became a cause for playful banter between her and her country boy suitor.

But Merle was not without his own admirers. "He was tall, slender, handsome. You could tell he was always thinking things out, and he always had this sly grin", reminisced one fan. Others remember the studious young man as social and fun-loving and was always seen as "a sharp dresser". Thinking back on his former pupil from Pleasant Plains High, Green's old principal would proudly emphasize that Merle:

...earned majors in English, mathematics, science, and agriculture. He was active in our physical education program and was a member of our basketball squad for three years. Mr. Green is a young man of clean habits and makes an unusually fine appearance as you will readily see from a personal interview. He has a good Christian-American home background. His actions will never embarrass his service organization. I think he will be a prominent member of any group with which he is associated. He has some flying experience. I do not hesitate to recommend him for any service.

Rose and Merle

Never one to overlook his resources, Merle was quick to lure Rose out to the farm where he proudly showed off his father's biplane. To his delight, Merle found the girl intrigued and it was not long before he and Rose buzzed off on what would be one of the many aerial adventures that led them to discover much of the countryside together. He would often coast just above the cornfields, clipping the tallest of the stalks with the plane's tires, leaving frustrated, cursing farmers in his showy wake. At other times he'd drop a wing and roll the craft a little too far, measuring his date's confidence and, at the same time, her stomach. Noticeably less than impressed, Rose always retained her poise, and while she was barely discernible above the whoosh of the engine, her displeasure was clearly relayed to the pilot. Still, just behind her the smirking flier sat, amused with himself and always content with being on the receiving end of any of Rose's attention. As his affection for the stunning brunette grew, Green found a cherished and captivating counterpart in Rose Marie. Merle's dogged pursuit eventually won out, and the couple's steady courtship swiftly evolved into a budding romance.

While Merle was entirely taken by the striking Denny girl, his mother did not share the same sentiments. Hattie, or "Vulture," as the couple secretly called her, did not appreciate the Catholic girl's hold on her smitten son. Being from hearty farming stock herself, Hattie would not hesitate to show her disapproval of the delicate, pampered vixen. Merle, undoubtedly, was kept busy as he worked to defuse his unimpressed mother while, at the same time, skillfully ushering off his equally aggravated best gal.

When the skirmishes between Rose and Hattie died down, the couple could be found rambling around the farm grounds or relaxing in the yard where they would hang on the sights and sounds of the countryside: the bubbling of the creek where the soft croaking of frogs arose from out of the cool twilight, the breeze whisping softly through the trees, the entrancing flickers of lightening bugs dancing in the garden, the livestock settling out in the dimmed light. The lovebird's conversations would shift to dreaming about their future together; thoughts of marriage and children and family and the farm. And then, of course, there was always the inescapable matter of war. Rose understood that, like her brothers and many of their friends, her handsome, idealistic beau was destined to enter military service before long, either by enlisting or through the draft. Volunteering early, they supposed, would at least provide Merle the chance to fly as those collected up in a draft would be slotted into positions dependent on the need of the Armed Forces. Furthermore, the steady pay of a 2nd lieutenant and monthly flight pay-income that was a substantial increase compared to anything either had known, was also an added bonus.

To fill the military training centers with the number of young hopefuls needed to man the nation's rising aerial branch, the US Army revised its pre-war entrance standards in January 1942. No longer required to have two years of college to be eligible for the US Army Air Forces candidate program, Merle made plans to visit the local recruitment center to take the service entrance exam. Before he could make the trip to the enlistment center in Peoria, however, Merle was struck down with a severe case of abdominal pain that resulted in hospitalization and culminated with an appendectomy. Recovery was frustrating in that it not only delayed his enlistment plans but adhering to the doctor's orders of maintaining a sedentary lifestyle necessary for healing must have been comical for the restless young man. By late Spring and finally fully recovered from his procedure, Merle was free to concentrate his energies on what would turn out to be the beginning of a great and trying journey.

Merle and Rose

4
AMONG THE ELITE

September 1942
US Army Recruitment Center
Peoria, Illinois

"To the best of your knowledge, are you sound and well?" prodded the questionnaire that had been slid in front of Merle on the 7th of September 1942 as he sat in the US Army recruitment office in Peoria, Illinois. Part of the military's entrance survey that probed everything from marital status, legal convictions, jail time, previous attempts at enlistment, civilian occupation, and his average weekly earnings, this inquiry was just one of many truly subjective and disconcerting questions presented to the applicant. Considering that this particular candidate was requesting to fly in one of the most inhospitable, unfamiliar, extreme environments known to man, it was arguably the most revealing, yet appropriate, query posed by the Army into the nature of the applicant. But perhaps the most absurdly amusing and downright distressing assessment was:

> *Have you ever used cocaine, heroin, morphine, marijuana, or any habit-forming drug or narcotic; since childhood wet the bed while asleep, had gonorrhea, sore on penis, convulsions or fits, or spells of unconsciousness; raised or spat up blood; had any illness, disease, or injury that required treatment at a hospital or asylum?*

Denying the aforementioned queries and sitting an ideal candidate for the Army, the 21-year-old's enlistment file recorded him as standing at 72 inches in height, with brown hair, blue eyes, being of a slender build at 165 pounds, and possessing 20/20 vision. He had completed four years of high school and listed that he was currently working for his father and "planted, plowed, cultivated and harvested crops such as corn, wheat, oats and a wide variety of garden vegetables". Under "skills" he reported that he "drove a tractor, [and] maintained farm buildings and equipment". The next day, onboard a bus bound for Nashville, Merle found himself surrounded by dozens of other enthusiastic young males who were not only destined for the same training camp, but equally as wide-eyed as himself. This was the new batch of the most desirable men who, as the Army required, "were young, uninhibited, [had] plenty of guts, and [had] no fear."

After passing through the installation's gates at the Army's Classification Center at Nashville, Tennessee, sharply dressed Army sergeants encouraged Merle and his fellows to disembark from the busses with haste. Once outside, the drill instructors began pressing into the bewildered herd in an effort to enthusiastically acquaint themselves with the nervous newcomers. The greeting was such that it was during these first few moments that many recruits would reassess their genuine level of desire to be an Army flier. Converting from civilian to soldier was entirely overwhelming to some but fortunately, there always seemed to be an attentive drill sergeant lurking nearby who was more than willing to educate any straying amateur, whose level of importance was now apparently that of the lowly "yardbird", with a few words of inspiration.

Shuffled to the medical station, the men entered the room just as they had entered life: completely befuddled and as naked as a jaybird. Inside, the candidates ran through a gauntlet of Army surgeons who poked, prodded, scraped, stretched, strained, and generally agitated the amalgamation that here now assembled from all corners of the Country. Along with the medical exam, the recruits were administered a multitude of tests including an exhausting three-hour written exam designed to assess each applicant's mental fitness, accuracy of perception, decision-making skills, mathematical understanding, reading comprehension, ability to function under stress, personality traits, hand-eye coordination, and mechanical aptitude. The candidates attended the Army Air Forces orientation and sat for a screening of the morale-building film, *Why We Fight*. They were also examined by a psychiatrist who scrutinized each man's character by conducting interviews that bordered an interrogation and through evaluating the men's ink blobs deciphers. The reasoning behind the intrusive and vigorous probing was not entirely clear to the recruits who felt they were being judged on matters ranging from bed-wetting and personal fears to experiences with the opposite sex, mother issues, moral attributes, and vices. In reality, the rationale behind the evaluation was to determine how well the individual would operate under the rigors of flight, while assigned to a team and in combat conditions but it also assisted the staff in measuring the candidate for classification as a pilot, navigator, bombardier, or whether they should be scrapped from the program altogether.

Throughout the Second World War, achieving the role of a USAAF aviator was an extremely ambitious, demanding, and time-consuming process. Of the half-million pilot candidate applicants entering service with Merle in 1942, fifty percent failed to pass the entrance battery. Of those remaining, forty percent would fall short of earning pilot's wings during classification and instead be reassigned to other training or schools. Some of these recruits would be appointed to the role of aerial gunner, and some destined to be "ground pounders"-an equally vital part in the military machine but absent the glamour of the swashbuckling image attached to the Air Corps. Other numbers were released during the pilot instruction programs that followed for a variety of reasons, and thousands more, 15,000 in fact, perished in training accidents long before deployment.

Awarded endorsement by the board of cadets, candidates would be sent to one of the three types of classification schools: bombardier school, the navigator program, or pilot training-the latter being the most coveted assignment. At the end of the frantic two-week-long classification process, the enlistees were summoned to the staff offices to learn of their fate. As each contender returned to their barracks, they were met by a swarm of their curious peers, eager to learn of the results. Many returned downtrodden but one cadet from Illinois arrived back at his bunk with a form that read:

#16-074-102 Merle D. Green Classification: Pilot

A few days later, a knock at the door at 1212 East Brown Street in Springfield accompanied the delivery of a Western Union telegram. Addressed to a "Miss Rose M. Denny", the cable was straight and to the point.

Rose,

Come Nashville immediately, urgent. Send reply now, call upon arrival.

Despite avoiding the plethora of illnesses that were carried to the classification center by boys originating from all over the nation, Merle came down with a highly contagious infection that was known to spread throughout the ranks of newly-christened cadets. It was known as "marriage fever," and Merle had developed a severe case. On October 31st, 1942, Rose Marie and Merle were married in Nashville by an Army chaplain. In attendance were friends, family, including Bob Green, and each of the couple's mothers, one of whom appeared notably less than enthused by the ceremony. After sharing breakfast with their guests, the giddy newlyweds headed off to Chattanooga for a swift honeymoon.

When Private Green returned from leave, he discovered that he had been affixed to the medical detachment at Thayer General Hospital as the Army was experiencing a dilemma of too many students-not enough training spots. Here, amongst the monotony of

Western Union Telegram

clerical work, Merle would first be exposed to the ugliness of battle as the hospital was accommodating hundreds of wounded and mangled soldiers and airmen recently returned home from the fighting abroad.

While he understood his duties were, undoubtedly worthwhile, the postponement of his instruction must have been painstakingly annoying for Green, who was eager to get into the scrap. "Still not in the cadets," he frustratingly wrote his mother. Luckily, Rose moved to Nashville where the couple rented their first apartment.

It wouldn't be until May of 1943 when Merle and a few hundred other cadets were packed into a chain of old, "vintage" Pullman passenger cars and chugged away from Tennessee. The troupe headed southeast for what would be an unpleasant 400-mile ride to Alabama in the dingy WWI-era rail mounted relics. Now outfitted in

Wedding day, Merle (center)

sharp, khaki uniforms and sporting the iconic patch of an air cadet-a vertical propeller flanked by outstretched wings, the cadets couldn't help but feel that they were part of an elite band of warriors.

Any air of prestige was soon deflated as upon their arrival at the training school, the plebes found themselves falling into line before a force of rigid saber-wielding, guidon-bearing senior cadets, who moved in crisp, synchronized motions and presented sharp, snappy salutes, glared at them from below visors drawn low over frozen, unimpressed faces. As a flurry of whispers ran through the edgy band, a flawlessly dressed senior cadet pivoted into the stunned faces of the gathering and commenced the schooling. "Get those heads and eyes front. You're at attention. This is not the GI Army. Chins in, chest out. Suck those stomachs in. Look proud, Mister, you're in the Air Corps!" Thus was their introduction to "Pre-Flight" at Maxwell Field.

The responsibility of "mentoring" the fresh pool of air cadets fell to the program's upperclassmen. The hierarchy created by dividing the men, it was believed, would aid in the successful transition of new students while, at the same time, empowering the senior cadets with the leadership opportunities required of an Army officer. In reality, for

The Green Wedding

many of the underlings the "mentoring" methods proved to be little more than downright hazing. Underclassmen were indifferently referred to as "zombies" and "dodos"; the latter a comparison to the flightless, dopey, unconditioned, and, if the upperclassmen had it their way, extinct fowl. If spoken to, the cadet would be expected to "hit a brace"-a position of exaggerated attention with chin tucked, chest puffed out, shoulders pulled back, and thumbs aligned along their pant seems. Even the best of "braces" was routinely met with open disgust from the superior class members who relished the opportunity to criticize, ridicule, or simply manhandle their incompetent pupils, although it was not unheard of for the upperclassmen to apply a combination of all three tactics to ignorant newbies. For the next four weeks, as many remembered, the "zombies" seemed to be in a perpetual position of attention. Deficiencies were remedied by awarding demerits which would be resolved by "walking a tour" while outfitted in their dress uniform and rifle. Without warning, the cadet's afterhours downtime would be interrupted by raids led by the seniors who burst into their bunkrooms, shouting for gas mask drills or "white glove" bunk inspections, all the while attempting to instill as much pandemonium into the scene as possible.

The blur of days and weeks to follow would continue to

challenge the overwhelmed freshmen to complete the strenuous induction process of endless marching, additional aptitude testing, squad drill, marching, small arms familiarization, rifle practice, marching, classroom lectures, formal parades, and, of course, there was more marching. It was the Army, after all, and with that association, the fledglings racked up mile upon mile of brutal, cadence-paced marches. These tramps left the men sweaty, dusty, aggravated, and entirely motivated to do everything in their power to avoid being cut from the flight program and naturally transferred to the infantry.

Pvt. Green (standing, left), Nashville Army Recruitment Center Basketball Squad

Every day, at least two hours were dedicated, whether through volleyball, cross country runs on the "Burma Road," or obstacle courses, to improving the physical fitness of the cadet cadre. They were introduced to "the school of the soldier", which provided the foundations of military structure, etiquette, courtesy, and drill. Further lectures were given, covering the escalating conflicts erupting in the various theaters overseas, but it wasn't the gore and lethality of combat talk that had the most sobering effect on the young men. Struck dumb, partially dismayed, and half-amused, the boys sat in silence as Army personnel stumbled through shockingly graphic sexual hygiene and disease-prevention presentations.

"Off we go into the wild blue yonder..." they sang as they high-timed it in-file to the mess hall. There, perched on the front two inches of their seats, Green and his companions ate "square meals": eyes fixed straightforward while they loaded their forks and lifted the food straight up from their plates before shuttling the chow to their mouths in silent, deliberate, ninety-degree movements. Following their refueling, the platoon double-timed to the classroom for lessons concerning biology, meteorology, Morse code, radio transmissions, first aid, engine mechanics, physics of flight, emergency procedures, and parachute operation. The students also memorized the silhouettes of aircraft and warships, both friend and foe.

Lodwick Aviation Military Academy

At the close of each day, the command staff addressed the squadrons before they dismissed the fatigued ranks for chow. Some evenings the hungry, depleted men were treated to a rousing sermon or patriotic speech from some officer who rambled on about the bastards in the Pacific or Hitler's supermen stomping across Europe. Following a long day of verbal abuse, mental acrobatics, and challenging physical demands, news of Nazi guns rumbling in Eastern Europe was of little consequence to that of the rumbling of the "dodo's" belly.

With four weeks of strict training under the tutelage of the senior class in his belt and with his pecking order greatly improved, Merle and his cohorts assumed the mantle and responsibilities as "upperclassmen". As such, one of the first duties assigned to Cadet Green was to march to the welcome portal with the other seniors to greet the next batch of "zombies". This new hatching of "dodos" were now the ones to be met with the dour instruction to suck in their gut, push their chest out, pull their shoulders back, keep eyes forward, and to "Look proud, Mister, you're in the Air Corps!"

In July, Merle promoted to flight school and traded the mugginess of Alabama for the sunshine and humid sea breezes of Florida. His primary school assignment fell under the direction of Lodwick Aviation Military Academy at Avon Park, Florida. Merle and his fellow cadets were housed in the sizeable three-story Colonial-style resort hotel arranged on a narrow strip of land between two pristine lakes. Known as "the Country Club of the Air", the academy had secured a fleet of fifty biplanes and staged the trainers at the nearby Lakeland Municipal Airport where the students could be easily ferried by bus. Excluding the rare parade up main street where cadets paced in perfect unison under the billowing banners of the school's

Lodwick Aviation Academy PT-17 Stearman trainers, Lakeland Public Library Collection

standards, the academy's relaxed environment was a much-welcome break from the strict military conditions endured up to that point. The local ladies' club commonly threw dances and socials, and the students were allowed off post when their training and classes allowed. Some days the academy unleashed the cadets at the local community swimming pool where the boys practiced treading water, learned life-saving resuscitation procedures, and practiced simulated parachute jumps into the water via a 15-foot-high diving board. In their free time, between games of baseball, tennis matches, and shuffleboard, the fliers enjoyed laying in the grass under the palmettos. Others went swimming or assembled bands of shirtless cadets, commandeered the rowboats that rested along the banks, boarded their crew, and pushed off into the lake where they did battle with other similarly manned vessels. They also roughhoused with the Academy's adopted canine mascot, aptly named "Washout," just as if they were playing with the family dog back home.

Above all else, the cadets were at Avon for one purpose: to learn to fly for Uncle Sam. The academy's civilian flying instructors, many of whom were "old bush pilots", were each assigned six raw trainees and charged with making each man proficient in ground and aerial operation of the aircraft and, with any luck, avoid killing themselves in the process. The first in a long line of objectives for the

BREAKDOWN OF TRIP TIME INTO CLASSIFICATIONS						REMARKS
INSTRUMENT	INSTRUCTION RECEIVE	DAY	NIGHT	DUAL	SOLO	INSTRUCTOR SHOULD ENTER IN THIS COLUMN THE NATURE OF EACH MANEUVER IN WHICH INSTRUCTION IS GIVEN, AND THE TIME SPENT THEREON, AND SHALL ATTEST EACH SUCH ENTRY WITH HIS INITIALS, PILOT CERTIFICATE NUMBER, AND PERTINENT RATING.
	0 44	0 44		0 44		STRAIGHT + LEVEL FLYING CLIMBING TURNS
	0 25	0 25		0 25		90+ 180° TURNS STRAIGHT + LEVEL FLYING.
	0 40	0 40		0 40		TURNS 90+ 180° GLIDING TURNS
	0 37	0 37		0 37		S TURNS, REC. COURSE BANK + SPIN
	0 38	0 38		0 38		FORCED LANDINGS STALLS + SPINS
	0 40	0 40		0 40		SPINS, S's STALLS + COORDINATION EXERCISES
	0 41	0 41		0 41		STALLS, COORDINATION EXERCISES RECTANGULAR COURSE, FORCED LANDINGS
	0 43	0 43		0 43		STALLS, SPINS S's OVER ROAD RECTANGULAR COURSE FORCED LANDINGS
	0 44	0 44		0 44		LANDINGS + TAKE OFFS
	0 43	0 43		0 43		LANDING + TAKE OFFS S's OVER ROAD RECTANGULAR COURSE
	0 50	0 50		0 50		LANDINGS + TAKE OFFS
	7 30	7 30		7 30		ENTER IN THIS COLUMN DETAILS OF ANY SERIOUS DAMAGE TO AIRCRAFT. IF MORE SPACE THAN THAT PROVIDED ABOVE IS NEEDED FOR ANY DETAILS OF FLIGHT INSTRUCTION OR AIRCRAFT DAMAGE, USE PAGES PROVIDED IN BACK OF BOOK.
CARRY TOTALS FORWARD TO TOP OF NEXT PAGE						

Cadet Green's Pilot's Flight Log

students was to familiarize themselves with the contraption they were to fly. Cadet Green felt right at home in the Stearman PT-17 "Kaydet", a fixed-gear, open-tandem-cockpit biplane. The newbies jokingly referred to the aircraft as the "washing machine" as it had a reputation for "washing out" scores of cadets, or the "yellow peril", owing to its brightly decorated exterior. The Army had chosen to paint the wings of most of its Stearmans a not-so-subtle "camouflage yellow", as acquaintances would say, the fuselage a soft blue hue, and the ship's rudder bore red and white stripes. The biplane's gaudy color scheme was the Army's effort to advise, or better yet, warn others that the equipment was a training plane and behind its stick, an amateur. On the contrary, the fliers were convinced that the lively paint job was chosen because it made it easier to find the craft's wreckage amid the swamps and forest.

During the first phase of their training, the instructors accompanied the students on flights, hopping into their cramped seat behind the student to teach their brood the essentials of flight. The fliers had only sixty hours of flying time to become proficient. By the completion of their training, cadets were expected to demonstrate confidence in solo flight, aerial acrobatics, and mitigating various simulated emergencies. "I wish you could come down and watch us fly," Merle wrote to his mother. "We have to do all kinds of maneuvers like stalls, spins, loops, "immelmanns", dives, and almost anything that you can do with an airplane. If we get through this, we should know how to fly with the best of them."

For the Midwestern cropper, Florida provided a thrilling setting to discover by air. The grand oak trees of home were replaced by cypress, citrus groves, and sinister-looking Spanish moss. Brick and panel, common construction materials back home, were traded for white stucco. The flyboy followed meandering rivers that fed stagnant marshlands, stretches where venomous serpents skimmed atop the murky waters and prehistoric-like swamp reptiles lay in wait. At night, these pools released relentless humongous blood-sucking insects that screeched faintly in the dark, searching for a tired, unaware victim who could be tapped for blood. Not too far off to the West, students could explore the Gulf where the waters cloaked the movements of preying U-boats, causing the expanse to be branded by the Germans as "the American shooting gallery". This was the rainy season where the cadets gambled to outrace the incoming storm fronts that would roll in each afternoon, bringing quick and heavy downpours, and then sunshine and humidity. When not deciphering the instruments, Merle continuously scanned the congested airspace in search of reckless amateurs, flights of fighter or bomber formations training for war and, all too often, oblivious buzzards. Instead of skipping over the top of Illinois crop fields, Merle buzzed orange groves and herds of cattle, now to the annoyance of Florida ranchers.

July 18, 1943
Sun. 9pm

Dear Mom,

I just got back to camp. We had open post last night and all day today. It sure was swell to get out and we had a swell time. I got your letter Saturday and was glad to hear from you and thanks for the show money and the ice cream money. Rose and I went to the show this afternoon and then got some ice cream. We said the treat was on you. This week we go to the airport from 9:30 A.M. until 12:30 and have classes in the afternoon. I have 7 hrs. 30 min dual flying time now and 25 landings. One of our upperclassmen cracked up Saturday and really demolished the plane. He overshot the field and tried to take off again, but he hit the fence at the end of the field. The plane went end over end and smashed it to pieces, but he came out with a black eye and a bloody nose. He was knocked out for a few minutes but was alright otherwise. I think it scared us worse than it did him.

While he was, by then, an experienced aviator, two days later, Merle completed his first official "solo" flight in the Army. Following tradition, Green could now wear his flight goggles on top of his head when not in use, signifying that he was no longer a "dodo" as those who had yet to solo continued to wear their goggles around their neck. After leaving his ride behind in the charge of a flight-line girl, he paid a visit to the canteen.

BT-13 Valiant, USAF

Bellied up to the bar, he and the other triumphant aviators sipped on Coke-a-Cola and bottles of chilled milk, a local favorite during summers at Avon Park. Before they could have their fill, comrades tugged Merle and his fellow swaggering soloists away from the smiles of the pretty female clerks posted behind the counter and rushed them to the lake. Struggling in vain, the flailing cadets were hauled by the rambunctious mob down to the end of the dock and then heaved into the waters for the ceremonial dunk in the lake.

Having completed his check-rides and fulfilled all didactic requirements, Merle graduated the academy on the 4th of September 1943 and was allocated to Class 44-A at Greenville Army Flying School in Mississippi. Here, the bi-plane trainers of primary school were replaced by the single-engine, low-wing monoplane, the BT-13 "Vultee

Cadet Green's 'first solo', July 20, 1943

Valiant"; an aircraft with a more powerful engine, retractable landing-flaps, variable pitch-controlled metal propeller, a two-seat enclosed cockpit, and a two-way radio. When Merle deliberately piloted the airplane into one of the hundreds of stalls required of his training, he found the craft would begin shaking violently; a distinctive trait of the aircraft that had earned it the moniker, the "Vultee Vibrator".

During this phase of Basic Flight Training, each student had nine weeks to complete seventy additional hours of flight, most of which focused on developing much-needed formation flying skills.

Greenville Army Airfield
Sept. 7, 1943

Rose,

Remember Sept 7, 1942? Yep, one year ago today I left civilization. I'm not sorry because what happened October 31 would never have happened. Another reason is that it shouldn't be long before I can show the Japs and Germans what a man can do when he really has something to fight for. They are really making us war conscious here. We have lectures from men who have seen action, picture shows and diagrams. For the first time I am realizing how close it really is. I miss you darling[,] more than I can tell you. I hope that I get the chance to make the Japs pay for every moment we are apart. I am taking this work pretty seriously because I am not going to be satisfied with just being able to fly and fight. I want to be able to make them yell, because I am dam[n]ed mad to think those little yellow devils can keep us apart. Another good reason is that I want you and 'Vulture' to sort of be proud of me. I still say that I am going to hand you the world on that silver platter- it may be sort of shot up when I get through.

While occupied with prepping for war and captivated with being able to acquaint himself with the newest air technologies, Merle, in his own playful style, always made sure to keep his wife aware of his fondness for her:

You are always telling me to do what I want to do. Why in the hell don't you tell me what to do? I wish you had never let me join the cadets-but no-you were big and told me to do what I wanted. Darling please don't ever let me do anything that takes me away from you anymore [,] promise?...do you think you could come down before too long? I love you, Rose, and miss you as equally as much. I'd give my right arm to see you tonight.

Neither Merle nor Rose could have predicted how ironic those few lines would become virtually one year later.

With another nine-week stage down, the remaining pool of fliers was dispersed to advanced flying schools. Merle, now an airman first class, received his orders and was disheartened to see that he had not obtained an assignment to any of the single-engine training schools where the Army was molding its ranks of fighter pilots. Instead, whether due to his height, personality, class rank, or, most likely, the needs of the AAF, Green was selected for multi-engine aircraft training: destined to pilot a bomber. Fortunes weren't all lousy as he was to be relocated to the program at Freeman Field in Indiana where his home, his parents, his friends, and his Rose were only a quick train ride away.

Advanced School at Freeman was designed to prepare the fliers for the complexities of controlling multiple power plants and handling larger, more complex aircraft. Many of these future combat fliers would soon be relying on the foundational instruction received at schools like Freeman, notably the talents required to keep their battle-mauled machines airworthy. In some cases, employing these methods would prove to be the difference between the life or death of both their aircraft and the men later to be assigned to their charge. The class pressed on with a furious pace, completing their check flights which included more night flying. As a finale to their training, each student executed a lengthy cross-country tour, requiring them to navigate by map during the day and by a chain of airfield beacons by night.

Following the oath of office on January 7th, 1944, the men, now officially commissioned officers, were turned loose upon their family and the crowd. Glowing mothers spoke softly to their sons through tear-filled eyes and proud

AT-10 Wichita, USAF

fathers extended an approving hand. Spirited youngsters bounced around their uniformed brother or father like an excited, playful puppy, and adoring sweethearts hung around the necks of their handsome suiters. After the ceremony, which was attended by his mother and wife, both of whom appeared presently committed to a truce and reserving the venom that they had for the other for some other time, the Greens promptly returned to Springfield as the Army had awarded the newly-commissioned 2nd lieutenant a few days' leave before he was to report to bomber transition school in Florida.

Lt. Green reported to Hendricks Army Air Field in Sebring, Florida eager to master his new aircraft, the B-17 Flying Fortress. The heavy bomber was enormous compared to some of the aircraft he had

Cadet Merle Green and Rose Marie (Left) with friends

flown during his time at the training schools, and once on the flight deck of the mammoth, the lieutenant found an astounding number of gauges, knobs, switches, levers, dials, throttles, tabs, and buttons. Merle got right to work, as can be seen by the entry in his flight log for January 24th; his first outing in the Flying Fortress. In the hour and fifteen-minute "orientation flight", Lt. Green was treated to a wild ride where the instructor, determined to remove any misgivings of the aircraft's capabilities and dangers, pushed the bomber near its limits, opened the throttles, and even forced the giant into stalls.

In nine weeks, Merle executed over one hundred landings and acquired equally as many flight hours in the Fortress. Tired training B-17s were taken up on flights in pairs and then in small groups where the airmen were rated on their capability to carry out the unique responsibilities demanded not only of a bomber pilot but of an aircraft commander. When not navigating one of the cross-country circuits between Jacksonville, Atlanta, and Miami, Green received additional

Merle D. Green Wins Commission In Army

Merle D. Green, son of Mr. and Mrs. Otto Green, Pleasant Plains, has recently been commissioned a second lieutenant and received his silver pilot wings at graduation ceremonies at Freeman army air field, Seymour, Ind. Lieutenant Green's wife resides in Springfield at 1212 East Brown street.

Lt. Green.

instruction on codes and signals, chemical warfare, naval vessel recognition, and bomb run training. Additional time was dedicated to practicing "blind flying" in the "Link Trainer"; a contraption that look a lot like an over-sized toy. Little did many pilots, including Merle, know how incredibly valuable their training in the funny-looking device would be.

Hendricks' flight program was staffed with combat veterans whose experience was invaluable in readying the new generation of bomber pilots born of the training schools in early 1944. The battle-tested expert instructors worked hard to increase their pupil's confidence, including showing them how to fly the bomber in close formation to produce a much more defensible unit. It was, in essence, teaching the uninitiated the concept of tightly "circling the wagons" in preparation for a gunfight. Cramped necks, exhausted forearms, and the sting from the sweat that rolled into the trainee's eyes during the tense flights were of little concern to the combat aviators who had witnessed lazy formations being picked apart piecemeal by the Luftwaffe firsthand.

While at B-17 transition school, Merle trained at heights up to 18,000 feet but during battle he would be required to pilot the bomber above 25,000 feet; an act made possible, in part, by the innovative addition of the turbo-supercharger. This device was incredibly

Merle, Cullen Goss, and Dale Gold, Drew Field, 1944

beneficial, especially during take-off and emergencies when circumstances called for the engines to operate at full "war power". As the "heavies" beat through the blue, they churned the air into a bumpy, jarring current of vapor producing a ravaging, corkscrewing whirlwind for trailing ships to brave and muscle through. To better appreciate the hazard, trainees practiced deliberately flying in the flow of prop wash-evolutions that could prove to be just as dicey in training as in combat. Crossing into the contrails, the plane slammed around the current, bouncing and vibrating harshly in the turbulent wake produced by the engine exhaust that trailed behind each ship. Amidst the maelstrom, fliers also became accustomed to air vortexes, atmospheric anomalies and the "venturi effect"; the latter encountered when one aircraft displaces the atmosphere around it, causing other nearby planes to be drawn towards it. During these exercises, pilots were exposed to this alarming phenomenon where helpless trainees cranked on their steering yolks, endeavoring to win control of their unresponsive aircraft as it drifted indifferently in the opposite direction. Clearly, bomber operation was a risky business.

Merle Green's USAAF Pilot's Wings

5
MERLE GREEN'S TEAM

April 1944
Third Air Force Training Command
Drew Army Airfield, Tampa, Florida

Shaping nine young men, most of whom were barely out of their adolescence, into a solid fighting unit and requiring them to bunk, eat, train, and prepare for war together created a unique undertaking for the twenty-two-year-old "Prairie State" crop planter-truck driver-turned military aviator. Furthermore, it was one that Merle had to complete in only four months. They came from the plains of the Midwest, New England river-valleys, the Allegheny plateau, the Bayou, the Lake District of the far North, bustling Mid-Atlantic metropolises,

Dixie deltas, and the Ohio-Valley Mountains. Along with the drawls of the southern boys, the Yankees brought entertaining and, at times, unusual accents that were frequently reinforced with obscure slang and colorful vocabulary. Three of the crew's families were recent immigrants to the US, having just dodged Hitler's takeover and the subsequent occupation of their homelands in Eastern Europe. Another gunner had grandparents originating from out of the southwestern region along Germany's Rhine River and still spoke German. A few of the boys were Catholic, a few Protestant. One was Jewish.

Rose and Merle, Tampa, 1944

Excluding black soldiers, who would serve in the US military during the Second World War in segregated units- many with distinction, the team was indeed a sampling of the nation's diversity and featured some of the finest youth America had to offer. Each brought his unique fears, prejudices, vices, technical skills, religious beliefs or lack thereof, physical capabilities, temperament, and personality. They were all strangers and all products of contrasting yet, simultaneously, similar upbringings. Like most Americans at that time, few of the men had ventured further than fifty miles from their childhood home before joining the Army and for a few, the military provided the first opportunity to handle a rifle, nonetheless a .50 caliber heavy machine gun. Moreover, a wide range of educational experiences existed among the fliers. Only a few had spent time at university, while others on the crew were not even a year out of high school. In the service, these airmen, many just teenagers, suddenly had access to tremendous responsibility, incredible technology, and good pay. For the first time in their life, the military experience awarded most servicemen a chance to be free of the rules, expectations, and constraints that their families and communities had expected of them during their youth and adolescence.

For all of their differences, they had assembled at Drew Air

Field, a replacement crew organization center located just outside of Tampa, with more than a few things in common. First and foremost, all had volunteered to fly. None were forced to fill the role and take to the skies where the battlefield was as extreme and intense as any that had ever existed-one that was, next to the occupation of a submariner whose numbers were minuscule in comparison with the Army Air Forces and thus suffering more significant losses proportionally, the most dangerous job in the world. At any time, whether during training in the US or while on the flight line in the moments prior to jumping off into combat, a flier could easily resign his flying status. Despite the opportunity to gracefully bow out, upon the team's assembly at Drew and beyond, the crew was absent any slackers or cowards.

Further commonalities existed amongst the team. They had had all passed the lengthy induction process and medical screening.

They had progressed through the succession of the USAAF's rigorous training courses, earning their wings along the way. Each had been successful in their school of specialty, out of which they emerged among the most highly qualified, best-trained aviators in the world. Not one among them was an automaton, none merely a body to fill a place on a crew. From the machine gunners who instantaneously calculated deflection and adjusted for the ballistics of their projectiles which would vary depending on a dozen minute details; to the bomb droppers who accommodated for factors like air pressure, even the weight and drag coefficient added by the paint that covered their bombs; to

Louis and Jane Lehere, Lehere Collection

the pilots who dueled with wake turbulence, the men, were experts, all. They skillfully operated one of the most innovative, high-performance tools of the era, but the team was essentially a capable, highly skilled, knowledgeable assemblage of youngsters. The final and possibly most significant unifying factor that existed amongst the group was that they were all patriots; each of them took immense pride in being a US airman.

Leaving behind the steel mill and a young wife in Butler, Pennsylvania, Louis Lehere enlisted in the Army Air Forces in 1942 and soon was shuffled through a network of technical schools. He ended up being delegated to the air mechanics program and once completed, moved on to flexible gunnery school. With stints in Texas, Florida, Washington, and Nevada, he was eventually allocated to a bomber crew, posted to the rotating plastic bubble arranged above and behind the cockpit of a Flying Fortress. Not only would he handle the turret's twin machine guns, but "Lou" also possessed an extensive knowledge of the B-17 and all of its systems. As an airborne mechanic-gunner, he could troubleshoot all issues with the aircraft, lay down a blanket of withering fire into the atmosphere above the airplane, and even assist the pilots with their flying tasks making the clever, 23-year-old sergeant an invaluable member of the crew. It didn't hurt that Lou also possessed Hollywood good looks, although, at the time he was the only married man on the team, aside from the plane's commanding officer (CO).

Oddly enough, at the time, a flier of 26 years would be considered old by the standards of his compatriots but Peter Aloysius Riley, charismatic and engaging as any, "pretty much made friends wherever he went". Hailing from Elmira, New York, "Pete" signed up in the fall of '42 and scored high marks in radio exercises, earning him a spot at the Army's radio school at Scott Field, Illinois. A jumble of dot and dash-packed weeks later, Riley was welcomed into the ranks of "the best-damned radio operators in the world", as the school boasted. On top of working the communication systems as a radio operator (RO), he

Peter Riley, Espinoza Collection

brought technical skills in navigation,

aerial gunnery, and photography. Furthermore, Riley was the crew's medical specialist.

George Ostrowski

The grandson of Eastern European immigrants, George Ostrowski had spoken his ancestral tongue of Polish since he was a child. Growing up, he had made a name for himself on football fields and with local hockey teams around Minocqua, Wisconsin. With his honest smile, slicked-back coif, and a stocky, muscular frame- a physique perfect for withstanding the physical demands and punishment in the turbulence and polar-cold at 20,000 feet, George was the epitome of the all-American athlete. In high school he had boxed, played baseball, and was elected homeroom treasurer of his graduating class. In 1943, Ostrowski traded his duties as a store clerk for a US Army heavy machine gun. In the Spring of '44, 22-year-old George was sent to Florida to fill in as a waist gunner for Lt. Green's crew. As the training progressed, he was designated the team's assistant engineer, working on the B-17's systems with Lou Lehere when needed.

In the middle of the aircraft, Paul Klekot was posted just opposite of Ostrowski and handled the left waist gun. Klekot's family had emigrated from Eastern Europe just before the German onslaught in the late '30s and settled in Woonsocket, Rhode Island,

Paul Klekot

a small industrial town where Paul attended high school. Before joining the Army Air Forces, he gained employment as a messenger and machinist at a local textile mill. Like Ostrowski, Paul also completed aerial gunner school before arriving at Drew and once allotted to the team, received further training to place him in the role of assistant radio operator. He was twenty-one years old when he joined up with the group.

Somehow, corporal Sidney Hatfield managed to cram his six-foot frame into the narrow space at the Fortress' tail guns. Perhaps,

when he considered the alternative of being folded tightly into the ball turret only to hang under the belly of the airplane, riding in the tail must not have looked too bad. At 19, Hatfield was let loose from the rolling foothills of Huntington, West Virginia, where his surname raised the eyebrows of many inquisitive sorts who were intrigued about his connection with one of the region's famous feuding families. Sidney joined up in '43 and, after attending basic military training in Kentucky, he was moved to Texas and familiarized on the Army's heavy, flexible machine guns. With little

Sidney Hatfield

more than six months past since his high school graduation, Sidney, also crew armorer, was wielding the "stinger" guns on a Flying Fortress.

The son of a baker, James Gegenheimer grew up alongside the Mississippi River in the tiny, close-knit community of Gretna, Louisiana. The family home had been converted into a bakeshop; "T. Gegenheimer Bakery", where his mother helped bake fruit for their delicious pies in between selling watches, candy, and other goods out of the front of the house. "If my daddy was on the side, everybody who'd pass the bakery shop would say 'hi Mr. Geg'-black, white, whatever nationality. Everybody was friends and that was a good feeling." As most Americans fought to cope with the financial

James Gegenheimer, Gegenheimer

collapse in the late '20s and well into the '30s, Terrance always tried to make sure those in his community would not go without. Habitually, he provided those in need with freshly baked loaves of bread, donated at the family's expense. Thinking back on his father, James would fondly remember that his father "...was a good old soul".

As a kid, James ran along the muddy drainage ditches where cattle crowded for water during the muggy summers. His stomping grounds included Front Street where businesses promoted their goods and services in front windows ranging from shoe sales and legal representation to "Magic Hoodoo Pesticides". Jim and his family had always taken pride in their German ancestry but as they monitored developments in Europe in the 1930s, the Gegenheimers couldn't help but feel alarmed. "We looked on it as, you know, here's a kook by the name of Hitler, how can he get backing of the people to do that the same way as they did in 1918 by Kaiser Wilhelm".

Shortly after his high school promotion, James joined the Army Air Forces. He was sent to Texas for basic training, eventually completing gunnery school in March 1944. Following a short leave, corporal Gegenheimer shipped out once again, this time for crew assembly at Drew. At 18, he was not only the youngest of the group but also the smallest and as such, suffering the fate of other airmen with similar stature, James was selected to man the cramped, precarious position in the ball turret. Lt. Green liked the gunner right away and the two struck up a good friendship. The feeling was mutual for "Geg"; "...I admired Merle as an extremely competent pilot and commander but even more importantly as a best friend."

Jack Williams, Hoy Collection

Twenty-two-year-old 2nd Lt. Jack Williams was the crew's bombardier-the man entrusted with releasing payloads of thousands of pounds of explosives that were destined to obliterate concrete, wood, and steel. Not long before, Jack was running track and dodging tackles on football fields around Wheeling, West Virginia. The Williams family was a part of the congregation of Vance Presbyterian Church and Jack was an active member of the local Fraternal Order of the Eagles, an organization that promoted the Ten Commandments and was rooted in community enhancement and the betterment of his fellow man. Determined to uphold "Liberty, Truth, Justice, and Equality", members went through an initiation process and used secret passwords; rituals akin to the induction process he would receive while at bombardier school at San Angelo Army Air Field, Texas in 1943.

Crew Assembly Training at Drew Air Field. Back Row (L to R): Louis Lehere, Merle Green, Peter Riley, Irving Metzger, Jack Williams. Front row: Sidney Hatfield, James Gegenheimer, George Ostrowski, Paul Klekot

The program aimed at creating "a new type of warrior", requiring candidates to complete coursework in geometry, trigonometry, and theory of flight, but Williams and his classmates received additional instruction in navigation, earning himself a dual rating in both proficiencies. Most importantly, the school introduced the trainees to the Norden bombsight. In the first days after he arrived at San Angelo Airfield, Jack and his peers took the "Bombardier's Oath", swearing to guard the secrets of one of the "country's most priceless military assets" with their lives.

In the training that followed, bombardiers were taught to dismantle and disable the bombsight to prevent the technology from falling into enemy hands. In combat theaters, the sight would be escorted to the bomber clocked and under armed guard. They were advised about the explosive thermite charge installed in the sight's mechanisms which could be set to self-destruct, if necessary. Prior to missions, some bombardiers would also be issued grenades to use, not necessarily against the enemy, but to ruin vital documents and equipment, including the Norden. Many years later, long after the conflict had ended, one 8th Air Force bomb-dropper was asked about the process to render the sight inoperable. The old airman hesitated, still holding to the constraints of his classified pledge that he had taken three-quarters of a century before, and replied vaguely, "Two or three bullet holes in certain areas would destroy the sight."

For a bomb slinger, one of the Army's "sharp-eyed daredevils", even a momentary loss of concentration or the slightest of miscalculations could prove the difference between putting an enemy airfield out of service, destroying a railyard full of supply-laden boxcars, halting the production of fuel and other war material, vaporizing adversaries huddled in their trenches, instantaneously eradicating an entire village of civilians, or blasting apart friendly ground units. Collateral damage, while unfortunate, was accepted as part of the deadly game of war and each man would internalize taking life differently. One bombardier based out of England explained:

> *I couldn't have any personal feelings for civilians, women, and children. As far as I'm concerned, every one of them was a German, an enemy, and I know that they looked at me the same way.*

As a fellow of the Fraternal Order of the Eagles, Jack had pledged to "make human life more desirable by lessening its ills and promoting peace, prosperity, gladness, and hope." Oddly, for Jack, it would seem that the way to accomplish such respectable aims would be by the use of the Norden's sighting devices-one of the most lethal inventions ever imagined. While Lt. Green made it a point to get to know each of his men, to fill the role of an older brother at times or provide counsel like a father figure when needed and still be able to pal-around with each of them, it was the pilot and bombardier that had established a noticeably strong connection and a mutual trust in each other.

Frank Jones, Jones Family Collection

It wasn't until June 1st that the team was assigned their navigator, a Flight Officer (FO) fresh out of San Marcos Navigator School. Frank Jones was the fifth of twelve kids born into one of the original farming families that had settled near Oak Hill, Alabama. As kids, the Jones boys went to war with boll weevils that would invade the family's cotton crops and left their knuckles covered in red welts. Nicknamed "Moon" by his family, young Frank was known to socialize with the girls in town by hurling "mud pies" in their direction. After high school, Frank hitchhiked to William and Mary College for a time but ultimately put his schooling on hold and enlisted in the fall of 1942.

It was said that to be a competent Army Air Force navigator one had to be a master of the past and present. In training, Jones studied star charts, memorized constellations, manipulated charting tools and instruments, worked compass readings, and familiarized himself with navigating by radio signals. To qualify with arguably the most selective of air candidate classifications, Frank accomplished over twenty navigational flights, many with the added stress of performing under the cloak of darkness. Jones was hustled to combat crew assembly in Florida straight out of the intense sixteen-week navigator program. The likable 22-year-old immediately fit in with the team and impressed both the enlisted men and the officers, including the crew's hard-shelled co-pilot.

Irving Metzger, Metzger Family Collection

Sitting at the controls on the right side of the cockpit beside Merle was a former salesman from Union City, New Jersey named Irving Metzger. At 20 years old, Irving was the lone Jewish member of the crew, and like corporal Ostrowski and corporal Klekot, his grandfather had recently abandoned Europe for the US. Before enlisting, Metzger had worked at his father's shoe shop while spending two years in college. When war was declared, his university experience helped him secure a spot in the Army Air Forces cadet candidate program where he planned on, like so many others, commanding his own fighter. Instead of entering into the single-engine program, Metzger was sent to bomber transition school, earning the rating of co-pilot, and selected by the command staff to assume the role of second-in-command of the Green crew. Metzger accepted the appointment less than enthusiastically as playing second fiddle aboard a slow, lumbering bomber was not his ideal assignment.

From the beginning, the men couldn't help but notice the differences that existed between their two pilots. Fresh-faced and standing at five foot five, "Irv" maintained a tough outward demeanor that complimented his stern leadership approach. He expected competence, embraced self-discipline, and, in keeping with military etiquette, frowned on the fraternization between the officers and enlisted men. While sometimes an annoyance for them to suffer, these qualities encouraged the men to, in large part, hone their skills, maintain focus, and ready themselves for the hardships of combat to come. Conversely, Merle was tall and lean, conditioned by a life of strenuous, manual labor and sport. A touch of Lindbergh and bearing a homespun charm and charisma that hinted of "Jimmy" Stewart, his small-town personable manner, laid back country ways, and modest yet self-assured bearing put those under his command at ease.

Outwardly, Merle presented a picture that seemed more suitable for handling his father's farm tractor than a $250,000 aircraft, being comfortable working in his coverall-like flight suit and ditching his "crusher cap" so favored by his contemporaries for a ball cap, fit with an upturned, jockey-like bill. Yet, each time the crew took to the air, Green was all business. His blue eyes flashed with excitement and brandishing his classic, roguish smirk, Merle enthusiastically led the team off to exercise for war. As admiration for their leader grew, the men endeared their bean-pole-framed CO with the nickname "Chief", with Lt. Metzger being referred to, consequently, as "Little Chief".

Standing (L to R): G. Ostrowski, P. Riley, L. Lehere, P. Klekot, Kneeling (L to R): J. Gegenheimer, S. Hatfield

Many years later, Gegenheimer would recall his first impression of the lead pilot:

> *I was immediately impressed, as were the rest of the crew, with his military bearing, his stately good looks, his ability to communicate and his insistence that, while he was the commanding officer, he would respect all of us as long as we all*

*worked as hard as he was willing to work to become a top-notch
B-17 crew. He reached out to us by making it clear that he was
not a fighter pilot who was on his own. From that moment on we
worked hard as a team, we had fun as a team, and we respected
each other as members of that team; 'Merle Green's Team'.*

Lou Lehere had a similar impression, explaining, "We had a
wonderful pilot[,] Second Lieutenant M. D. Green. He was Dandy!...I
had all the faith in the world in him."
Looking back at his time during crew
assembly, Gegenheimer recollected that
"Merle was an excellent pilot" and that
when the landing was as smooth as
glass-a "grease job", there was no doubt
that Green was at the wheel. George
described his commanding lieutenant as
a "nice guy, responsible" and, mirroring
the sentiments of his teammates, "one
of the best of pilots." With Lt. Green at
the helm, the men believed that while
their destiny was uncertain, the
lieutenant would do everything in his
power to see them through the most
trying of odysseys. More than anything
else, with his focused desire to get into

Tampa, 1944

the fight, they knew they would soon have the chance to show what
they were made of. While slightly older than the team's average age of
21, and even though two of his fliers were senior in years, for the rest
of his life, Merle would refer to the crew as "my boys".

The months leading up to the completion of crew training saw
the men fine-tuning their abilities and developing team cohesion. The
schedule was relentless, requiring the boys to complete three morning
flights, three afternoon flights, and a trio of night flights, one per day,
before earning a much-needed day off, only to then repeat the cycle.
The crew conducted so many simulated attacks on Atlanta and
Jacksonville that they grew bored, although the enlisted boys, perched
in the open windows midship, enjoyed the scenery whenever they
passed low over the crowded beaches of Miami and West Palm Beach.
Countless large, evil white circles, simulated bombing targets scattered

around the training zone, met their demise at the hands of Lt. Williams when he let loose his load of sand-filled dummy bombs. While Frank navigated his pilots over gulf waters, the gunners practiced unleashing their .50 caliber machine guns, peppering aerial tow targets and various objects left floating as simulated prey. Naturally, competitions arose among the crew to see who was the best at wielding the Fort's heavy fifties. Even Merle couldn't pass up the opportunity to take part in the contests and was known to, without warning, rise from his chair on the flight deck, manipulate the dazed engineer into the pilot's seat beside Irv and, with a playful grin, set off towards the chuckling gunners.

Rose, Tampa, 1944

As aircraft commander, Merle understood that he was obligated to prepare his men for combat but also for a variety of difficulties. Despite their innocence, their boyish exuberance, and their inclination for the lighter-hearted ways of life, they were together a polished machine. Regardless of how callous the process of preparing for battle was, Merle had grown to love and appreciate his men. Though when all was said and done, as CO and leader of nine promising young lives, Green knew that one day, very soon, he may have to issue an order that could essentially send these young men to their demise.

Rose joined her husband while he was stationed at Drew and while the crew buzzed off on their training flights, she was left to enjoy the warmth of the Florida sun and cool gulf breezes. Having obtained some nursing experience, she gained work at a nearby healthcare facility, but her favored vocation was assuming the role of crew mother. As the CO's wife, Rose wrote to the crew's families, making sure to keep their loved ones informed of their airmen's status. She enjoyed doting on the youngsters and treated each as if they were her own brothers. Some of the most enjoyable experiences for the team were the weekend gatherings at the Green's rented house in the military block. Rose would happily play the charming hostess and "the boys" would take over the couple's living room. Conversations, inevitably, would follow, covering the training for the week, many making sure to remind each other of their goofs and gaffs, and, as empty Coca-Cola and beer bottles manifested about the den, talk would change to the more important matters: their looming deployment, the War, and most significantly, the opposite sex.

During this period, Jim Gegenheimer's lovely girlfriend, Mary Lee, made the trip from Louisiana to visit her airman and meet his brothers-in-war. After presenting her to his companions, Gegenheimer commented to Mary Lee about how he thought the Greens were "the most beautiful couple". Mary Lee countered with,

Klekot Wedding, July 2nd, 1944

"What about us?" "Okay," the perceptive gunner replied, "they are the second-best looking couple, after us."

With only days remaining before their deployment, the gang celebrated the wedding of one of their own. Valerie Novak and Paul Klekot married on July 2nd in the presence of family and the entire crew. Klekot, whose face was permanently plastered with a large love-drunk smile, posed for pictures with his radiant new bride. Much to the embarrassment of the newlyweds, nine troublemakers paced off-camera, gesturing over the photographer's shoulder, and awaiting the sign of completion that, when it finally came, unleashed them upon the bride and groom. The gang managed to compose themselves just long enough for a few crew photographs to be snapped before returning to the celebration that would rage on well into the evening.

Graduation from the Replacement Crew Overseas Training Course on July 15th was bittersweet. Time was running short and although the crew was awarded leave, orders had been issued requiring Green and his men to reassemble back at Drew Field on the 24th. As the men raced off and hopped trains bound for their hometowns with instructions to withhold all details about their travel schedule or destination, it was still unclear where the team would be sent. The leave was brief and culminated in tears, embraces, and pats on the shoulder as ten somber scenes played out at train station platforms, around dinner tables, and on front lawns from the Midwest to New England as the fliers tendered their farewells with their nearest and dearest.

In Pleasant Plains, family and friends of the Green's gathered to see the young lieutenant off. The farewell was as to be expected. Hattie was worried but kept busy entertaining the guests with Zenobia while Bob beamed about his dashing older brother. Thoughtful of his own brother's experience in Western Europe in 1918 and knowing full well what war does to young men, Otto did his best to restrain his anxieties. He knew that, similar to the eternal cycle in his fields, Merle was among the new crop of America's boy soldiers and now it was his turn to be harvested to safeguard freedom. An acquaintance of Merle's that day remembered:

> *He liked to be in the service and wanted to be the best pilot that he could. He wanted to get rid of the Germans 'cause they were doing so much bad. He left for overseas…and then we didn't hear anymore.*

6
ENGLAND AND THE EIGHTH

(L to R) Standing: Louis Lehere, Irving Metzger, Merle Green, Frank Jones, Sidney Hatfield. Kneeling: George Ostrowski, Peter Riley, James Gegenheimer, Paul Klekot

30 July 1944

"The following named crew WP [will proceed] by air in the aircraft as indicated below at the proper time from Hunter Field, Savannah, Georgia, via North Atlantic Route to the European Theater of Operations, London, England, reporting upon arrival therat, to the commander, 8th Air Force Service Command, Air Transport Command Terminals of Arrival, British Isles, for further assignment and duty with the 8th Air Force."

2nd Lt.	Green, Merle D.	(Pilot)
2nd Lt.	Metzger, Irving	(Co-Pilot)
F/O	Jones, Frank M.	(Navigator)
2nd Lt.	Williams, Jack O.	(Bombardier)
Sgt.	Riley, Peter A.	(Radio Op.)
Cpl.	Lehere, Louis E.	(Engineer)
Cpl.	Gegenheimer, James N.	(Ball Turret Gunner)
Cpl.	Hatfield, Sidney I.	(Tail Gunner)
Cpl.	Klekot, Paul	(Waist Gunner)
Cpl.	Ostrowski, George	(Waist Gunner)

From the embarkation point of Hunter Air Field, Georgia, Lt. Green, now piloting a factory-new B-17, steered north and began bounding along the network of airfields that sat spread along the eastern seaboard of the United States. All had gone according to plan but as the Fortress coasted closer to Goose Bay, Labrador, the Green gaggle found themselves socked in and flying blind through an unexpected storm front. Frank Jones had tried his best to keep on the projected flight path but soon found that despite his best efforts, and even with the assistance of Pete Riley who sat monitoring the wireless transmissions and radio beacons, the crew was unable to confirm their location. With the looming possibility of being blown off course deep into the desolate Canadian wilderness, Merle called back over the intercom system for Pete to extend the plane's copper trailing wire antenna in hopes of boosting signal reception. Meanwhile, Jim Gegenheimer was relaxing in the radio room, slumped up against the transmission box, and observing Riley as he worked. "I was just resting in the radio room, sitting behind the radioman, sitting with my back to the wall and there was a wooden floor there," Jim reported. "All of a sudden, we got hit by lightning". Finding himself with a literal fire lit under his posterior, Geg shot to his feet and began "jumping up and down" as red-hot embers rained about the cabin leaving both himself and the radio operator singed and flustered. Thankfully, the remainder of the flight to Labrador turned out to be uneventful. Upon landing at Goose Bay, however, electrical damage to the generators caused the crew to sit idle for the next few days as the base mechanics performed a complete overhaul of the new Fortress' wiring system.

Following their stay at Goose Bay, the "big push" over the next leg of their migration to war was to be a long and tedious flight. To forgo a stopover in Greenland for fuel, extra gas tanks had been fixed in the B-17's bomb bay, dramatically increasing the bomber's range. After cruising approximately 1,535 miles over open water, the weary bunch landed in Iceland and took pause for two days until, windswept and chilled, they pressed on for the USAAF Ferry Terminal at Valley, Wales. It was August 7th.

At Valley, the Boeing was taxied to the staging area where the officers and men dropped out of the bomber and into the dreary, wet English climate. While the others made a beeline to the barracks to stow their kits and bags before heading out in search of hot chow, Green, holding a ticket to over a quarter-million dollars in US government funds and with instructions to relinquish the bomber to Valley operations, hunted down officials to pawn off the pricey responsibility. Though, disappointed by the loss of the glistening, brand-new Boeing- excluding the refurbished electrical system of course, the crew's griping wouldn't last long as the team and dozens of other new arrivals were shipped to the 11th Combat Crew Replacement Center (CCRC) at Bovingdon, England.

The CCRC had been established as a "finishing school for combat" and indoctrinated US airmen to military practices and life in the English warzone. The facility was embedded along "buzz bomb alley", as the pulsating robotic drone of V-1 rockets were frequently heard as they zoomed past. At Bovingdon, training staff revisited fundamentals with the latest assortment of inexperienced replacement crews including high-altitude hazards, hypoxia warning signs, and oxygen system troubleshooting. The men were directed to report to the flight surgeon in the event of coming down with a cold or respiratory infection as flying at altitude when sick could result in painful headaches or ruptured eardrums. Even the importance of shaving was underscored as combat fliers had found extended mask usage greatly irritated unshaven skin.

Victory ("V-Mail")

One seminar that did capture interests was a presentation conducted by recovered and returned downed Allied fliers. As the former evadees described being shot down over hostile lands, surviving crash landings or precarious parachute jumps, as well as their calculated, odyssey-esque trek from behind enemy lines, the intrigued newbies absorbed the details in silence. Conversely, intelligence officers had to fight to keep the men awake during one lecture that covered the rights and expectations allotted to prisoners of war.

With the War now seeming to be creeping towards the beginning of the end, many airmen found that the safest option before them was, if capture was inevitable, to turn themselves into a German in a green uniform-the *Wehrmacht*, or, better yet, a blue outfit-the Luftwaffe, and wait out the conflict behind barbed wire. They were to avoid surrendering at all costs to anyone in a black uniform-the garb of the *"Schutzstaffel"*, the "SS"; an organization known for their barbarism against Allied prisoners. The men were even cautioned about making contact with German civilians as surrendering to angry farmers or bomb-blasted villagers came with its own risks. What was certain was that if they were captured without identification tags, airmen could be detained, imprisoned, forced to suffer interrogation that may utilize harsh physical encouragement, or simply shot; the latter a consequence of being a "spy". While US air personnel were expected to act in accordance with the Geneva Convention's guidelines related to internees and directed to respect the military rank and structure of their adversary, 8th AAF command made it clear that it was expected that every man captured had a duty to try and escape. Suffering from the naiveite of untested youth and betting on their self-assured belief in their immortality, most novice crusaders passing through CCRCs were primarily unimpressed by such lectures. The indestructible bunch were dismissed with the understanding that, if captured, "name, rank and serial number" would be all that they were required, and expected, to concede to the enemy.

The amateurs were shown recent Allied target strikes and sat for classes on RAF rescue processes including cold-water survival techniques to be used in the event of ditching and having to tread the chilly, lethal, unforgiving North Sea waters where countless downed combat teams had perished in only a matter of minutes. Two full days of indoctrination training were devoted to examining the history of the Luftwaffe and the progression of the opposition's tactics and strategy. Also covered was the evolution of the enemy's defense systems; mainly lectures focused on "flak"; German anti-aircraft fire, smoke screens, and radar. Unlike confrontations with enemy fighters, US bomber boys felt nearly powerless at guarding against German anti-aircraft fire. Unaware of the exact figures at the time, when Merle and his band sat in attendance at Bovingdon that fall of '44, 8th AAF flak-related casualties were on the rise and would, in fact, spike during that month of August.

To assist in their transition to live amongst the English; a resilient people who referred to the Yankee buildup that would see nearly three million pass through their country during the War as the "friendly invasion", the Americans were given pamphlets detailing how to conduct themselves while in their host country. English phrases, sports, automobiles, history, religion, customs, coffee, and, of course, women and beer were covered to help smooth interactions and public relations between the two nations who were considered cousins-in-culture. The English considered the "Yanks" boisterous, brash yet polite, lacking in social etiquette, and generally "overpaid, oversexed and over here", as the popularized saying went. In response, the Americans declared that their hosts were simply "underpaid, undersexed, and under Eisenhower."

While at the replacement center, Lt. Green received the following letter, condensed into the typical shrunken "V-Mail" ("Victory Mail") template:

August 16th '44

Hello Sweet. I have you again. For all of your big business you tell me you miss me and love me. That I go for. You sound very busy and excited. That news about your missions and our anniversary is heavenly. But my darling, I pray that by then it will be over and that I can keep you for always and not just a leave. For I'm afraid you'll have to accomplish all that I know you will in this trip over there because the next one you will have company. How is your bombardier smelling these days? Do please be careful. Member our Hail Mary! Thanks for wanting me around still.

All my love,
Rose

After a week at Bovingdon, as the four officers were ushered off for additional instruction, the gunners were shuffled to "the Wash", located near King's Lynn on the chilly, damp, gusty East coast of England. The purpose was to give the men additional gunnery practice, but one 8th Air Force airmen who passed through the site recalled that "the Wash"…

… was generally a dangerous place to be, because a bunch of undisciplined youngsters, with no supervision, will act like

hoodlums. And there was no disciplinary force in the crew tent area. No base personnel ever penetrated there as far as I know. I don't blame them.

During the Second World War, the US Army qualified vast numbers of aerial gunners from a handful of specialized training schools in Nevada, Arizona, Texas, and Florida. Some of those 200,000 candidates had mustered at enlistment centers after viewing the Army's successful recruitment film featuring one of Hollywood's leading men, Clark Gable, and his exploits as an aerial gunner in the 8th during 1943. The flexible gunnery curriculum was hectic and over six weeks the airmen advanced from wielding pellet guns to shooting skeet with shotguns from the back of moving jeeps. They learned how to determine range, memorized dozens of aircraft silhouettes, studied the effects of flight on bullet trajectory, troubleshot equipment malfunctions, and familiarized themselves with turret operations. Students sat behind camera-linked dummy guns at training device stations and tracked projections of "enemy" aircraft as they passed by

(L to R) Standing: Ostrowski, Hatfield, Gegenheimer, Riley.
Kneeling: Klekot, Lehere

on a series of screens. A rudimentary precursor of present-day virtual reality and immersion training, the set-up allowed the students to practice tracking and firing on moving targets, honing the skills necessary to beat off any challenger's aerial advances.

The mainstay defensive weapon systems deployed on the "heavies" during the War was the .50 caliber heavy machine gun. Virgin

fliers were not only reminded of the importance of governing their bursts to prevent burning out and warping the barrels-a skill rooted in regulating both their emotions and the number of rounds sent downrange, but they were also cautioned about the possibility of their weapons freezing up in the extreme cold of the troposphere. The shooters were also informed that their weapons, while capable of reaching longer ranges, were most accurate and effective at distances less than six hundred yards. Their projectiles, they were told, could punch through anything that the enemy defenders could throw up at them, an

Jack Williams, Hoy Collection

assertion that was discovered to be only partially accurate, as when face-to-face with the Luftwaffe, many gunners would watch their rounds bounce harmlessly off the armor-reinforced engine cowlings and steel-plated bellies of the attackers.

Between range time, the gunners practiced fieldstripping and reassembling the weapons for time. Then, they rehearsed the process while blindfolded. Before qualifying for flight status and being endowed with the much-fancied combat aircrew badge, students certified by hopping into the open gun station in the back of a training aircraft and were swiftly buzzed up to altitude. There they would let loose bursts from their machine guns upon harmless tow targets, pulled by defenseless machines manned with apathetic, newly-minted 2nd lieutenants in the dry air and tranquil skies above the barren ranges of the American "Old West".

Now, at "the Wash", the gunners practiced firing their fifties at targets set in the bay from shoreline revetments. One youthful American gunner who had been transferred to the site to ready for battle reminisced that "…what we were hitting out there was whales and porpoises." As the bored, aspiring warriors soon grew tired with the business, they busied themselves by finding impromptu targets to test their .45 caliber pistols. As an additional precaution, before shipping off to combat, many airmen were issued a handgun, carried in shoulder harnesses, and awarding them the look of what one USAAF flier described as "Chicago gangsters". Despite the added firepower, a considerable number of downed airmen would hastily discard their sidearms-if they even brought them along on missions at all, in the harrowing moments leading up to their capture so as to not add to the chaos of their detainment by jumpy or vengeful German soldiers.

Upon retiring to their tents at day's end while at "the Wash", more than one gunner used his allotment of ammunition for much livelier purposes. Mischievous gunners were known to set rounds on the face of red-hot stovetops and while the shells rapidly heated toward their ignition point, pandemonium ensued as a stampede of giggling youngsters made a profanity-packed mad dash to clear the shelter before the round popped off and zipped through the air. The tomfoolery was not to be contained to the grounds of the facility though. More than once, a neighboring English farmer was reimbursed by the US Government for the loss of a sheep or pig, although the perpetrators were never caught. Coincidentally, some "Wash" alumni reported tolerating the dreary squalls rushing from off the sea by enjoying the occasional impromptu feast of barbeque pork.

Meanwhile, back at Bovingdon, Lieutenants Green, Metzger, Williams, and F/O Jones were being familiarized with the 8th's operating procedures. As their training finally wrapped up and they sat anticipating assignment to their home airfield, the officers enthusiastically took advantage of a pass for leave and set out to explore the peculiar and fascinating war-beaten land. London of August 1944 presented many fascinating sights and sounds to the small-town Americans. Pairing up, Jack and Merle visited all the famous locations they had read about in their textbooks in school: the 900-year-old Tower of London, the Thames River, Buckingham Palace, Trafalgar Square, Big Ben, and Westminster Alley. Knowing that his wife would appreciate hearing of his excursion to St. Paul's Cathedral, Merle studied the enormous dome which still stood firm and, miraculously, intact above the roofs of the battered capital. By day, Piccadilly Circus was a bustling hub filled with liveliness and color but overrun each evening by the legendary female commandoes; "ladies of the night" who bore the district's name. The "tube", which had shielded Londoners through "the Blitz", provided easy access around the city and eager taxicab drivers offered exceptional and inexpensive tours of the ancient metropolis and its endless dazzling, historic sites. The pubs were plentiful but so were the "GIs"; the American soldiers and airmen who flooded the establishments, drinking the taps dry and, most times, vastly outnumbering the women.

Though stunning, great sections of the city had been wrecked, first by aerial bombings that began nearly four years before, and more recently, by the first of the Nazi's vengeance weapons. A blackout was still in effect, windows were reinforced and boarded up, and most of the buildings were encased in walls of stacked sandbags. Having had their fill of the scene, Jack and Merle shored up in one of the many Red Cross (RC) Clubs that had blossomed throughout the great urban labyrinth. These establishments offered facilities, recreational activities, beds, and a base of operation for the never-ending flow of US servicemen who visited the capital during the War. However, some of the most invaluable services that the men found available at the RC Clubs were a good cup of coffee, warm doughnuts, and a little slice of home: an all-American hamburger and a Coca-Cola.

August 27th.

Dear Rose,

Jack and I went to London with Mowers the other night. He is a member of the '400 Club', which is one of the nicest places in town, and also is in the club that used to be the hangout of the famous 'Eagle Squadron'. Jack and I are going to join it the next time we go back to town...

Notwithstanding his exciting explorations, it was all too apparent to Rose that her impatient partner was itching to get into the War. Merle sent another note home to Rose. In it, the pilot vented to his wife that he and another friend from advanced pilot training in the US, Cullen Goss, had been split up when he was "shipped out".

"About this action," she penned her husband, "take it easy Bub, you'll get around, you always have."

Unknown to Lt. Green, orders were being drafted at that moment that would grant him his wish. When he returned to Bovingdon, Merle dashed to the assignment board and skimmed over the postings in search of the crew's designation number. Then he saw it: "Crew AE-35: US Air Station #468." He and his crew were to assemble immediately for assignment to the 410th Bombardment Squadron of the 94th Heavy Bombardment Group.

7
KING EDMUND AND THE WOLF

20 November, 869 AD
Haegelisdun Wood, East Anglia

Edmund, King of East Anglia, had been defeated in battle by an army of invading Danes and upon being captured, he was led to the Haegelisdun Woods and bound to a tree. After attempts had failed to coerce Edmund into denouncing Christianity, Danish archers loosed their flight of missiles at the King, riddling his body with arrows. The invaders continued their conquest but not before severing the King's head and casting it deep into the forest. As the story goes, followers were unable to recover Edmund's head until they were alerted by a wolf that had been standing guard over the slain King's crown. Once reunited, the skeleton was taken to the village of Beodericsworth and buried. Edmund was later canonized as the original Patron Saint of England, while his shrine became a pilgrimage site for faithful souls from all over Europe. Centuries after his death, a stone abbey was erected at the village that would later be renamed, "Bury Saint Edmunds".

In the early 1940s, cement and steel began replacing broad swaths of East Anglian farmland as military installations sprouted up amongst ancient structures and picturesque hamlets. This included "Bury" where, seventy miles northeast of London, Flying Fortresses of the 94th Bombardment Group (BG) buzzed over the village's cottages, manors, hedgerows, pastures, stone wall-lined lanes, and Norman-esque cathedral tower as they headed off to war. A former RAF aerodrome, the footprint sat on nearly eight square miles of stunning forestland and farm fields between the communities of "Bury" and "a little wide place in the road", named Rougham. The 94th, later to be one of the crack outfits of the 4th Combat Bombardment Wing of the 3rd Air Division, had assumed control of "Rougham Field",

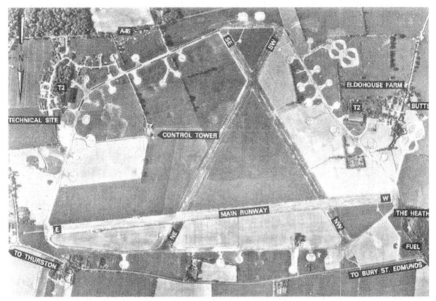

USAAF Station #468

designated US Air Station #468, in June 1943 and by the fall of '44, the Group was acting under the command of Colonel Charles Dougher. Enclosed by over three miles of perimeter track, the main runway cut a 6,000-foot long, 150-foot-wide swath through the center of the complex. Two shorter strips transected the main runway and, together, formed a large "A". A two-story, box-like control tower, designated "Chairleg", orchestrated the flow of the Group's "heavies", organized into four squadrons: the 331st, 332nd, 333rd, and 410th.

When not directing their tonnage on the Nazis, the B-17s could be found loitering on the fifty concrete hardstands that budded along the perimeter track. There, the bombers were tended to by teams of masterful mechanics and support personnel but for those planes needing more specialized attention, a pair of enormous maintenance hangers squatted at the field, able to shelter three of the fleet's tired and battered birds simultaneously. The Group's Fortress were fed their iron-encased bombs by armorers who ferried the explosives from revetments at each squadron's bomb dumps, which were staged well away from the flight line and adorned with camouflage netting. The site had a post office, a military police outfit, fire apparatus, an ambulance unit, an RC organization, a chapel, recreational facilities, engineering shops, petrol dumps, a mess hall and cookhouse, a PX, a quartet of Headquarter buildings and an operations block, all of which were dispersed amongst a sprinkling of technical tents and shanty huts. Within this small city existed an army of 8th AAF electricians, photographic personnel, fuse setters, weathermen, intelligence officers, truck drivers, Women's Army Corps personnel, record keepers, medics, Red Cross girls, and sheet metal workers, as well as British civilian contractors; all just a sampling of the myriad of support organizations and staff that buoyed the flight crews and made the combat endeavors possible. The 94th's unifying sense of duty was clearly stated in their adopted unit motto, "Results Count".

Huddled among beautiful ancient groves and thickets, the combat men bunked in Nissen huts. These crude, half-cylinder, prefabricated, corrugated aluminum shelters rested atop bare concrete slabs and were bricked up at both ends, one of which framed a door. Each shack bore a unique name like "Lacka Nookie Lodge", "12 Mad Sergeants", "Swoon In", "Scrubbed Mission Manor", "Hangover Heaven", "Flak Home", and "The Busted Onion-Come in and Weep". Beside the entrance, two small windows had been engineered but were concealed behind thick blackout curtains, hung there in place to stifle out all interior light. The dwellings leaked when it rained, trapped in the stale heat during the summer, and only partially shielded its occupants from the frigid Suffolk winters. To keep the chill away, the men would gather around the hut's small iron stove and burn their meager, rationed allotment of coke. Each hut typically housed two crews, as well as all the odors that come with dirty laundry, stale bedding, sweat, gasoline, and other aromatic masculine scents. From the arced interior walls, uniforms hung above scratchy wool blankets, each concealing lumpy mattresses set on metal-framed bunks, arranged in two rows, one on each side of the hut. Festering in the corners and permeating from beneath the cots, lay ripe piles of unwashed clothing. Letters from loved ones, sweethearts, and admirers lay on the bunks and salvaged ammunition boxes or shipping containers, repurposed as makeshift side stands. Then there were the pin-ups; colorful posters depicting patriotic, albeit, scantily clad damsels, many of whom were painted to appear more determined to sock a punch to Hitler then they were to locate their misplaced undergarments. Copies of the US Armed Forces' newspaper, *Stars and Stripes*, lay open on tables, relaying news from the home front and reporting on the War's progress, although most readers went straight for the sports or comics section.

Floating in the background, the chatter of British Broadcasting Channel (BBC) radio programs and the blaring newscasts of the Armed Forces Network intertwined with the serenades of Sinatra, Miller's jazz, and Crosby's baritone. On rare occasion, the voice of "Lord Haw-Haw" filled a corner of the hut where the men chuckled disconcertedly over the projections that the German propagandist customarily forecasted. However, the most notable nemesis of the airwaves, undisputedly, was "Axis Sally". The Nazi villainess' broadcasts were hauntingly provocative to the airmen, being composed of a mixture of the most popular tunes of the day-virtually all American artists, and truly startling insights into the men's day-to-day activities. Poignantly, many of the musicians and singers featured were talented Black jazz musicians, all of whom were considered "degenerate", per Hitler, and declared "verboten". "We used to listen to her almost every morning as we were getting ready to board the aircraft for the flight," reminisced one young Rougham flier. The most discomforting moments came when she would welcome fresh aircrews by name or confirm the crew's target for that day's mission-particulars that most of the non-coms were not even privy to even after their briefings. "They knew when we were going, what our target was, and when we were supposed to reach it", detailed the airman. "We weren't supposed to listen, but she'd say, 'Hello, Joe. No need to worry today. Your girlfriend is dating this guy', and all that junk."

Plank walkways linked the huts with one another but proved only somewhat effective in keeping the men out of the muddy soup that seemed to dominate the landscape most of the year. While each squadron had its own latrine and set of showers, the distance between the living quarters and facilities proved quite the hike, especially to worn-out airmen who, when they did make the venture, found that the water was seldom warm. Just outside of the huts, the crews staged their fleet of bicycles. Airmen posted to the site could purchase a bicycle at a shop in town but, on occasion, one could be obtained by winning the pot at a card game. Whatever the method, having a bicycle proved to be essential for getting around the base, not to mention for ventures around the countryside. A jeep could be obtained at the motor pool if fliers had the time, and many used their wheels to set off for "Bury", Rougham, or any of the dozens of nearby lovely hamlets. Needless to say, the stock was in high demand as scores of off-duty GIs looked for any chance to break free of the installation and galivant around the English landscape. The predicament had led those who had negotiated a vehicle from the transportation sergeant to find their ride covered with a swarm of thirsty, lonely, and adventurous associates bound for town. In August '44, after many complaints had reached Group

Landing approach, Fold3

command concerning the men's driving habits, the Colonel issued strict orders to cut out any horseplay. The directive was only a temporary deterrent and mostly fell on deaf ears as joyriding American boys were still seen clinging to the outside of speeding jeeps as they raced down the narrow stone fence-lined lanes, dodging horse carts and startled pedestrians along the way.

In the fall, the men formed softball teams and battled it out in their own World Series competition. They also improved an area next to the administrative huts and held tryouts for "Dougher's Eagles", the 94th's formidable football crew. For those who wanted to spend their downtime pursuing other hobbies, the men could attend foreign language classes, view one of the latest films at the movie theater, pay a visit to the skeet range, or lounge at the Aero Club. In the communal building, the men were free to study the gigantic operations map that was plastered on the wall, kept current by the Group's intelligence staff. Most, however, chose to avoid any hint of the War during their downtime, if even possible, deciding instead to unwind with a game of billiards or by skimming through magazines or losing themselves in a novel pulled from the Station's extensive library. Others sat reclined in easy chairs and were treated to the classical works of Bach and Beethoven- ironically both German composers.

B-17s of the 94th BG in action over Fortress Europe, Fold3

Resting among meadows and cottages, the tails of some of the 94th's bombers, each adorned with a black "A" set inside a white square-hence the unit's "Square-A" moniker, towered out over country lanes creating an enticing temptation for the local youngsters. Most of the time, the base's military police shooed off the children before they could infiltrate too far past the perimeter of the installation's barb-wire fence line, but other, more determined lads managed to evade the security personnel. The game of cat and mouse was alluring as the Americans were keen to buy up apples, plums, and various other fruit from the sprats. Frequently, the sergeants doled out treats to the children who returned to their homes with their spoils of chewing gum and candy, chocolate for their mothers, and American cigarettes for their fathers. Regular interactions with ground personnel prompted some crews to adopt the curious schoolboys as was the case for one adventuresome local, Clifford Hall. The Bury boy became so well-liked by a ground crew from the 332nd that the men invited him up into the bombers to sit alongside them in the co-pilot's seat while they worked through instrument checkoffs. As time went on, Hall found himself first airborne with the Americans, gliding over his neighbors' hayfields and neighboring villages during maintenance test flights. Afterwards he joined the airmen for meals in the mess hall. While Hall preferred his mother's cooking over the Army-issued fare, he and other Bury kids cherished the friendships they had developed with the young American lads: their surrogate brothers.

At first, the townspeople had been put off by the raucous, swaggering Americans who piloted the giant war machines that roared low over their heads, "...shaking everything in the area...", drying up their cow's milk and scaring the eggs out of the hens. "They frightened the life out of everyone," remembered Hall. Despite the intrusion, locals quickly found a genuine love and respect for the Rougham boys, youngsters who had come to fight off the Hun advance and pound the "Krauts" back into their den. They invited them to their homes for supper, serviced their uniforms, and rented out rooms to airmen on liberty. Some even lent out their horses for the more equestrian-able men to tramp around the countryside. When the Americans visited Bury, they frequented establishments like the King's Head, the White Lion, the Nutshell, and Ma Café. After nearly drinking the pubs out of business, the men settled their bill, bid goodnight to the kind barkeeper, and then wobbled outside where they attempted to mount their bicycles for an interesting and highly comical trek back to the aerodrome. Several well-oiled 94th fliers would later tell of being molested by Bury's briar bushes upon their tipsy return to Station #468 along the seemingly uneven lanes outside of the village during many a-lively late night. So many men had been injured on bicycles that Rougham fliers joked that the apparatus was actually "Hitler's secret weapon". Having observed German bombers passing overhead on their way to blitz Liverpool or London earlier in the War, by the fall of 1944, locals were used to seeing the airspace above East Anglia heavily saturated with US airships, all heading off to hammer target Germany.

They took comfort in the sight and knew that those bellowing monsters that bore the big "Square A" were from their airfield, and inside, manning the massive crafts, were their beloved Rougham boys.

Having survived "the Wash", Paul, Lou, Pete, Jim, George, and Sid were jounced along the ruts of Suffolk backroads in lorries bound for Station #468 while the officers arrived in Bury St. Edmund by rail. Merle Green's team was one of the two new replacement units selected for the 94th BG on August 29th, 1944. These untried fliers were undoubtably a new generation of combat men. The airmen who had been shredded in the fall of 1943 above Regensburg only to limp on to seek harbor at airbases in North Africa, those who earned the Group Presidential Unit Citations: first for destroying the aircraft factory at Marienburg in '43 and then again for their bravery over Brunswick the following winter, the fliers who sweated it out over Berlin during the first attacks on the Nazi capital, the kids who were battered during "Big Week", the stalwarts who went toe to toe with the best of the Luftwaffe in Spring skirmishes, the ones who helped blow open the Normandy coastal defenses-most of those fliers were all gone now after completing their tours or having been lost in combat. It wasn't until the late summer of 1944 that the number of downed and missing aircraft and, in turn, fallen aircrews, saw a noticeable decrease. Although flak was becoming more of a lethal threat and rumors of Nazi jets abounded, the men's spirits were improving considerably. Allied ground forces were pushing hard at the Axis Powers on the continent, opening, at last, a second front in Northern Europe. The advance also created opportunities for stricken bomber crews to seek refuge at a series of friendly landing fields, recaptured and scattered across France. Even the ordinarily touchy Northern European weather was proving uncharacteristically agreeable. Notwithstanding the turnover, the 94th was packed full of expert combat men. Along with the veterans who did remain, the raw additions began to believe that the worst of the air war might indeed be over. It appeared as though the Green crew had arrived at Rougham at the perfect time.

Two days before Merle's arrival, the 94th had flown its 200th mission: a deadly jaunt to Berlin. The combat fliers had returned to Rougham that afternoon following a nightmarish, near-fatal encounter. Not one Fort had expelled its payload as clouds, not fighters, had prevented the entire Division from reaching their objective. Nearing the target, visibility was so dismal that, as one sweating crewman recalled:

> *We couldn't see, at times, our outside wings, beyond number one and number four engines. That's how thick the clouds were, and you combine that with the heavy flak that they were sending up, and you've got a very ticklish situation.*

Knowing that other bombers, completely hidden in the cloudbank, were bobbing and sliding around just feet from their wingtips only compounded the precariousness of the undertaking. Finally, the formation "started to come out of it...and there were planes all over the sky," recalled Morton Kimmel who, on that day, jerked along in his Fortress, *Dorothy V*. The bedlam was incredible, and many, like Lt. Kimmel, would echo that the experience, not fighters or flak, was "the most frightening thing I have ever been through."

94th BG and 'flak over Munster', 1943, Fold3

Although the crews were disappointed that they were unable to liberate their bombs on the heart of "Hitlerland", the ground teams and armorers were equally as letdown when they discovered the birds were still saddled with their iron eggs upon their return. Many of them had scribbled personalized messages to "Der Fuhrer" and his cronies in chalk on the sides of the bomb casings just before they raised the load up into the bellies of the ships earlier that morning. All letdown was soon to be overshadowed as, in commemoration of the 200th mission milestone, an extravagant celebration was slated for the 15th of September, just two weeks away. The organization and preparation that followed was nothing less than extraordinary. The logistical coordination displayed by the men of the 94th in organizing the event was astonishing and conducted with the same precision and thoroughness that was devoted to launching an operation into enemy territory. In a show of gratitude, headquarters had secured the popular songstress Dinah Shore and Glen Miller's band as entertainment for the evening. The plan was for the party to be held inside the cavernous expanse of hanger #1, where steak would be on the night's ticket and, if that weren't enough, beer would flow freely. Most vital to this mission, buses were to be reserved- commandeered if necessary, to ensure the shuttling of what would turn out to be a crowd of over seven hundred English girls from Bury and neighboring villages. Along with locals and friends, General Doolittle himself would attend the gala and pay tribute to the unit which had been instrumental in the war effort with their spirited "contribution to the Allied cause." "It was unreal," recalled a flier in attendance that night. "What a time we had!" Harsh weather would scrub the mission scheduled for the 14th of September, the day before the celebration, but it was beer, dancing, and English lasses that happily put the 94th out of action the day following the festivities.

At Rougham, Green and his crew were attached to the 410th Squadron, introduced to the command staff, advised of their schedule for the days to follow, and issued additional flight gear. Upon being led off to their quarters in the 410th's area, the crew weaved past a sign displaying a charging black Pegasus hitched with a salvo of bombs- the squadron's battle insignia. Frank, Jack, Irv, and Merle were steered to the officer's huts where they introduced themselves to their roommates: Basil Pullar and his fellow raiders. The non-coms found bunks that they too shared with other men from the squadron, but apart from learning that they were fresh "flak bait", the newbies were mostly ignored by the veterans, as was custom. As they unpacked their kits and began organizing their racks, they discretely eyed the war-worn combat men who kept their distance and doubted that these rookies recognized that each of the empty bunks that they were now filling signified the departure of a good companion, a dependable colleague, or a fallen brother.

Before being authorized to fly in combat as a crew, each man on Lt. Green's team would be attending ground school; more dull classes that lasted up to ten hours each day. Once signed off by the training staff, the ten airmen would be individually assigned to a spot on an experienced crew's aircraft where each man would fly their first combat missions under the mentorship of tried experts. The Group had mastered close-formation flying and Merle and Irv would have to demonstrate their proficiency to their Squadron training officers. 94th

Basil Pullar (kneeling left) and crew, Anderson Collection

legend William Cely frustratingly expressed the feeling he had upon his initial arrival to the unit nearly a year before: "We had to learn to fly all over again...". Cely would go on to complete a full combat tour loaded with exhilarating, and sometimes nearly unbelievable, adventures. This included the time he piloted his steel-peppered *Frenesi* through German flak fields and back, all the while suffering strafing runs and rocket volleys by enemy fighters who had managed to shoot off his plane's tail turret, dislodge an engine, and punch multiple gaping holes through the aluminum shell of his aircraft. Despite being separated from the Group and piloting a lame airship, Cely managed to get back to his home field with "the most battle-damaged plane ever at Rougham". The performance not only amazed "the brass," but the tale also captivated reporters and journalists from London to the US, Stars and Stripes and Time Magazine. Even "Axis Sally" made mention of the incident, taunting Cely and his crew that they would not be so lucky the next time.

On August 30th, the men of crew #35 scarfed down a breakfast of powdered eggs, toast, and coffee before gathering around "Chairleg" to watch the incredible spectacle of the bomber force coming to life. It was an impressive demonstration, commencing with the ignition of more than one hundred and thirty-two engines that whined, belched, and coughed to life. The earth trembled as the soul-clenching pulsation of the force's heartbeat enveloped the field, penetrating all who were in witness. Roused from their hibernation, the "heavies" plodded onto and then along the perimeter track, and then onto the runway. Each bomber paused for a brief moment as they mustered the entire magnitude of their strength before speeding down the gray strip and launching off into the sky. The sight of the hefty dreadnoughts clawing into the air and then vanishing into the gray haze fascinated Green and his crew.

By mid-afternoon, the peace that had overtaken the land following the bombers' departure was disturbed as the din of engines began rolling over the patchwork of farmland around the airfield. Again, Merle and the crew joined ground personnel and the other uptight combat fliers unassigned to the day's labors around the tower to take tally of the returning 17s. All kept their eyes towards the horizon, scanning southeast,

William Cely (Right), 1943, Fold3

excited to catch the first sight of the silver and green slivers that grew steadily on the horizon and rumbled louder by the minute. Soon the bombers began letting down into the landing pattern, and as each Fort dropped into orbit to await clearance for approach and touchdown, the men watching below assessed the birds for battle damage. Regrettably, it was routine for aircrews to observe their comrades closing in on Rougham in shattered ships or with engines floundering, barking, and vomiting oily smoke trails. At other times, men spied significant wounds in the bombers' skin; mutilations arranged by a determined opponent that had severed off sizeable chunks of the airframe. The most disturbing of any homecoming was the sight of a red flare: the signal to alert the waiting ambulances, the "meat wagons", that there were casualties aboard.

From their position on the green beside the control tower, the officers and sergeants strained to read the tail numbers of the incoming planes, some chuckling at a clever nickname or cartoon character painted on the side of the airship's noses as they passed by. That day, Merle inspected *Tuff Teddie*, *Reno-vation*, *Puddin'*, and *Morgan's Raiders* as they circled in a wide loop around the field before lining up for final. A bark of the wheels stroking cement signaled each giant settling back onto the earth. As Merle ogled the procession, another silver bird roared overhead, completed its lap, and flared down onto the runway. As she groused past the tower, the name *Daring Doris* could be seen on its cheek and beside the letters, a voluptuous seductress stretched out in a provocative, come-hither pose. More Forts were coming in now, thirty-three in all. One among them, an older ship, noticeably weathered and wearing a sun-beaten green drab coat, thundered in and as Green and his crew followed it, they could just make out the name of the warbird: *Erie Ferry*.

Merle and his team sat idle for the next few days as the English weather worsened, grounding the crew, and scrubbing all training flights. Green wrote home:

Sept. 3, 1944
Sun Nite

Dear Rose,

No mail today and no flying either. It seems as though I'll never get off the ground. Oh well, I guess I'll grow old on the ground. If the war keeps up at the present rate we won't get our thirty-five missions in. Please send some candy.

On the 5th, and despite not being deployed with the Group to hit German batteries dug in around the French harbor town of Brest, that Tuesday in September was a momentous day for the crew. After months of delay, promotion orders had finally come through for Gegenheimer, Klekot, Ostrowski, and Hatfield. While Lehere and Riley had been promoted to technical sergeants before leaving the States, the others had been impatiently awaiting a change in rank, and with it, an increase in pay. They also saw the upgrade as a likely indicator for being released for combat as it was well known that the USAAF had an alternative reason to award the rank of sergeant to its enlisted fliers. The Geneva Convention had restricted prisoners of war with a grade of three stripes or higher from being obligated to perform manual labor while detained by the enemy. In the likelihood of the men being lost to the Germans, the airmen's rank would, in theory, afford them better living conditions while a guest of the Third Reich. For now, however, with the thought of being captured not given even the slightest consideration by the reinvigorated bomber boys, the promotion was nothing but cause for celebration. No one was prouder than the crew's commanding lieutenant.

The celebration proved bittersweet, as Lt. Green was requested at Operations and informed that one of his waist gunners, Paul Klekot, was being transferred off the crew. In both aircraft and operating procedures, the 8th had evolved much since its trial by fire in 1942. By late summer of 1944, one change included stripping a waist gunner from each aircrew for reassignment elsewhere. The presence of the Luftwaffe was growing increasingly scarce, while the demand to fill new bomber crews was on the rise. As such, Bomber Command determined that fielding only one waist gunner was an acceptable gamble. It is unknown why Klekot specifically was chosen but as the newly-married gunner was given transfer orders to the 15th Air Force in Italy, the remainder of the Green crew, dejected after losing a brother-in-arms, received their assignments for their induction to combat.

A millennia after King Edmund's trial, the English were again battling another determined aggressor who was also bent on their destruction and total submission. Nazi arrows had been unleashed upon the English, many causing significant ruination. Just as the Wolf had done at the death of Edmund, it now seemed as though it was the

Americans who would stand guard beside the battle-worn, yet resilient English. Although they had come close, unlike the King, the Brits had not succumbed. Instead, they held firm and rallied, and now, stiffened by a new ally with bite, they had beaten the invaders back, first across the English Channel waters and then towards their homeland. At last, with the Germans now reeling from the combined Allied offensives on the ground and in the air, Bomber Command was positioning itself to administer the final death blows on Nazi Germany.

8
"NOW A COMBAT MAN"

Again the town of Mainz, which has the important tank manufacturing plant and also the flying bomb assembly,... to be attacked by this Group. On 1 September this target was assigned to this Group, but due to adverse weather the mission was abandoned.

-94th BG Mission Orders for 8 September

08 September 1944
0837 Hours
Station #468, Rougham Aerodrome
Bury St. Edmunds, Suffolk, East Anglia, England

Climbing away from Rougham, one by one, the Forts of the 94th edged through the grey abyss. With each foot gained in altitude, tension increased tenfold; a palpable uneasiness grinding its way through the guts of all those who sat aboard the bouncing birds as they blindly spiraled upward, instinctive like. There had already been a deviation from the plan of the day: always an ominous sign in a business where the difference between success or disaster was frequently measured by only a few feet and mere seconds. Dense fog, capped by thousands of feet of heavy cumulous, squatted over the airfields, mandating that the bomb groups complete the assembly above the heavy bank of clouds. To keep on schedule, all twenty-six ships of the 94th were now required to climb more drastically and much faster than anticipated, adding concern to the already risky maneuver. Through the vapors, pilots struggled to keep a visual on their wingman but were careful to prevent drifting in too close. It was all too easy, they knew, to clip a friend and cause both ships, maybe more, to be vaporized in a brilliant red-orange cracking blast; the life light of twenty souls literally flashing out in an instant. Between straining to see past the clouds whipping over their wingtips in the dreary murk, eyeing their instrument panels, adjusting airspeed, holding a consistent climb rate, regulating engine rpms, confirming headings, and staying on course, the aviators kept their heads on a swivel, leaned into their seat harnesses, and held their yokes firm.

Strapped in on the right of Lt. Merritt Fausnaugh in the co-pilot's seat of one of the Group's Fortresses, Merle breathed a sigh of relief as the clouds finally burst open before him and the ship broke out above the grim murk. It had been eighty long minutes of navigating through the turbulent gloom and now Green abruptly found himself rising into the brightening blue above, his heart still hammering away. As the undercast steadily fell away, Merle watched as the rest of the bomber force breached from out of the sea of clouds below him. First, their big tails were spotted, seen slicing through the vapors like a large, dark fin. Then, emerged the long, tapered cylindric fuselage. The

Merritt Fausnaugh, Fausnaugh Remembrance

massive, outstretched wings surfaced next, each rigged with a couplet of engines. Each engine was fixed with a yellow-trimmed translucent grey circle: a trio of propellers pulling through the thinning air. Meanwhile, thorns on the brutes' noses and flanks twitched and swiveled and the spikes sprouting from blisters on their heads and bellies twisted and flexed. In addition to the swarm around him, further beyond he recognized more of these creatures, hundreds of vessels, all broaching free of the phosphorescent blanket of pink and orange, lit by the morning sun, lying below and now gathered in packs and fanning out in assemblages as far as the eye could see. Spellbound by the display of such might, Merle realized he was witnessing the entire 8th Air Force apparatus gather for battle, and it was the most fantastic assembly of airpower that he, and most others, would ever see.

To create a strike force worthy of penetrating Reich airspace, the 8th's Bomb Groups would be required to gather their aircraft into coordinated, tightly-compressed organizations. 94th Group assembly

A group of B-17s gathering in formation, Fold3

looked like this: two bombers would file into position behind a lead Fortress; usually a ground-scanning radar-equipped ship known as a Pathfinder, each slightly behind and off to one side of the leader to form an inverted "V". These three-ship assemblies, called "elements", often tucked their massive machines in so close that the tip of their wing would overlap the space a few feet behind the trailing edge of the leader's. Four of these "elements" formed a

squadron and assembled into an even larger inverted "V" configuration and flew in similar proximity and orientation, but with varying altitudes. One squadron flew fifty feet higher than the lead element and one, fifty feet lower, with the third fifty feet beneath that, creating a staggered profile. Expanding the process even further, a bigger formation, known as a "flight" -sometimes used interchangeably with "group", was produced when all squadrons from the unit combined. These "flights" were labeled "A", "B", "C", and so on, depending on the number of planes dispatched for the mission. By mid '44 onward, a triad of squadrons, sometimes a quartet, was the typical group-size deployment. The "high" flight situated its bombers one-hundred-fifty feet above the "lead", off to starboard and up to a mile in trail. "Low" flight cruised below and off to the left of the spearhead and followed at the same interval as the bombers in the "high" flight. Once amassed, this "combat box" formed roughly a 1,000-foot front, was 1,600 feet in depth, and flew stacked over 600 feet high. This formation construction, consisting of 24 to 36 "heavies", not only improved bomb-strike patterns but enabled the units to field an incredibly formidable defense of overlapping fire from over four hundred heavy machine guns against enemy fighter assaults.

After the unit completed the assembly, the Rougham bombers settled into line with three other bombardment groups, each in duplicated design, and together formed the 4th Bombardment Wing. Once Wing formation had collected, it moved on to the next navigational objective point and united with the other similarly assembled units of the Division, five wings in all. Finally, when the three Air Divisions merged, a process that could take up to three hours, the 8th was poised and, at last, ready to head off to the continent. When packed and formed, these immense combat formations were known to stretch well over eighty miles in length. By late 1944 these assemblages were fielding over one thousand bombers and nearly the same number of fighters; a force of upwards of ten thousand men aimed toward the enemy and let loose.

By 1006 hours, the 94th BG had crossed over the French shoreline, rendezvoused with their "little friends," an escort of P-51 Mustangs, and began streaming east towards the heavily defended Rhineland. Executing a deviation left at the IP (initial point), the location where the Boeings would begin the bomb run, the fleet started its ten-minute approach on the Gustavberg tank assembly plant. With the remainder of the Fortresses fanned out behind, the pathfinder crew took a fix of the target area and shepherded the Americans towards the objective. During the last moments of the bomb run, the lead ship, whether due to frozen motors or a mechanical failure, was unable to open its bomb bay doors. Seeing that the entire Group was readying to discharge their loads at the first sight of their bombs, the radar-equipped B-17 had no choice but to relinquish command and fell back out of formation, leaving the deputy leader to take over the approach just seconds before they were above the goal. Scrambling its way to the front of the pack, the delegated Fort attempted to align itself, but under the gun, the brevet lead bombardier, frantically adjusting his levers and tweaking his dials in hopes of recalculating his aim, struggled to get his crosshairs onto the mark. The 17s dumped their payload anyhow, casting off thousands of pounds of explosive freight through the broken undercast. Predictably, as the force turned away from the facility, the Group's shooting was believed to be poor. Aerial photographs taken later that day recorded the drop was, in fact, ineffectual, as most of the bombs had fallen on strategically trivial adjacent structures and in the fields to the west of the intended point.

The Squadrons had experienced light flak while engaged on the run but upon navigating towards the rally point, the "RP," following "bombs away," German gunners found their stride as there was a noticeable improvement in the accuracy of the shelling. "Quite a bit of 105 and 150 mm" fire encouraged the pilots to execute some evasive action but not before the quest down the shooting gallery had caused damage to eleven of the 94th's machines. Several thin vertical smoke trails, four according to eyewitness accounts, were spotted lancing skyward from the area around Mainz, and seven more were spied near Kaiserslautern to the south. Apprehensive, but captivated by the unusual sight, the boys from Rougham followed the trails as they stretched higher and arced toward their formation. Upon rising to their elevation, these "telephone pole"-like objects hissed through the ranks of the 94th, somehow passing through the multitude of bombers without connecting, but completely unsettling the men anyhow.

What the crews of the 94th were witnessing was something fairly new in aerial warfare of the age: the unification of an ancient technology fused with the most modern of science and defensive military tactics. Reinforced by flak nests, which blasted 20lbs iron shells up to 30,000 feet at supersonic speed, the German defense system had employed anti-aircraft ground-launched rockets to rid the skies of Allied bombers. It was well known that the Luftwaffe had hurled rockets at the "herds" from racks fastened underneath the wings of their Focke-Wulfs, Junkers and Messerschmitts during aerial brawls since first contact two year before. Some German fighters had even released bombs into the horde of Fortresses and Liberators from above or towed long steel trailing wires through the bomber boxes, leaving them to whip and slice through American aluminum and flesh; but reports of ground-to-air missiles only began to surface in after-action interviews in early-1944. On the Bremen run on August 30th, Lt. Stephan Hoza's men reported "11 rockets-observed...at 25,000 feet." Robert Hall's team also claimed to have seen at least one of these missiles in the target area that day. "Reed's Rowdies" spied "4 ground rockets" rise through the thick cloud bank to greet them when the Group, flying at a precariously low altitude of approximately 10,000 feet, wasted entrenchments around Brest four days later. As the Battle of Brest slugged on, the 94th was sent back to level fortifications around the vital Brittany port city on September 5th, where "about 4 rockets" were reported by navigator Lt. Richard "Dick" Bishop of the Charles Duda crew.

Beginning that summer and continuing well into the winter of '44, many other 8th AAF bomb groups passed on accounts of contact with ground-launched rockets while on approach to their targets. Among the most common zones to be engaged by these, precursors of surface-to-air missiles, included the airspace around Brunswick, Osnabruck, Bielfield, Munster, and Berlin. As if the spectacle of the product produced by the 385 heavy anti-aircraft cannon immediately surrounding the synthetic oil facility at Leunawerks, near Merseburg, wasn't concerning enough, the diary of one navigator from the 94th BG recorded that on one visit to the refinery the airspace above the plant "was covered with rockets and the usual heavy flak." In fact, numerous post-mission interviews make mention of this so-called "rocket flak" and note that the exhaust trails "looked a lot like our smoke bombs"; the comparison being made to the phosphorus smoke marker bombs that were released by lead bomber crews as a signal that the unit had reached the bomb run's zero hour.

Fortunately, all missiles failed to strike any of the Group's aircraft on the 8 September effort to Mainz. The crew of a/c [aircraft] #653, better known as *Erie Ferry* and co-piloted by Lt. Green, reported their near-miss noting, "at 1128 hours a rocket came right behind the tail." Perched in the nose of the *Lucky Rebel* for one of his combat initiation flights, Jack Williams stared at the salvo with the veterans of the Morris crew who reported spotting a total of "6 rockets in the target area."

By mid-afternoon, all of the 94th's aircraft had settled back on hard ground at Station #468, despite being fired upon by English defense batteries posted along the Thames estuary. Most likely, the justly-edgy Brits mistook the returning Rougham fliers for a German marauding party who were known to try and sneak into English airspace among retiring Allied bomber groups, in essence hiding in plain sight. The Group had returned unmolested, although the flight proved to be a rough one operationally. With his first crusade complete and excited by the prospect that he would soon be leading his own team on attacks into the Fuhrer's lair, Merle wrote to inform his family that he was, "…now a combat man."

Dear Mom,

*Well at last I got my chance to get a crack at the Germans.
Grandma told me to "kill every dam[n] one of them" before I
left and yesterday I got started. I don't know how often I'll go
now, but I hope its every few days. I can't give you all the details
of the mission, but I'll be making a book of them and I'll be
home in a few weeks with more stories than uncle Henry. One of
the boys here finished up his 35 missions today. Boy he sure is
happy! The trip I made yesterday was with an old crew. I have
to make another one with them before I take my own crew out.
I'll be glad to see how they act when the flak starts cracking
around them. I'll admit I was scared, but I was too busy to worry
too much. Well mom, that's about all the news for now.*

Love,
Merle

09 SEPTEMBER 1944

*Your mission is to supply 2000 to 3000 Frenchmen who are
waiting to be armed for the purpose of delaying or cutting off the
Germans retreating thru the Belfort Gap. The plan is for these
frenchmen to join a force of Maquis and to attack the Nazis as
they withdraw to Germany. Identify target by bonfires, people
waving red flags and possibly a large square piece of white cloth
on ground. Bonfires visible for 5 miles. No known flak on entire
course. Dijon on right going in is still in enemy hands and is
defended by 20 guns.*

The men of the 3rd Air Division awoke at 0300 hours for their
briefings on the 9th and learned that this day they would execute a
secret sortie into eastern France. Lt. Green was not selected to fly, but
Jack and Sidney discovered they had been penciled in to join the other
94th crews for the special assignment. Designated "Operation Grassy
Messenger," this would be the fourth and final supply drop flown by
the 3rd Air Division to equip French resistance fighters, known as the
"*Maquis.*" These "mercy missions" had kicked off in late June with
"Operation Zebra," just as Allied ground forces pressed inland from
the landing beaches along the Normandy coast. The bombers had also

previously delivered containers to the partisans during Operations "Cadillac" and "Buick." Both of these runs had a tremendous impact on enabling the Maquis to put up a dogged opposition against the Germans and eventually regain control of many regions throughout their country by early fall. By the conclusion of the "Grassy" affair, the 8th had coordinated the transfer of nearly three million pounds of food, munitions, medicine, and weapons to the resistance, and the 94th had taken part in all four missions.

Twenty-five miles south of Bresacon over the Vercors Plateau, the Forts of the 94th, gliding at an altitude of five hundred feet, lowered their landing gear and extended their flaps, slowing to just above stalling speed. Operating at reduced airspeeds and dropping their payloads from such a low height was necessary to avoid damaging the ten-foot-long-supply-laden aluminum containers in the turbulent

Supply pod deployment by the 94th for the Maquis, Fold3

process. At 1047, and guiding on the smoke of signal fires, the Group released 814 supply containers by parachute onto the pastures selected as the target zone with nearly flawless results. "When the supplies were dropped it was a beautiful sight," remembered one 94th airman flying that day. "All the chutes were colored which lent a carnival air to the whole episode. The Maquis were out in the open waving to us, and it made one feel good to be able to help those courageous people." One of the Group's B-17s managed to miss-drop its haul into what was thought to be territory still under German control. Not to be left for the withdrawing German army, the valuable cache was promptly strafed by a pair of hedge-hopping Mustangs from the Group's fighter escort.

After eight hours and ten minutes in the air, thirty-three tired combat crews returned to England without a loss and only minor flak damage to a few of its aircraft. Nonetheless, the actions of 9 September are fondly recognized by the 94th's veterans as one of the most memorable and fulfilling missions of the War. To the French, however, the material that was floated down by their friends in the Forts passing above them represented much more. For them, the supplies helped to reinforce their resolve, boost their capacity to endure the terrible difficulties that they were experiencing at the hands of their German occupiers, and continued to infuse hope to their resilient people.

10 SEPTEMBER 1944

Well-positioned to launch a fierce defense against Allied menaces now threatening from airbases in England and Italy, Giebelstadt Airfield became high priority for Allied Bomber Command. The aerodrome, positioned approximately 250 miles south of Berlin, was one of the oldest airfields in Germany and; by 1944, it was considered one of the most strategically important bases in the Reich by both sides. A 9,100-foot enhanced runway provided optimal footing for any of Goering's fighters or bombers, including the newest

Me-262, Impact Magazine

aerial prototypes in the Nazi arsenal. Operations at the facility were kept classified, even to German military units who were unable to pinpoint the location of the facility, or even the name of the nearest village, on their maps. When US forces secured the field in 1945, troops stumbled upon a secret railway line, explicitly constructed for the Fuhrer. Such great effort would be taken to camouflage the site that authorities painted the runway to blend in with the pastures surrounding the airfield, even going so far as to paint a "herd" of sheep on the tarmac.

In April of '44, Hitler's swept-winged twin-engine turbojet fighter, the Messerschmitt 262, began nesting at Giebelstadt field. The "Schwalbe," or "Swallow" in English, could operate at well above five hundred miles per hour and spit cannon shells and blast rockets at bomber formations with devastating effect. Rumors of this top-secret, technologically advanced Nazi wonder weapon had scattered among unnerved US crews, but there had only been limited intelligence on the jet and even less interaction, that is until early fall. "We saw strange planes coming at us," remembers Morton Kimmel, who observed a few of these machines firsthand in August. "We found out at debriefings that they were jets. I didn't know what a jet was." Antolin "Al" Algorri, navigator on the 94th's *Ice Cold Katy*, a B-17 aptly named due to being the "…coldest ship on the field, no heating system…," jotted down one encounter with a Me 262 in his war diary:

> *We spotted a jet-propelled enemy fighter climbing straight up going about 300 mph-started at about 10,000 and ended up about 40,000' [.] Hell it was going straight up as fast as our fighters fly level.*

Outside Bury St. Edmunds, those who had found a few hours of sleep amongst the muttering of engines being pre-flighted far out in the darkness were awakened long before dawn on the 10th of September. Rising grudgingly from their bunks after being roused by the most hated man on the base; the Charge of Quarters sergeant, the chosen dressed in silence, doing their best not to disturb any of their tired roommates who had the luck of having the day off. The men collected up their shaving kits and rushed off to the latrine, returning to the hut a few minutes later clean-shaven and slightly less shabby, having washed the previous day's grime from their faces and passed a comb through their matted hair. Outside in the squadron area, small groups of fliers, clad in leather and sheep wool flying jackets, had already begun flowing between the shacks. Swept up in the murmuring procession and surrounded by the tiny flickering flares of cigarettes, the men tramped through the blackness towards the mess hall where those airmen scheduled for the day's "ball game" would enjoy fresh

Antolin Algorri, E. Algorri Collection

eggs–not powdered–for breakfast. As they soundlessly sipped on their hot coffee, many contemplated the plethora of disturbing knowns and unknowns that they would soon face, knowing that some in their company, perhaps even themselves, may fail to return to these tables for dinner. Not surprisingly, many airmen made sure to visit the chapel, connecting with the Chaplain to receive Absolution before setting off into combat. "Briefing at 0330," wrote 94th bombardier Al Algorri, "but before briefing received the Holy Communion. Felt much better. I'm all over my flak worries now."

Mission overview briefings were conducted for every flight. Security was tight; no man whose name was absent from the assignment list was allowed access to the conference. The briefing commenced when the tense, chattering pack was called to attention just as the command staff strolled into the room. Taking his place at the head of the congregation, the Group commander—at the time it was Dougher—or another delegate would address the tense masses with something like: "Gentlemen, the target for today is…." The map would be uncovered as he spoke, revealing the unit's flight path, denoted by a long, thin blood-red ribbon stretching from the launching fields in England and angling to the day's objective. Commonly, when the target was unveiled, a collective groan would swell amongst the crowd. This response was typical; only the degree of moaning was known to fluctuate from day to day depending on the objective. A few profane words could faintly be heard punctuating the commotion of whistles, energized murmuring, and nervous chuckles. It was clear that there would be no "milk run" today. As the veterans deliberated Bomber Command's decision, the less experienced among them, Lt. Green included, sat absorbing the mood. The men would quickly compose themselves, and the briefing would resume as the flier's attention fixed back on Dougher. The Colonel would then remind them of the significance of their assignment and encourage the crews to keep their elements tight and conserve their ammunition. He customarily closed the address with a "good luck" or "God speed" before turning the floor over to the planning staff, referred to by the combat fliers as "the wheels."

The remainder of the session was conducted by members of the intelligence staff, aka the "inspirational" officers. These "ground grippers" gave a quick summary of the battle plan, bomb loads and type, target identification, anticipated opposition, arrival times and distance to control points, flare colors, Flight and Group assignments, and Wing formation type and position. The "weather guesser," the meteorological officer, followed and disseminated the sum of his discipline to the group. The more disillusioned airmen believed the reports to be more of a faux science considering that weather reports were, primarily to no fault of the planners, frequently erroneous. Nonetheless, the Weather Officer made sure to relay the projected forecast along the route, wind direction and speed, and estimated temperature over the target area. To close, the communication officer revealed the mission's call signs and start-up and taxi code words for the flight. Lastly, when prompted, all in attendance synchronized their watches, the "time hack," vital in harmonizing the fleet's schedule.

At the conclusion of the briefing, it was customary for the

crews to break off to attend meetings regarding their specific disciplines before completing their final tasks prior to the "call to stations." While the sergeant gunners filed out of the briefing room, flowing first to the dressing hut where they donned their battle trappings and then towards the armaments shack like a long, muttering, smoking river, thirty-six of the Group's radio operators funneled into a conference hall for their own meeting. Inside, they were advised what radio frequencies were to be utilized that day, as well as various passwords to be employed in the event of having to confirm a recall order or transmit an emergency notification. Additionally, as a radioman, or "static chaser" as the ROs referred to themselves, he was given precise instructions on deploying radar countermeasures. Precursors to "chaff," and known as "window," thin strips of aluminum would be chucked from a small hatch in the radio compartment when needed. Calls of "make it rain" could be heard over the RO's headset as they commenced to release the tinsel-like technology. The metallic deluge would continue at interval until the order was given to stop and "dry it up."

The bombardiers would also regroup for a special brief of their own. They meticulously studied aerial reconnaissance photographs of the four-mile diameter surrounding the selected "mean point of impact," the desired target, making sure to note geographical prompts and memorizing characteristics of neighboring structures. Taking particular note of bridges, spans of rail tracks and junctures, and waterway intersections, bombardiers knew that details as small as the shape of a cluster of forest would alleviate the need to refer to their notes and maps while over the objective. Not only was the primary target thoroughly examined by the flying grenadiers, but secondary and tertiary targets were analyzed as well.

At navigator's briefing that morning, Frank Jones and his fellows began marking flak positions, escort rendezvous locations, and hostile airfields on their maps and in their logbooks. The fickle Northern European climate was always of particular concern as, no matter how far-advanced the science, the bomber force was largely at the mercy of the elements and "ill winds." Underestimating air currents over the continent could cause the attackers to be pushed far off course, soon to find themselves miles from their goal. Dreaded crosswinds were nullified by coordinating with the pilots who combatted the effect by "crabbing" the aircraft along the flight path.

Headwinds could hinder progress, delay arrival at objectives, burn up fuel loads, and require the navigators to continuously re-calculate gas consumption rates. Likewise, overlooked tailwinds had been known to shove bombers toward treacherous storm systems or into the crosshairs of anti-aircraft cannon, complicate their convergence with other Allied units, or prevent it altogether.

Like the bombardiers, navigators were required to identify the adjacent countryside and recognize the infrastructure and landscape within a ten-mile diameter of the target. Each man studied his "flimsies," edible rice paper sheets handed out each morning depicting the day's classified flight plan. Furthermore, Jones was also prepped on escape routes and evasion protocols; both could prove to be invaluable for the crew's survival in the chance of getting separated, downed, or beaten away from the Group. Before leaving the conference of navigators, Frank collected his kit of notebooks, "flimsies," and briefcase. Inside his satchel were the tools of his trade: a slide ruler, Weems plotter, pencils, triangles, charts, and maps. Prepped, briefed, and armed with his instruments, the Flight Officer took a deep breath, pivoted, and then exited the briefing room to hunt down his crew for the day.

9
THE UNINVITED

"We'll show those filthy bastards how the 94th can hit."
-94th Bomb Group Anthem

Robert Hall crew photo, Hall Family Collection

Mission #208 launched at 0707 hours on the 10th of September 1944 and saw two flights from the 94th sent to hit the German airfield at

Giebelstadt. The trek would be Lt. Green's second checkout flight and, upon successful completion and return, the final assessment before being released to lead his own crew into combat. Also climbing onboard Green's assigned aircraft, #773 dubbed *The Uninvited,* was his navigator, Frank Jones. Adding to the stress of his first flight into Germany and having to perform with an unfamiliar team, the seven-hour and thirty-minute, 1,400-mile round-trip haul would present quite the test for the Flight Officer. Now playing for keeps, Jones knew that any slight miscalculation on his part could have catastrophic consequences.

Hosting the neophytes that day was 1st Lt. Robert Hall and his crew of battle-tested flyboys. While he was, by then, the quintessential veteran bomber pilot, two years before Hall's aviation aspirations were nearly dashed before they began. When asked what role he desired to play upon enlisting in the Army, Robert was almost laughed out of the recruitment office when he countered that he wanted to fly B-17s. Only officers or those with college educations could qualify for the Air Corps, berated the enlistment sergeant. The criticism didn't discourage Robert one bit and after scoring exceptionally high marks on the Army's college equivalency exam, he was accepted into the glider pilot program. Hall's road to combat would divert once again when he and half of his graduating class were scrapped from the ranks due to a surplus of the so-called "canvas coffin" drivers. Not willing to let their investment, nor the man's talent go to waste, administration went about looking into options as to where to shuffle the gifted flier. Before a decision was made, Robert, once again, requested assignment to B-17s. Once again, he found that his answer drew more chuckles from the "chairborne troopers," men who would remain delegated to administration deployments entrenched behind desks in the US while airmen like himself were endeavoring to try not to get their rear shot off in the ETO.

Months before, prior to setting off on his first combat operation with the 94th BG, Robert felt inclined to attend the group prayer service in the base chapel. Although he had extended an invitation to all his crewmates, only a few took him up on the invite to what was the pilot's first but soon-to-be ritual pre-mission tradition. The absentees had elected to forego the sermon and last rites afforded to the Group's combat-bound boys on that day, their first expedition into the jaws of the enemy, only to be found sitting front and center before their second combat flight, heeding the chaplain's addresses, and hanging on every one of his words. If the flak had, indeed, failed to pluck Hall and his crew from the sky, the anti-aircraft fire had at least lit the spiritual coals of his team.

Heavenly Comrade, Hall Collection

Unquestionably, Robert Hall was a man of faith, but he was also deeply entwined with fate and destiny. Some could write off Hall's knack for survival as chance—a random fall of the cards—but the man himself saw it much differently. Even before his first scheduled flight against the Germans, he found himself counting his blessings, having survived a crash landing after the B-17 that he was ferrying to England experienced mechanical issues on the flight over the Atlantic. The brutal confrontations in European skies would only further reveal the direness of his circumstances, but with it came a strengthened conviction.

While the ground crew of *Heavenly Comrade,* Robert's primary aircraft, went about their repairs following one notably hot engagement, the crew chief approached the pilot, asking if he could show him something in the plane. Although the lieutenant was dead-tired following the day's work, he happily trailed his trusted crew chief back to the flight deck where the B-17's windscreen hung cracked in its mount. Nearing the target just a few hours prior, the Group had jockeyed through a box of heavy cannon fire. At one point, smoke had filled *Heavenly Comrade's* flight cabin and when the air cleared, Lt. Hall noticed that a metal splinter had snapped through the glass just inches directly in front of his face. If that weren't proof enough of providential intervention, one of many indications that Hall would receive during his tour in the 8th, what the crew chief revealed next would dispel all doubt. Bringing Hall's attention to the bulkhead just aft of the pilot's chair, the sergeant pointed out a cavity that had been carved out in the wall behind where the lieutenant had been posted. After breaking through the reinforced windscreen, the chunk of fragmented metal had shot through the cabin and come to rest, lodged in the crevice. The crew chief commented how lucky the pilot was to have been out of his seat when the flak shard penetrated the cockpit. When Robert informed the mechanic that he had been far too engaged in handling the aircraft and had never moved from his perch during the flight, the flabbergasted sergeant was left lingering in stunned awe as the pair analyzed the flak splinter that, due to its trajectory, should have passed right through the pilot. Inexplicably, Hall had returned to Rougham without a scratch.

Something was special about Lt. Hall and the men; not only his own crew but others in his sphere of influence sensed it too. Superstition held a firm grasp over many airmen. Routines and pre-combat rituals were, in their own eyes, just as essential to their survival as were the flak vests, armor-reinforced battle positions, life preservers, parachutes, and the crates of ammunition that were loaded into their ships before start-up. To circumvent misfortune, for example, the thirteenth mission of a man's combat tour was commonly designated "12 B." Men pulled on lucky socks, or carried with them mementoes of girlfriends, or, despite vigorous protest by others who shared the same living quarters, refused to wash their charmed pair of long underwear as, to some, the slightest unorthodoxy or deviation from habit could be their undoing. It was no wonder that anxieties ran high when one on Robert's crew was required to complete a make-up flight after coming down sick and missing a mission. As a result, the man reluctantly motored away into English skies, temporarily attached to another crew while the Hall team took a day's rest. Later that afternoon, Robert was shaken from his cot and driven out to a hardstand where he was asked to help identify his crewmate who was suspected of having been killed in a random explosion while over the base. Hall was, in fact, able to recognize the man, though all that was left was a finger that still bore the familiar ring of his friend.

During his deployment at Rougham, many would seek out

Hall's advice. He had assumed a spot as one of the exemplars of the 410th and would later fly as an Element, Flight, and Deputy Group Leader, and as such, his chums and strangers alike were naturally drawn to him. Some looked for mentorship or acceptance; others sought to be reassured; and, while he would lend an ear to many during his time deployed, Hall couldn't help but notice a morbid pattern emerge. Decades later, long after victory was secured in Europe and the Pacific, Hall revealed to his family that all of his comrades who had foreseen their impending demise and expressed such apprehensions to him had failed to return from errands over the continent. To a man, all had been shot down or killed. "The brass" was unaware of these statistics but, without question, would have cared little even if enlightened of the fact, as it was Robert's remarkable composure while under fire and sheer grit that interested them. Thus came a promotion and, with it, additional responsibilities. This included coaching up the Squadron's new pilots and ushering the probies through the inferno.

Once airborne, F/O Jones concentrated on his charts and began confirming the headings with his pilots who reared *The Uninvited* through a slow, deliberate, circular ascent towards 14,000 feet. Known as "threading" or "shuffling the deck," hundreds of aircraft, fully loaded with fuel, bombs, ammunition, and men, would begin to organize over Norfolk and Suffolk counties each morning. Commonly, assembly was accomplished in total darkness, in the drizzle of rain or snow flurries, and customarily complicated by the abominable English soup that would completely sock in the fields. With dozens of Forts from the Group fighting to gain altitude and stay on schedule, each flight team had to work as one to keep their aircraft on the correct headings and keep pace with the mandated climb rates. Along with help from the radio operator, Frank remained intensely focused on identifying the network of navigational aids used to assemble the 94th's strike force. "Buncher 12" was Station #468's navigational beacon and was instrumental in helping the 94th navigate during their time "screwing" up into their assembly pattern. Bearing in mind the Group's six-mile diameter orbit pattern around the "buncher," and knowing that the epicenter of nearby aerodromes were as close as twelve miles distant from their own, the pilots could not afford to wander too far from Rougham's guidance beacon signal as friendly but unbending sister assemblages simultaneously wound upward nearby in the chasm. Other radio-guidance transmitters, known as "Splashers," were used nearer the coast, drawing together several bomb groups to the locus where the growing flotilla would unite before crossing the Channel.

Carefully, in the inky pre-light, Frank's pilots tightened up their spacing by guiding on the lead ship's colored assembly flares. Isolated in the bomber's stern, the tail gunner of the ship flashed the Group's identifier into the shadowy void by Morse code with an Aldis lamp, signalizing to the other titans banking and ascending out in the blackened expanse. Those on the team who were forced to sit and wait out the lengthy process with little to do sat huddled in the radio compartment, praying that the men behind the control columns of both their vessel and the pack's other Boeings stayed sharp and that the new, unproven navigator's math was spot on. Remarkably, this heartrending assembly routine would be replicated every mission and was always accomplished under strict radio discipline and without radar assistance. It was no surprise that for most 8th Air Force combat men assembly was often the most nerve-wracking component of a mission.

Moving past 16,000 feet, where readings registered temperatures of -15 degrees Celsius, the B-17 edged into its designated position in the Group assembly. The process took the 94th sixty-six minutes before the unit was able to sail on to the Wing rendezvous point at "Buncher 13" and attach themselves to the steadily expanding task force. Passing the control points, the 94th departed the English coast six minutes ahead of schedule at 0917, more than two hours since the first ship set off from Rougham. As he tracked the progress of *The Uninvited* on his maps, Jones took a moment to document his status, including the aircraft's course: 157 degrees, magnetic heading: 172 degrees, airspeed: 185, altitude: 20,000 feet, drift and wind direction: +3, distance from the last control point at Southwold: 72 miles, time from previous control point: 21 minutes, and estimated time of arrival at "enemy coast": 9:45.

Tucked into the forward compartment below and in front of the flight deck, Jones hovered over the charts he had sprawled out over a small wooden table that protruded from below a pair of windows in the port side airframe. The personnel based inside this tiny cabin, the navigator and bombardier, were forced to move about the cramped compartment on their hands and knees. When not occupied with their other duties, these men crouched behind one of the two forward machine guns that protruded from the Fortress' cheeks. Both had a small chair; the navigator's chair was bolted into the bulkhead alongside the table, while the bombardier's stool was rooted on a raised platform at the front of the compartment, directly behind the clear, conical-shaped plexiglass nose cone. There, the bombardier swiveled between his gyroscopic sight and bomb release levers and the chin turret's electronically remote-controlled firing handles, which, when not in use, could be locked against the starboard wall, out of the way. A plexiglass astrodome bulged out of the roof above, granting Frank an alternative view to navigate using his sextant if needed or, if working at night, by the stars. As all crew members wore many hats, navigators were also observers and taught that even the most minuscule details of the flight could prove invaluable to the Allied war effort. They were expected to keep a log of intelligence ranging from the time of arrival at predetermined points throughout the flight, the loss of any aircraft, fuel consumption and, if applicable, the number of parachutes, enemy

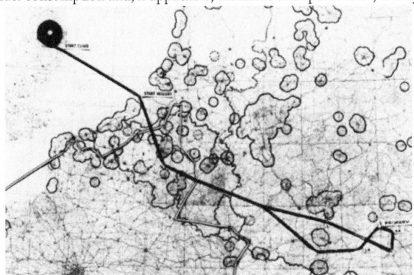

10 September mission plot map with flak zones, Motz/National Museum of the USAF

aircraft type and markings, anti-aircraft barrage zones, flak fire characteristics, bombing results, and countless other particulars.

As the Rhine River was crossed just before 1100 hours, Jones watched as black mushroom-shaped clouds began to sprout up in the sky far outside of the formation. "Germersheim at 21,000 feet, out of range, tracking and meager," Frank entered into his log. With just a few millimeters of aluminum separating the navigator from the blue abyss, atmospheric temperatures had now plummeted to 57 degrees below freezing. Along with the other squadron navigators, he visualized heavy barge traffic on the waterway heading east. He noted the construction of a large, suspicious complex of buildings, recorded barrage balloons at Germersheim, and described smoke clouds blossoming from oil fires near Cologne, set off by a British bombing raid the night before. As the crew approached Kaiserslautern, Jones identified a chain of locomotives, seventy-to-eighty railcars lying in tandem. Reminiscent of the previous days' incursions, the appearance of the familiar thin, vertical columns of rocket smoke could be seen emerging from out of the fields laid out before them, although none of the missiles posed a threat.

Reaching the IP at 1114 hours and initiating the bomb run, the flotilla wheeled left into line. For the last few months, the 94th, replicating the habit of the 8th USAAF at large, had been outfitting only a limited number of its aircraft with a bombsight. Up until early 1944, each "heavy" had been allocated a Norden and a bombardier who, flying in tight formation with the other ships of the squadron, would then attempt, individually, to sight in on the target and subsequently release his explosives when he deemed best. The product of such a strategy had habitually resulted in scattered loads and, in turn, highly ineffective, wasted attacks. It wasn't until the bomb groups implemented the method of dropping on the lead bombardier's mark that results improved drastically. The effect reinforced Bomber Command's confidence in the tactic, and by the midpoint of '44, with few exceptions, policy saw that only bombardiers posted in the nose of the lead and deputy lead PFF aircraft would be given the device and delegated the job of keeping the crosshairs of their sights fixed on the target. The plan evolved once again as the US Air Forces began replacing bombardiers, certified officers with the rank of lieutenant or higher, with "toggliers"; enlisted personnel tasked to "toggle" off their loads upon the appearance of the leader's smoke "sky marker" bombs. War had changed the USAAF apparatus; and, as time went on, the organization, like the aircraft themselves, became more streamlined and efficient. Now, complemented and reinforced by "Mickey" radar operators, lead bombardiers, working their Norden bombsights, would do the shooting for the entire group.

While the lead bombardiers, faces pressed to the sight's optics, contemplated the enemy aerodrome inching closer through bursts of "ack-ack" (Anti-Aircraft), the crews remained vigilant and did their best to ignore the precariousness of their situation, a feeling of being dangled over a bed of hot coals. Ordinarily, the gunners gained a brief intermission while on the bomb run, as hostile fighters rarely dared to engage the bomber boxes while over the objective where the flak storm typically intensified. But dangers were ever-present. Operators rooted in the ball turrets kept a lookout for any errant 17s that may have unknowingly drifted into the path of their bombs below them. Likewise, the top turret gunner scanned for strays in the airspace overhead and promptly notified the pilots in case of an impending

Miss Donna Mae II, May 19, 1944, Fold3

crisis from above. The airmen flying aboard *Miss Donna Mae II* of the 94th BG had fallen victim to this type of mishap on May 19, 1944, when their ship slid out of position just before "bombs away" and had its horizontal stabilizer hammered off by a friendly's 500 lbs. bomb. The aircraft's final tragic moments, with her ten-man crew trapped inside, can be seen, captured in the famous stills that were taken by their horrified associates observing helplessly in the Fortress overhead.

At 1122, a salvo of bombs wobbled free from the hold of aircraft #643, the Group leader. A stream of colored phosphorus trailed off behind the first pair, followed closely by six fat and very lively 500-pound high-explosive bombs. At the instant they were alerted by the trails of the "sky marker" smoke bombs, the remaining twenty-five Flying Fortresses sent their payloads tumbling earthward. Cruising at a height of 20,000 feet, the release had been made two miles before the ships would be directly over Giebelstadt airfield. Countless eyes followed the explosives down, ogling the green cylinders as they rained from the bellies of the Boeings and jostled against one another as they became smaller and smaller until, at last, disappearing completely. Having sunk away towards a grouping of administration buildings, rows of hangars, fuel storage tanks, prized Luftwaffe fighter and bomber aircraft, and runway, the bombs reached near-supersonic speeds. Small, quick flashes sparkled around the complex, the hellholes blinking like long strings of giant firecrackers, each issuing a concussion halo that expanded and accelerated outward from each orange-red flicker. Smoke churned out of each blast, entombing the bulk of the facility in thick smog that continued to billow as the B-17s began their retreat home, leaving the field wrecked, pitted, and ablaze.

Flying his second assignment as aircraft commander, Charles "Chuck" Duda was sitting at the flight instruments in the cabin of B-17 #153 named *Daring Doris*. Today, Duda's ship was arranged in the exposed and vulnerable #3 spot in the Group's rear, outside element. As the Forts ahead lurched upward– the result of rapidly separating from 6,000 pounds of steel and explosives–Lt. Duda realized that Doris hadn't responded in kind. In the nose cabin below and in front of him, his togglier, Sgt. John Caro, was frantically engaging the bomb release toggle switch. Although he had flown a series of training sorties during his brief period in England, it was Caro's first time operating in

Charles 'Chuck' Duda,
Buehler/Colangelo Collection

ship #153. *Daring Doris* was outfitted with an older release system, and while he was trying his best to lose his bombs, the sergeant couldn't sever his haul until well beyond the target. When the payload was finally released, Caro had only succeeded in blowing the hell out of a few acres of fertile farmland.

Moving off the target, the Group executed a hard turn, descending abruptly, to try and throw off the aim of the flak gunners below, and flew on to the RP, where all of the Squadrons dressed up their formation and hunkered down for the long return trip back to East Anglia. While the fighter escorts were seen to chase off a group of hostiles that had been posturing on the distant horizon, the Luftwaffe was practically a no-show. Merle would write that his business that Sunday was "uneventful," most likely because "the Jerries were in church."

94th BG 10 September 1944 Smoke marker and bombs away

One peculiar incident occurred as the 94th was pushing ahead upon the return leg northeast of Mannheim. From the Fortress, *My Ideal*, a lone B-24 Liberator was seen approaching the rear of the formation. Multiple crews cautiously eyed this "stray" bomber that "joined just after target" but then had, inexplicably, "left formation at Worms where flak started." About twenty minutes later, at 1220, a "beat up" B-17 F bearing the markings of a sister bombardment group slowly slid in closer to the 94th and shadowed the formation for the next thirty minutes. The enigmatic aircraft flew close enough for machine gunners on the Fortress *Bouncin' Annie* to observe that both the top and bottom turrets were unmanned—a peculiar detail especially while over hostile territory. When the Squadron attempted to make contact by transmitting a challenge message to the mysterious "heavy" over the VHF, the bomber immediately banked away from the Group and vanished into the clouds.

Kampfgeschwader 200, also known as "KG 200," was a Luftwaffe special projects unit tasked with carrying out a variety of covert operations. Organized into multiple squadrons and deployed throughout Nazi-controlled territory, the outfit flew various models of both German and captured Allied aircraft, including numerous Liberators and over twenty Flying Fortresses. These salvaged airships, still bearing USAAF markings and squadron colors, were used to infiltrate American bomber boxes under the guise of being a separated or stricken ship seeking the protective refuge provided by the formations. It was common, after all, for lost or straggling Allied bomber crews to attach themselves to any friendly unit to improve their odds of safely returning to Allied territory. Seeing an excellent opportunity to exploit, the Germans implemented the "Trojan horse"-esque tactic not with the aim of shooting down unaware American bombers, an act that would undoubtedly see their invaluable aircraft blown out of the sky by overwhelming numbers, but to reconnoiter. With precise knowledge of altitude, heading, speed, and formation arrangement, the stealthy German ship could act as a "spotter" and transmit firing solutions to the waiting anti-aircraft batteries. The guns could then generate an even more exacting curtain of hot iron and fire that the attacking force would have to pass through. Whether the bombers seen by the 94th that day were some of KG 200's captured aircraft remains unclear, but it is interesting to note that one *Kampfgeschwader* unit operated out of an airfield located alongside the route flown on the 10th of September just outside of Frankfurt. In any case, Rougham's Intelligence officers readily took note of the unusual interaction.

The remainder of the incursion was uneventful as the Group reversed itself along the flight path they had used earlier to infiltrate Germany. When returned to Rougham, the pilots taxied their goliaths down the perimeter track, each veering off as they arrived at their assigned hardstand. Beside them, ground crew personnel marched alongside the purring aircraft, examining its form, and taking note of any battle scars or structural deficits. A flurry of screeches from grinding brakes followed as the B-17s pivoted back into their roosts.

Upon killing the motors and with it, the deafening noise, the propellers swept through the last of their revolutions, ticking to a stop and leaving only the faint tapping and knocking sounds of hot engine metal as they cooled and settled into a much-deserved slumber. The combat men dismounted, stretched, and passed on attaboys and concerns to the indispensable technicians who helped keep the plane airworthy. After the handoff, the airmen lugged their bags toward the waiting transport buses as maintenance personnel swarmed about the aircraft.

Having flung their flight suits into lockers in the equipment hut and returning their parachute bundles to the "chute shack," the disheveled combat crews began ushering through the doors of the Ops hut where intelligence staff, "S-2," commenced with the post-mission interrogation process. Wearing the look of both predator and prey, and wanting only to fill their hollow stomachs, relieve their throbbing bladders, and return to their soft beds to escape into a deep sleep, the men, reeking of sweat, cordite, coffee, and cigarette smoke grouped around the tables, pushed back their matted coifs, and began relaying the details of the day. To remedy their jitters and loosen their tongues, an administration of medicinal Scotch, "nerve tonic," followed. Other boys, hoping to work out the chill that still hung in their bones, sipped on hot coffee, or chatted energetically with buddies, reliving thrilling moments of the flight. Commonly they would snicker at morbid observations and other comments unfit for civilized society—an unconscious attempt to combat the mental wounds that they had suffered with their usual gallows humor.

At his table, Jones relayed his list of headings and computations to the intelligence man, noted the time of bomb release and detailed the crew's experience sweating out the flak. The bombardiers were questioned on the transfer of their ordinance, gunners about the type, number, and identifying characteristics and the color of markings brandished by the opposition, in tandem with the kind of tactics that were employed. Any "kills," claims of any downed assailants, had to be confirmed by a witness before the shooter received the credit and, with it, bragging rights. Once satisfied, the S-2 officer dismissed the crew who then shuffled into the next room where Red Cross personnel had set out hot chocolate and arranged stacks of sandwiches. After attacking the refreshments, most returned to their quarters where they abandoned their bags beside their bunks and promptly disintegrated into their beds.

Frank returned to his berth that day, flooded with relief and euphoric but unsettled. Six and a half hours earlier, he had set off to face the enemy, largely uncertain of all of the perils awaiting him. He returned that afternoon confident that the enterprise before him, thirty-four more flights into combat, would be complex and trying and marked with long, indistinguishable periods of boredom, punctuated by a few seconds of remarkable terror. Many combat fliers would tell that they became even more frightened after their initial expedition, as it wasn't until then that the hazards of their dangerous business were truly realized. This sentiment seemed to hit one individual appointed to Lt. Duda's team particularly hard; as, upon his return from Giebelstadt that day, the ball turret gunner refused to fly any further combat missions. When word of the man's resignation reached Squadron command, the sergeant was speedily separated from his fellows and transferred off base. As an associate from the 94th perfectly summed up the experience of first seeing combat: "When we took off on this first mission, I wasn't too afraid, but after this one, and for all of those thereafter, I was scared to death!"

10
BOEING 42-31653

November 1943
Boeing Company Plant #2
Seattle, King County, Washington

204 days. Thus was the lifespan of a Flying Fortress operating with the US 8th Army Air Force in late 1943. Factoring out maintenance hours and non-operational days, a B-17 was projected to fly nineteen combat missions before being shot down or suffering destruction by one of the seemingly endless dangers that were likewise faced by the combat fliers themselves. One of the nearly 13,000 Flying Fortresses built between 1935 and 1945, B-17G #42-31653 rolled off the assembly line of Seattle's "Boeing Wonderland" assembly plant in November of 1943. Reined into line alongside a dozen identical warbirds, the titan sat in silent attention on the cement apron as chilly sea breezes swept the early morning haze back out to sea. Before her towered the camouflaged walls of Hanger #2, whose roof masqueraded as twenty-six acres of ordinary Seattle neighborhood. The immense, 1,776,000 square-foot structure sheltered multiple state-of-the-art assembly lines, untold millions of dollars in material, and the most advanced assembly technology of the time. The building also housed 30,000 expertly-skilled employees, most of whom were women; thousands being black women, and just a portion of the 20 million-plus "Rosie the Riveters" caught up in the fight across the Nation. These indispensable workers—patriots all—augmented the US war industry and, indisputably, helped win the War.

Wrenched free from the bauxite ore mines of the South to the smelters of "ALCOA Island" in the Pacific Northwest and finally to the "Fortress Factory" on the Puget Sound, the B-17 had come a long way, as had the evolution of her kind. As a "G" model Fortress; the final, most advanced, and best-equipped version of the aircraft, this bomber was the product of nearly a decade of design and three brutal years of combat trials. Tried and tested in all theaters of combat, the origin of many of the alterations and evolutions engineered into the Fortress would come at the insistence of the battle veterans themselves.

B-24 Liberator, USAF

When assembled, her fuselage measured over seventy-four feet in length. Outstretched, she spanned 103 feet, wingtip to wingtip. Four, 1200 horsepower, nine-cylinder Wright Cyclone intercooled radial engines, each capped by a three-bladed propellor with an 11-foot diameter, would help the 32-ton beast get into the air. With the assistance of state-of-the-art turbo-superchargers, the aircraft could cruise at an astonishing maximum speed of over 280 miles per hour and travel nearly 2,000 miles and bear a payload of up to 6,000 pounds. With every hour in the air, it guzzled four gallons of oil and consumed two hundred gallons of fuel–the latter drawn from stores in its large fuel tanks and several self-sealing "Tokyo tanks" housed in the wings.

While the aircraft featured an abundance of the most innovative technologies of the day, perhaps the Flying Fortress's most valuable and unequaled feature was its capacity to withstand an unbelievable amount of structural harm. The American B-24 "Liberator," the Fortress' four-engine sister, flew further and could haul heavier loads; but it was the B-17's ability to tolerate severe abuse that made it the more endeared airframe among the fliers. Compared to the twin-tail B-24, known as the "Lumbering Lib" and the "Flying

Boxcar" due to its angular, crate-like profile, the Fortress was sleeker and, overall, more aesthetically appealing to both combat crews and the public alike. This led to the B-17 to being dubbed "the Hollywood bomber." Appearances aside, both the Liberator and Flying Fortress, the "aerial battleships," were the tools most capable of answering the call of the USAAF for strategic, high-altitude, daylight, precision-bombing activities. These "heavies" could lift the tonnage, execute the long-range assignments, thrive at extreme heights, and bring the flying men home only to repeat the merciless work, day after day.

Sleek as she was, with thirteen heavy .50 caliber machine guns, the Flying Fortress, nevertheless, packed quite a punch. Although its predecessors bristled with an assortment of weapons that led the Japanese to refer to the massive aircraft as the "four-engine fighter," it was the addition of the "chin turret," engineered under the bomber's nose, that gave the B-17G its unmistakable brutish profile. It was found that by adding not one but a pair of "fifties" to the aircraft's frontal defenses—an improvement that, along with the two cheek guns—bestowed the snout of the Fortress with the look of the barbels of a catfish, albeit with a much more potent sting. Many of the Luftwaffe's audaciously lethal "12 o'clock high" head-on attacks were checked by this adaptation, contributing, in part, to cause some Germans to develop what they called *"vier motor schreck"*—the "four-engine fear."

When not planted at his table behind the bombardier in the same confined space of the nose compartment, the navigator utilized two heavy machine guns installed in the aircraft's cheeks. Just behind and above the flight cabin where the two pilots were posted, the flight engineer controlled a twin gun, electrically-operated, plexiglass-capped rotational turret. Aside from his other duties, this sergeant was entrusted with sweeping the airspace above the bomber, although the radio operator, found in his alcove just behind the bomb bay and poised with his own weapon angled high to the rear, also helped scan and

Cheek guns and bombardier turret, Kay

clear the skies overhead. On the underside of the aircraft hung the Sperry ball turret—a round shell of steel and glass that was able to rotate 360 degrees and pivot its dual Brownings straight down, thereby generating a wide cone of fire below the B-17. To bring the weapons to life, the man elected to this cramped orb would drop into the electrically-powered turret when the aircraft was in flight. There he would remain for the majority of the mission, only extricating himself when on return over England.

Further astern, in the mid-section of the ship were two additional gun stations, manned by a pair of non-commissioned officers, "non-coms," and designated as waist gunners. Another improvement seen in "G" models, these battle positions were staggered, allowing more functional space for the gunners who previously stood back-to-back and pivoted their heavy machine guns around each other, protecting the flanks. The addition of windows, through which the guns traversed, spared the men from the turbulent, freezing slipstream.

Secluded under the towering vertical stabilizer was the tail gunner's station. The airman assigned to the position, another "non-com," sat facing rearwards and straddled a small seat. Entrenched behind ballistic glass in a narrow compartment below the rudder, the man wielded two more heavy guns. This "stinger" position could throw out a concentrated hailstorm of lead and was vital in dissuading any threats approaching from the rear.

During the final stage at the Boeing plant, the bomber's 4,200 square feet of surface area was painted. The upper surface was coated in a dark, olive drab, while the aircraft's belly was covered in a neutral grey–a transformation to help disguise the $258,040.00 aircraft while it sat vulnerable, resting on the ground. A white star, set in a blue circle flanked by short white horizontal bars, the roundel birthmark of a United States Army Air Force aircraft, was added to both sides of the fuselage just in front of the staggered waist windows. Two more of these insignias were painted on the ship, one on top of the port wing and the other on the bottom of the starboard wing. On both sides of its large tail, a series of yellow numbers were stenciled, advertising the machine's serial number. In total, thirty-five gallons of lead-based paint covered the Fortress, decreasing airspeed by roughly five miles an hour and adding up to three hundred pounds of additional weight. Far from regulation, it was not uncommon for a few ounces of ink to be added to the extraordinary machines before leaving the assembly floor, as many of the workers themselves left their mark, quite literally, on the aircraft. Upon assuming a newly-assembled bomber, some aircrews

Justin R. Burke

discovered that many of the "Rosies" had penned their names to the interior surfaces of the plane, some even adding their home address.

Released for handover to the USAAF, #42-31653 sat poised and ready to add her contribution of the 640,000 tons of ordnance that would be discharged by B-17s onto Nazi Germany during the conflict. Departing the Boeing complex, the mighty bird spent the following fortnight stretching its wings, slow-timing engines, and hopping through a series of modification centers in the Midwest for final adjustments before being deemed "fit for flight." At Kearney Army Airfield in Nebraska, the bomber was matched with a newly formed, battle-bound crew who readily accepted the dazzling new warbird to fly to the troupe's assigned theater of deployment in England.

From Kearney, the flight path took the B-17 over America's heartland, first passing over great expanses of rolling plain, fertile farm fields, and then beyond. The drone of the B-17's powerful motors soon filled Hoosier kitchens and then resonated in Buckeye living rooms, transported there by soft breezes that, on occasion, tenderly lifted the red, white, and blue fabric of US service banners. Over coal country, the aircrew examined the land's craggy highlands and valleys, every now and then noting the scars from a century of mining operations. Further east, the crew counted the bridges that spanned a trio of converging waterways: the Ohio, Monongahela, and Allegheny Rivers, where the "Steel City," Pittsburg was diligently generating its daily contribution of what would add up to be a total of ninety-five million tons of steel produced by War's end.

Over eastern Pennsylvania, the pilots began their gradual descent, crossing over into New Jersey and swinging the aircraft back over the Delaware River to line up for the approach to New Castle Army Air Base. There they remained "wheels-down" for the night for rest as the Air Transport Command's Ferrying Group continued coordinating the logistics of moving apparatus, equipment, and personnel to their terminus in the British Isles. On the 19th of December, the Boeing and her crew arrived at the jumping-off point of the North Atlantic Route, established at Presque Isle Army Air Field, Maine, and staged overnight before lifting off of US soil for the last time the next day.

Navigating north, the ship traversed the vast, frigid Canadian wilderness where signs of life were sparse, at best. The Flying Fortress set down in Labrador at Goose Bay Air Base, a huge installation whose icy 7,000-foot-long runway was almost eternally hedged in by walls of snowpack. Surrounding the base existed nothing more than the utterly remote, undeveloped, secluded Canadian frontier. Departures were dictated by the weather as conditions in the area and systems over the Atlantic were, in many instances, entirely unforgiving. In 1944, an average of twenty ships per day were pulling away from the frosty field at Goose Bay, destined for one of the multitudes of bomb groups in Britain.

Following a bone-chilling layover, 42-31653 was cleared for take-off with orders to navigate 780 miles northeast to "Bluie West One" at Narsarsuaq, Greenland. While there was no debating Atlantic weather fronts, flight control released aircraft at irregular intervals. Though each machine was inevitably destined for the same embattled isle far off to the East, each crew was directed to fly a slightly different flight path as the demand for secrecy and employing deceptions was necessary. Prying eyes were everywhere, no doubt, and the battlefront was getting closer with every mile. As the cruising altitude was reached and the rage of the radials settled into their characteristic, tranquilizing drone, the non-coms, when not amusing themselves with estimating the untold numbers of icebergs that drifted by below them, settled in for a lengthy flight filled with card games and intermittent sleep. Some crews who started the journey during the evening hours became entranced by the pink, green, yellow, and purple hues of the Aurora Borealis that danced out in the immense expanse of the heavens. This fleeting moment of insight into the divine hung in sharp contrast against the infinite expanse of murky, biting seawaters below whose abyss concealed countless fallen crusaders and their ships of war, sunken supply vessels, and, of course, Hitler's hungry steel wolf-pack of U-boats.

The Atlantic crossing, "the Northern Route" as it was known, was notorious for being a treacherous, exacting, and highly fickle pilgrimage. It not only challenged the skills of the navigators and pilots but commonly required daring and, at times, quite literally, blind faith. Over the ocean, temperamental weather systems could hinder visibility, requiring aircraft to fly at exceptionally high or uncomfortably low altitudes—deviations that produced further hazards. Climb too high and ice would subtly accumulate on the leading edge of the airfoil. Those who failed to recognize the peril and quickly descend to warmer altitudes would find their airship had become too heavy to maintain stable flight and plunge into the sea. On the other hand, fly too low and pilots risked slamming into whitecaps and crashing into the ocean where the ship, and her men, would be dragged down into the dark nothingness. North Atlantic headwinds slowed progress and burnt up precious fuel, while crosswinds were known to blow crews further south and consequently away from land. It is thought that as thousands pushed along the route in 1943, up to ten percent of the teams were lost in the chilly waters of the Arctic and Atlantic Oceans. With the possibility of rescue considered improbable at best, most efforts were not attempted. In the end, with the wheel-of-war grinding on, the occasional sacrifice of machine and personnel became an acceptable cost by the US Air Transport Command.

While at Goose Bay, the crews had been given lengthy briefings on the unusual approach to the unique airstrip in Greenland known as "Bluie West One." Upon reaching the mountainous coastline, aircrews first had to pinpoint the correct fjord that led into an unforgiving labyrinth of towering stone. Flying low and slow, 42-31653 finessed her way between twenty miles of bluffs and rocky cliff walls, some socked in with haze and, at times, rising hundreds of feet above the Fortress. With no room to maneuver and plentiful dead-end pathways, the pilots would not get a second attempt at their run up the narrow valley leading to the airfield. Shooting the stony corridor, her wingtips passed within feet of clipping mossy-covered rock faces as the men inside were jostled about while the big bomber negotiated up, over, and around craggy outcrops. As the B-17 emerged from out of the corridor, the worn-out pair of pilots, countering brutal wind gusts with flexed forearms and tensed backs, executed a quick turn, lowered the landing gear, extended the flaps, nudged back the throttles, and immediately lined up for a swift, final approach on the solitary runway laying between them and the bay waters just beyond. After landing, the white-knuckled pilots guided 42-31653 onto the steel-mat apron, shut down her engines, and hurriedly went about securing the aircraft in temperatures well below freezing. After a detailed meteorological and navigational briefing following a few hours of much-needed shut-eye and nourishment, the Americans once again took wing and fixed their heading on Keflavik, Iceland, 748 miles distant.

Having navigated above the icecap for the previous five hours, the B-17's propellers ticked to a stop at Meeks Field, where the team was greeted by a bitterly icy breeze, a tranquil stillness, and the striking

131

beauty of the "Land of Fire and Ice." "People all pro-Nazi, unfriendly, backward, seems 30 years behind US in civilization," documented one unimpressed flyboy passing through Meeks. Other accounts from transient fliers refer to the locals as "fish heads," due to their heavy seafood diet, or inaccurately as "Mos"–a derogatory contraction for Eskimos. They also nicknamed the local girls who became bewitched by the presence of the handsome, well-dressed Americans as "Stukas"–a playful reference to the ill-famed shrieking German dive bomber. Setting off from Meeks, Prestwick, Scotland, terminus of the "North Atlantic Ferry Route," would be their next and final stop on their march to war. Blessed with a bird's-eye-view of the terrain, they first winged their way over vast lava fields and black sand beaches of Iceland's beautiful, yet haunting, southern shores before pushing out into 845 miles of open ocean where the arctic conditions worked against the tired crews.

Most navigators heading to England executed their duties superbly, despite the many risks, the extreme environment, a limited knowledge of the weather systems and atmospheric conditions, and the sweat-inducing pressure to perform. To circumvent catastrophe, these route finders were encouraged to trust in their training and tools and work in close contact with their flight team and radio operator– the man who kept the aircraft "on the beam" by deciphering navigational radio frequencies. A lot of deviation could occur over 2,400 miles, the distance between Goose Bay and Prestwick Air Field; and there was ample opportunity for a U-boat or high-powered German radio tower to bait complacent aircrews further south over open waters or lure them into bearing left, bringing them back toward isolation on the enormous arctic ice cap. To complicate matters, flight time to Nazi-occupied Norway was virtually identical to the Meeks-Prestwick leg.

Reaching the Firth of Clyde, the aviators let down through the overcast and confirmed landing instructions with Prestwick control. Upon approach, the bomber glided low over the bustling water traffic, where troop transports slid up the river with their loads of warriors and tools of destruction destined for Greenock, or perhaps further on at Glasgow where the whine of pipers greeted the sea-legged Yanks as they disembarked. 42-31653 touched down on Scottish soil and rolled to a stop at its allocated position on the apron. Sitting alongside were rows of Liberators, Mitchells, Skytrains, Mosquitos, Lancasters,

Hudsons, Mustangs, Spitfires, Thunderbolts, Lightenings, and of course, more Flying Fortresses–just a small portion of an immense assemblage waiting to be organized and set loose upon the adversary.

On top of a reorganization that increased the size of its four squadrons, the 94th Bomb Group had suffered the loss of nine aircraft in the month of November 1943. Five more followed in early December, each with their complement of ten young men, and it was obvious that replacements in both personnel and machine were needed right away if Command wanted the unit brought back up to fighting strength. Of the nearly twenty "green" Flying Fortresses sent to the station in December 1943, only two would survive until the fall of '44. One would miraculously return to the States after the end of the War, only to be converted to scrap metal. The other was 42-31653: Rougham's Christmas delivery.

The ground crew and mechanics at Rougham Airfield were among the finest in the 8th, but the addition of untested machines always presented them with new challenges. Factory fresh aircraft were seldom fit for service right out the door. In reality, the ships had to be "broken in" to a point between being "green" and "bent." Upon arrival to Rougham, final modifications and numerous adjustments would be made to get the Boeing battle-ready. The projects included adding supplementary oxygen cylinders, upgrading her antenna and radios, replacing her windscreens with bulletproof glass, and, in a move to prevent the plexiglass nose cone from being splintered by the concussive blasts, fitting eighteen-inch blast barrels to the machine guns in the chin turret. One of the most appreciated endeavors effectuated by the maintenance crews was the addition of steel sheeting to the battle positions throughout the aircraft including the seat bottoms where the armor was thought to shield the most precious of the boy's cargos. During the conversion process, ground personnel painted "GL": "George Love"; the identification marking of the 410th Bomb Squadron, on each side of the airframe just aft of the roundel. "Victor" was the new bird's unique code letter, and a large "V" was added on the tail, arranged under the aircraft's yellow serial numbers. Lastly, a large white square was painted on the top of the vertical stabilizer, the sign of the 3rd Bombardment Division. Stenciled inside the square, the addition of a black letter "A" made it official: The bomber was now a part of "the Big Square A"–the 94th Bomb Group.

Throughout her time at Rougham, hundreds of men would

'Bombs Away', Fold3

entrust their lives to this incredibly resilient Fortress. While it would be assigned to numerous crews during 1944, the aircraft was tended to by only a few dedicated ground personnel and maintenance staff. These often-overlooked men were essential in preparing the aircraft for flight and combat maneuvers, and each squad attended to the machine as if it was their own. Upon meeting a new team of combat fliers, many crew chiefs would be sure to emphasize that although the airmen would fly in it, the aircraft belonged to him. These men prided themselves on their work, labor that began even before the bomber squealed to a stop on its hardstand following the day's pursuits. Applying their mechanical know-how, they could address any issue with the ship and would toil day or night, in snow, sleet, rain, and freezing conditions. These sergeants patched up holes the size of basketballs in their ship's aluminum skin, scars that she had earned in skirmishes with the Luftwaffe or driving through fields of flak. The maintenance team could replace her giant radial engines with such speed and efficiency–a base all-time-high of 81 was changed out in September 1944 alone–that most instructors could not match even in the sterile training environments back in the States. While revolutionary and of the latest design, the power plants had been engineered with farm boys in mind allowing them to take to the motors with the same ease and familiarity that many had developed with their father's tractor.

Some of their procedures could be accomplished while the plane hunkered on the hardstand; but if needed, the bombers would be moved into the cavernous hangars where new or salvaged parts, many recovered from other battle-weary Fortresses known as "hanger queens," could be fitted onto the mangled aircraft. One of the far less glamorous jobs never depicted on Army recruiting posters, it was the ground crew who was also given the unsavory duty of washing out the gore and the various human bodily fluids expelled deliberately or inadvertently on violent forays over enemy lands that could last more than eight hours in length.

The maiden combat flight for the virgin Fort, now listed on Group formation charts and assignment boards as "653," would come mid-January 1944. Being hot off the line, #653 was awarded to the lead crews of the 410th Squadron. On multiple occasions, when veteran Lt. Daniel Riordan led a pack of the 94th's raiders into battle that winter, he and his men flew in "653." "We named this aircraft 'Margie' for Dan's girlfriend in the States and who he married when he returned to the US. We flew it nineteen times," recalled Riordan's replacement bombardier, Adolph Del Zappo, in a post-war letter. "We never did get the name 'Margie' painted in bold letters on its nose but my engineer did scrawl it in small writing near the right window of the cabin," wrote Del Zappo in 1994. When the Riordan crew carried out their final flight of their tour, twenty-five still being the number required by some veteran crews flying in March of '44, they returned to England in mystified astonishment, knowing they had beat the odds and cheated death countless time; and they had done it with "653."

To celebrate the accomplishment of surviving hundreds of hours in tightly-massed bomber boxes, passing through the sights of Luftwaffe pilots and sailing past the hot guns of German anti-aircraft gunners, some pilots, upon arriving over their home field, were remembered to have slipped their airships out of the traffic pattern only to gun their engines and execute an unauthorized low pass over the tower and just above the heads of their cheering comrades for the final, celebratory "buzz job." Others, like Riordan's bunch, "...peeled off firing flares from the nose, tail, and waist as fast as we could," showering the field with colorful balls of light. As tribute for their service, Riordan and his team were presented with a "Lucky Bastard Club" certificate. In the decades that followed, the den in the Del Zappo home would be adorned with memorabilia from the 94th. Included in the collection was his own framed certificate with the following inscription:

> *On this 28th day March nineteen hundred and forty-four the fickle finger of Fate finds it expedient to trace on the roll of the*
> **LUCKY BASTARDS CLUB**
> *The name of Adolph Del Zappo "Margie" Who on this date achieved the remarkable record of having sallied forth, and returned, no fewer than 25 risky times, bearing tons and tons of H.E. [High Explosive] Goodwill to the Fuehrer and would-be Fuhrers, thru the courtesy of Eighth Bomber Command, who sponsors these programs in the interest of the Government, "of the people, by the people and for the people"*

Remembering those incredible days past in a conversation with friends, Del Zappo ended a letter recalling his time in the 8th with, "The #42-31653 brings back many pleasant though awful memories of the vicious air battles we fought over Europe."

Upon assuming the role of squadron lead, Lt. Fred Koval and his veteran crew were relegated to the now broken-in bomber. It was considered bad luck by some superstitious aviators to rename an aircraft; but Koval, a pilot who would end up completing two European tours and one in the Pacific Theater before War's end, was determined to christen his new Fortress. Believing that his friends back home would get a kick out of their connection to his explosive enterprise of hurling tons of American iron on the Reich, the lieutenant chose to name the Boeing in honor of his hometown. "He was from Erie, Pennsylvania…just named it like their job was to 'ferry' bombs to the target," remembers Koval's son in a 2019 interview with the author. In between a run of winter operations, Fred secured the services of a creative maintenance sergeant and had the aircraft's name painted on the port side of her nose. She would be called *Erie Ferry*. As was typical for all combat teams, the lieutenant and his nine crewmates flew at least five different ships while based at Rougham, each with its unique "personality" and many of which proved to be unreliable and far less rugged. When *Erie Ferry* was on the mend after one particularly tough mauling, Lt. Koval found himself courting the vexatious *Lucy Valves* into battle. "He named it that as he always said it was the noisiest airplane he had ever heard," explained Koval's son, relaying that his father "was concerned that it would shake itself apart."

After a handful of jobs with the Koval crew, 653 was re-assigned to yet another Keystone State aviator named George Kacsuta, when he lifted off to knock out Nazi shipyards along the Reich coast. Kacsuta had been flying with the 94th since the previous fall and was considered an experienced, competent combat pilot. Despite the German's best efforts, George had successfully brought several battle-bruised bombers back to East Anglia, each time, amazingly, with an unscathed crew. Although she would continue to be referred to as *Erie Ferry* on the 94th's Group records, when George grabbed the reigns, his boys took to calling her by a new nickname: *Kac's Flak Shack*.

The air battles of early '44 were unforgiving on 653, and every run into Luftwaffe hunting grounds took a toll on its airframe. After casting a load of incendiary bombs onto the sub pens at Wilhelmshaven, the 94th, *Erie Ferry* among them, bolted for the open sea where a sleet storm pounded the Group, making close formation flight impossible. With each frozen Fortress nearing ruin at the storm's icy grip, the Group Leader transmitted an emergency order instructing each crew to break formation and fend for themselves. As the entire force began letting down through the storm, chunks of ice could be heard breaking loose from the wings and pinging off fuselages and horizontal stabilizers. During the turmoil, one Boeing from the Group nosed into the rear of another, sheering off the tail guns and the unfortunate sergeant gunner with them. The disorderly flight broke free of the clouds at no more than two hundred feet above North Sea waters.

As a/c #653 screamed onward through the broken sea fog, accompanied by a disbursement of B-17s from the Group, the unit discovered that they were racing over the enemy-held Frisian Islands. When the haze abruptly dissipated, the Rougham men gazed down upon a company of German gunners who, apparently just as surprised by the chance encounter as the Americans, made a mad dash for their gun positions. With German 20mm cannon opening up on the intruders, the 94th's gunners returned the favor and hammered away with their .50 caliber Brownings. At such a low elevation, the fliers could clearly see pillars of sand erupt along the ground as lines of their colored tracer rounds skipped and ricocheted along and among the battery entrenchments. One 94th Fortress gunner later wrote that as his Boeing passed through the shooting gallery, stocked with enemy troops, he "saw about twenty go down like rag dolls."

On February 20th, the first missions of "Operation Argument" and what would later be referred to as "Big Week," Major Roger Stevenson was to lead the 94th's "B" group and took ship #653. Each time the battle-tried B-17 returned from a successful trip over the continent, a yellow bomb icon was painted on the side of its nose and for every enemy aircraft destroyed, *Erie Ferry* was marked with a small swastika. By late Spring 1944, #653 was proudly displaying her war paint: three bombs for Frankfurt, a pair for Brunswick, two for Brussels, and one for Wilhelmshaven, Rostock, Leipzig, Saint-Andre-de-L'Eure, Enclavelles, Chartres, Diest, Politz, Halle, Augsburg, Behen, Aulnat, Monceau-le-Waast, Chaumont, Boulogne, Wimereux, and Eperlecques. Many more would follow. A few of the symbols also signified jumps across the English Channel to the "Robot Coast" on "Crossbow" missions–assaults aimed at extinguishing V-1 rocket launch sites. One bomb, tallied after the March 3rd adventure, held a particular significance for the Boeing. That day, she was introduced to Berlin, better known as "Big B," on what would be her first of many pushes on the Nazi capitol.

In May, the Koval and Riordan teams rotated through assignments on #653, racking up even more missions to the aircraft's total. *Erie Ferry* was nearly lost when, on another visit to the Reich capital, the force was recalled over the coast of the mainland after reports of exceptionally dense and elevated cloud formations made their way to Wing leaders. With hundreds of Fortresses and B-24s simultaneously turning back for England, the units lost all cohesiveness. As the "heavies" attempted to navigate blindly through the clouds, the move inadvertently caused many groups to run a collision course with trailing formations. When the clouds finally parted, it became instantly apparent that *Erie Ferry* and a sister Boeing had decided to occupy the exact same airspace at the exact same moment. Quick thinking, evasive action, and sheer luck prevented a cataclysmic event, and #653 was fortunate to return to her home field, astonishingly brandishing only a dented wing. Late in the month, in anticipation of a possible German night raid, 94th Bomb Group mechanics, crew chiefs—even riveters—were employed with additional and unfamiliar responsibilities. Leroy Kuest, a well-liked, accomplished mechanic from the 331st Bomb Squadron revealed, "We are now guarding our ships each night with Tommy Guns as if we are afraid of a Nazi Paratroop invasion."

During its stretch at Rougham, *Erie Ferry* saw action in some of the 94th's costliest undertakings, but she also partook in a few uneventful "milk runs." Some days she would close in to her squadron position beside one of her sister Fortresses like *Good Time Cholley III, Frenesi, Grin and Bear It, The Shady Lady*, and *Nine Yanks and a Jerk*. Flying along with *Hard-to-Get*, she had pounded Bremen, sailed to Friedrichshafen alongside *Idiot's Delight*, and struck Nuremberg with *Filthy Hag, Dog Tired, Tuff Eddie*, and *Northern Queen*. Covering the flank of *Fortress McHenry*, 653 tucked in with *Mighty Warrior*, winged with *The Gimp* to Konigsberg, and made a call on Stuttgart, Hamm, and Brux with *Red Hot Riding Hood, Flak Buster, St. Christopher's Kids, Friday the 13th*, and *Ordinance Express*. At other times, 653 was selected as a "spare" for the day and would be left to recuperate on her hardstand, earning a short respite as the rest of the Fortress colony embarked upon its explosive, diurnal migration cycle.

By June, nearly a dozen freshman crews had winged into combat aboard Boeing 42-31653. At that point the bomber was considered sturdy and dependable, but aged. As veteran crews were allotted new, unpainted, gleaming Fortresses just off US assembly lines, the older B-17s—the ones that were left—were now set aside for the inexperienced, unproven squads. "We started out flying an old olive drab-colored Fortress named the *Erie Ferry*. It was number '653'," one gunner on the Verner Wertsch crew recorded. The lads on the McKeekin, Fleming, Morcan, Harpootl, Weston, Haller, Cummings, Fausnaugh, Wall, Morris, Brooks, and Thomas teams would also takeoff and return safely to Rougham after their first missions in the maturing queen. By then, the "ghosts" had been exercised from the machine, all the "gremlins" worked out of her system, and as the veterans moved on to newer airships, superstitious greenhorns sensed that this Fort, although time-worn, was blessed with good fortune.

D-Day would see the 94th fly three assignments to Normandy, beginning with an assailment on the Caen coastal defenses three hours before Allied troops hit the beaches. *Erie Ferry* contributed to the

A Luftwaffe fighter approaches from six o'clock low, Fold3

destruction on the ground and returned to Rougham on the morning of that momentous day without incident. The ship was refueled, re-loaded, and returned to Northern France where it struck the marshaling yards at Alencon. On 25 June, *Erie Ferry* and two squadrons of the 94th carried out a supply drop near Vercors Plateau for "Operation Zebra." Instead of bombs, the force released parachute-equipped supply pods bearing munitions and provisions for the *Maquis* partisans.

As the sorties piled up, Bomber Command continued to bolster Allied ground efforts in France and turned much of its focus east towards Germany. That summer, the 94th BG joined in more strikes on objectives near Berlin, Regensburg, Bremen, and Leipzig and discharged even more stocks of supplies for French resistance fighters across the Channel. For three consecutive days, *Erie Ferry* flew to Munich with the Group, fought through the ferocious flak storm that habitually simmered over the city at the presence of the bombers, and inflicted a devastating blow to the historic Bavarian metropolis. As Axis and Allied ground armies continued with their clashes in France, the US Army's aerial arm, along with the RAF, was not only wrecking Nazi industry, transportation, and fuel production plants across

Northern Europe but now, it pounded at the heart of Germany itself.

Lt. Merritt Fausnaugh sank into the left seat in the cockpit of *Erie Ferry* on one Friday in early September. The run for the day, the 8th, was a relatively short hop to Mainz, Germany, where the bombers were dispatched to thrash an important tank assembly factory. For Fausnaugh, one of the 410th's "old-timers," his obligations this day included mentoring a fresh arrival for what would be the pilot's inaugural baptism by fire. Although the Rougham 17s were hit with some severe, concentrated flak, the flight went well. After dismounting 653 once back at Station #468, the new, blue-eyed lieutenant listened attentively to Fausnaugh's critiques. The stranger then shook hands with the crew, glanced back over his shoulder at the old sun-bleached warhorse whose battle scars were now pockmarked with various shades of aluminum patching, and loaded into the transport truck that would drive him and the team to the operations block for their post-flight interviews. Seemingly impressed, Fausnaugh was satisfied with the young man's attention to detail, adherence to Group standard operating procedures, and overall performance under the stresses of combat flight and withering enemy fire, and signed off on the new pilot.

The following day, *Erie Ferry* was summoned into the air once again. For the fourth time, supply pods fell from ships of the 94th and descended under full parachutes onto a plain in a French valley to arm the resistance. On the 10th, the mechanics charged with preparing *Erie Ferry* for war were kept busy through the night and well into the early pre-dawn hours of the 11th to ready the Fort for her next job. In the calm before daybreak that Monday, the same new, slim, blue-eyed lieutenant would return to #653's hardstand but this time he brought other unfamiliar characters. This day, he would pilot the "heavy" as the aircraft commander. As the airmen pulled themselves up into the plane, the ground crew chief skimmed over his check sheets for one last final confirmation. He scanned the nine new names listed on the form. Typed on the "ship no." line was the familiar "#653," but the pilot had scribbled something different in pencil next to it. Apparently adding his mark, the aviator had jotted down the Fortress' new nom-de-guerre; the *Green Hornets*.

11

11 SEPTEMBER 1944

11 September 1944
0725 hours
Rougham Aerodrome hardstands
Bury St. Edmunds, Suffolk, East Anglia, England

Behind the two-inch-thick bulletproof windscreen of their B-17, Irv and Merle sat silently in the shadows of the Fortress' cabin, mindful of each second ticking off of their wrist watches, and scouring out into the blackness, waiting for just this moment when they would finally catch sight of the guiding light. Then, following what seemed like an eternity, suddenly they saw it: a streak of emerald cracked from out of the darkness and rose rapidly into the softly lit sky. The comet hissed skyward, encircled by a glowing halo; and, as it reached its zenith, it stalled and then suddenly ruptured with a pop, transforming into a brilliant orb of green. The report echoed over the hazy fields just as the flame arced over to one side and fell back into the murk, burning out above darkened thickets of oak. After the flare collapsed into itself and flickered away, the command "Daisy" scratched over the pilots' headsets, breaking the early-morning quiet and sending a jolt of adrenaline surging into their guts and igniting a blaze in their chests. At the sight of the signal, the duo initiated the routine they had been practicing and refining together for the last six months: "Start engines, fireguard posted, batteries on, hydraulic pump auto, flaps up, cowl flaps open, master switch on, gyros caged, inverters on, parking brake on, fuel quantity check, bomb bay doors closed...clear left." Posted in the right seat for what was to be his first combat flight, Lt. Metzger confirmed the items on his checklist, swiveled his frame towards the starboard wing and reported back, "Clear right."

In the command pilot's station on the left side of the cabin, Merle pivoted and glanced down out of his open side window where a ghost-like mist wafted silently over the cracked, oil-stained cement pad. "All clear...starting one," announced the lieutenant as he shot his arm out of the window. Catching the attention of the ground crew waiting below, Green raised a finger and made a whirling motion with his hand. With the throttles set, the starter switch for the #1 engine was engaged, bringing the ship out of its hibernation. Both officers studied the propeller as it began to rotate–whining, clicking and knocking into action. Smoke belched from the engine ports as the motor chugged, hesitating for just a moment before resigning to the prompts issued from the masters on the flight deck. Following a few sluggish revolutions, the engine caught, abruptly sending the big blades charging through a few more cycles before the trio jerkily accelerated and converted into a whooshing, transparent gray, yellow-ringed circle. The pilots redeployed their attention back on their instrument panel as they reacted instinctually, balancing pressures, adjusting mixtures, and setting engine revolutions. When satisfied, the pair repeated the procedure, one-by-one, with the other three power plants, each time being rewarded with the same response.

Sgt. Lehere had assumed his post between and just behind the two pilots and as he listened to the guttural growl of the engines, his eyes darted between the gauges on the instrument panel and the choreographed movements of the officers who methodically walked down another page of their check sheets. Even warbling at a fraction of their total potential, the powerful motors triggered the entire aircraft to vibrate, shudder, and sway. The aviators had provoked the monster and now it sat straddling its concrete slab, growing in agitation as the resonance of her engines melded into the humming chorus spreading across the field. The crescendo continued to swell until the entire fleet sat poised on their launching pads, radiating a collective snarling roar of more than one hundred and four engines into the fog and lowlight. All united, the bombers literally shook the earth.

All through the night, long before the flight crew's arrival, the ground echelon: the mechanics, fuel tenders, armorers, munition specialists, photo lab technicians, drivers, and ordnance personnel, had labored to get the fleet ready. At each cement pad, armorers had heaved allotments of heavy wooden crates into the planes and situated them for take-off. The boxes, holding twenty-seven-foot-long ammunition belts, each containing hundreds of .50 caliber rounds, would later be moved to the battle positions by the gunners and charged into the machine guns. At the bomb dump, the iron explosives were loaded onto carts using a combination of cranes, hoists, and human muscle. Then, being transported to the flight line on trailers, the bombs were fused and prepped by technicians, raised into the bomb holds by the loaders, and, at last, secured on their racks. Before the "witching hour" earlier that morning, the Nordens had been fetched from the "bomb vault" and installed in the ships by a few, specially vetted personnel. Convoys of trucks ferried gas to the hardstands where thousands of gallons of fuel were fed to each of the Group's thirsty birds. While the mechanics and crew chiefs fluttered around the aircraft, testing magnetos and exercising engines, technicians ensured the plane's oxygen stores were full and filled the portable bottles. Elsewhere on base, medical orderlies stocked their ambulances, and the firefighting company made ready their crash trucks and water tenders. Military Police soldiers not only continued to monitor the operation room and command huts but patrolled the perimeter of the installation and stood guard at the access points. At the mess hall, while attendants organized the stock of utensils and trays, an army of cooks whipped up massive batches of fresh eggs and toasted bread and began brewing a seemingly infinite supply of coffee. This was the crucial business carried out night after night, all while the combat men slept, huddled deep in their wool blankets.

Hours later, when the combat team arrived at #653's dispersal pad, the sergeants passed the Brownings off to the ground crew who helped the edgy airmen yank their tools out of the oil-soaked cloths and clean away any remaining traces of lubrication. If not removed, the oil would cause the guns to freeze up at altitude. Lastly, they fixed the weapons into the gun ports, manipulated them through their ranges of motion, and blessed them with wishes of good shooting. While the gunners helped the ground crew walk each propellor through a dozen revolutions-necessary to prime the engines and work the settled oil from the motors, Lehere busied himself with his own pre-flight practices. Surveying the ship, he examined his notes, looked over the aircraft's maintenance sheets, confirmed the fuel load and aircraft weight, and periodically scribbled down details as he trailed after the doting, harried crew chief. Soon after, the clamor of another heavy truck rumbling to a stop in front of the Flying Fortress signified the arrival of the officers.

As the flight engineer and crew chief linked up with the pilots to confer and relay the plane's diagnosis, Frank and Jack scampered up into the bomber via a shaky ladder that had been set up under the forward access hatch, located just behind the nose on the port side of the aircraft. Once inside the bomber's nose, Frank stowed his charts at his station, crammed his parachute alongside,

Norden bombsight, USAF

scanned over his guidance instruments, and set about reviewing the course particulars and heading data. In the meantime, Jack had hauled himself up into the B-17 and tossed his bag into the nose cabin before turning astern. Plodding rearward, he had to concentrate on his deliberate footfalls, ducking railing, and being careful not to hit any of the hard, unforgiving metal edges that formed the cramped interior of the front of the ship. Managing to dodge all obstacles and averting the tragedy of earning a painful, swollen knot on the top of his head, Lt. Williams stepped through the aperture just past the top turret platform and onto the slender beam that spanned the bomb bay. There, poised on the narrow catwalk, Jack stood within his nest of ten, 500-pound explosive eggs. When satisfied with his evaluation of the payload, bomb racks, and release mechanisms, Jack retraced his route to the front of the craft, moved ahead through the hole in the forward bulkhead, crawled towards his stool, roosted himself in front of the bombsight, and began fidgeting with his sight's settings.

With his preparations complete, Jack slipped out of the B-17 and wandered up beside Merle. The two friends stood together,

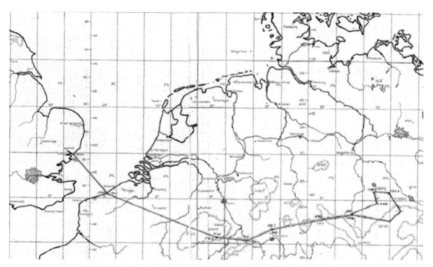

94th BG mission plot map for 11 September 1944, NARA

pausing to commit to memory the misty stillness and knowing that within only a few minutes' time, the peace would be stirred by the ignition of the great machines, charging the air with their mechanized battle cry. A few inspirited words were exchanged, along with some nervous glances, before Frank and Irv joined the duo. With the lieutenants following along, the navigator drew his finger across the face of his map, reviewing the specifics of their flight route, destination points, and arrival times. The day's odyssey was apparently a lengthy one, as had been indicated by the topping-off of the Boeing's fuel tanks, but only the officers were privy to the day's objective and its location: the Braunkohle-Benzin AG synthetic oil refinery, "*Bohlenwerks*," located far inside the gut of the Reich. The target was considered high priority, not only because it was a manufacturer of enormous quantities of synthetic fuels but because it was well known that the Luftwaffe was highly reliant on this site, in particular for its production of aviation gasoline. So vital was the complex that great efforts had been taken by the Germans to protect and conceal the site. This included the construction of a "dummy refinery" located adjacent to the actual complex, the latter ringed by a series of smoke generating towers and units equipped with mobile smoke pot generators, not to mention the deployment of some of the densest concentration of anti-aircraft batteries in all of Germany. To complete the lengthy raid, the crew would be on oxygen for nearly seven exhausting hours.

Ready and prepared for the call to battle stations, the sergeants began to assemble nearby under the nose of the aircraft. At first, each eyed the ensemble of officers from a distance but then began slowly edging in towards the small conference, trying to overhear the strike plan and burn off the restless energy that permeated the scene. Catching a glimpse of the curious band, Lt. Metzger motioned them over and distributed the escape packs and medical kits. Tucked inside the escape and evasion parcel was a silk map, a small compass, various foreign currency, matches, a needle and thread, a razor, water purification capsules, and a small box of malt tablets. Stuffing the kits into the pockets of their flight suits, some of the boys fired up one last smoke. A few broke away from the group to relieve themselves in the grass at the edge of the hardstand, although more than one used the chance to try and breathe away the faint hint of nausea that twisted in their stomachs. They paced aimlessly, fidgeted with their gear, and tugged at the sheepskin collars of their heavy leather flight jackets, hoping to fend off the morning chill or whatever it was that was icing up their spine. Inevitably, as the team waited, someone's hand settled on a companion's shoulder, prompting a hushed dialogue in the low light. Most exchanges culminated with an uneasy but pleasant smile, a forced chuckle, or nothing more than a long drag on a Lucky Strike.

That morning, "Chief" made a point to connect with each member of the team, especially Jim, Lou, and Irv, as today would be the trio's inauguration. He greeted "his boys" with a heartfelt smile, held their gaze while words were exchanged, and offered encouragement, making sure to emphasize to each man that he depended on them. Subtly, he studied them, his "Green Hornets," carefully searching the young faces in an attempt to measure each man's resolve. Nervousness was expected, even welcomed, as he knew that the stress would only help heighten the crew's senses, making them more vigilant; but those a little too far on edge would require a slight degree of reassurance to be eased back into line. All the while towering over the scene, the old bird-of-war patiently crouched, sheltering her new crew as they prepared under her enormous, outstretched wings.

With the number of anxious glances at wristwatches becoming more frequent, at last Merle looked at the young faces around him, nodded, turned back to the Fortress, and hauled himself up through the small access hatch. It was the sign that the team had been anticipating. All went into motion. The officers imitated the pilot, filing to the ladder under the tiny access portal where the trio meticulously tramped up the wobbly steps and disappeared into the ship's jowls. The gunners, burdened by their hefty flying outfits, funneled under the plane's belly, lining up in front of the hatch in the starboard side of the bomber's waist. Cigarettes were flicked away, the chatter decreased; and, while a couple just gazed at the ground as the line filed aboard, a few among them could be seen bringing a few fingers to their brow, then move them to the center of their chest, then to one shoulder and finally the other. One by one, each man propped a heavy boot upon the base of the door, clutched onto the frame, and hiked themselves up into the Boeing.

When the second signal flare surged skyward into the brightening haze, the taxi code word "chain" crackled over the VHF. Off in the distance, Lt. Green spotted the 410th's Flying Fortresses easing off their pads and beginning their roll along the perimeter track towards him. "Hotshot Pink," the Group's "B" flight leader's codename for the day, rolled by first, and as the procession moved past, Irv studied the numbers decorating the vertical stabilizers, waiting

A group of B-17s during taxi, Fold3

for 653's place in the queue. Some of the 94th's hardest-hitting warbirds had been scrambled for the day's fight, including *Dorothy V,*

Gremlin Hotel, Texas Mauler, Sally, War Weary Vulture, Bouncin' Annie, Second Hand Express, Mission Bell, Puddin', Ice Cold Katie, Lady Anne, Duchess, Renovation, The Big Wheel, House of Lords, Trudy, Going My Way, and *Daring Doris.* When *Sassy Suzy* ambled past, Metzger relaxed his footholds on the rudder pedals, releasing the brakes, and assisted Merle in nudging the throttles forward, easing over 60,000 pounds into motion.

Lt. Metzger merged the *Green Hornets* into its spot among the bulk of the 410th and joined the squadron in weaving down the taxiway. As was customary, the co-pilot would handle the Fort during the taxi, although it would take the combined teamwork of Green and Sgt. Lehere to usher the cumbersome bomber along the path. The B-17's inverted tricycle landing gear configuration caused the bomber's nose to angle high, awarding her a look as if she were sniffing the air, already judging the winds, searching for the scent of her prey. While this gave her a regal, yet predatory-like profile, it prevented her handlers from being able to visualize the path directly ahead. Moving the aircraft along the track in a snaking motion—winding back and forth—allowed the pilots to judge the spacing between the behemoths. The drivers rode the throttles with caution, summoning up just enough power to keep up with the pack but making sure not to boost themselves into the tail of the Fortress ahead, all while endeavoring to anticipate the aircraft's momentum and avoid burning up the brakes. Ever present during this delicate process, just off to each side of the road, lay the potential to blow a tire or become mired in the mud. Both were undoubtably humiliating and frustrating mission, not to mention reputation-ending catastrophes. The pachyderm-like parade to the runway was an arduous exercise in of itself but also exceptionally noisy at that. The sound of the big bomber's brakes rubbing and squealing as they progressed, combined with the relentless blaring buzz of the engines, was near deafening.

At 0740 hours, the first of the 94th's rumbling herd of B-17s grudgingly lifted off the runway and lumbered out into the glowing mist where the 8th had already begun gathering. In each bomber's belly, 5,000 pounds of explosives hung fixed, destined to pulverize the Hun barbarians. In their wings, 2,780 gallons—17,514 pounds of fuel—were stored in several self-sealing compartments, and, lastly, thousands of pounds of gear, instruments, ammunition, and flesh and bone were added to the load. When fully burdened, the Forts would struggle just to get airborne and then labor to gain enough altitude to pass over the canopies of the monsters of oak that stood guard at the end of the runway between the airfield and Bury. As Lt. Green's element leader's Flying Fortress advanced down the runway, the officers pivoted #653 into the center of the strip, locked the tail wheel, applied the brakes, and heeded Lou's countdown from thirty, the designated interval between the initiation of each aircraft's take off. The seconds ticked away at a tormentingly slow tempo, but Merle knew that the spacing was not only crucial for the assembly process but also necessary to avoid the possibility of disaster resulting from being overturned by the prop wash blast of preceding bombers. Discipline was a necessity for all fliers, but especially for the pilots. Clutching the throttle in his right hand, the 23-year-old harnessed an incredible 4800 horsepower. In his grip he held command over the devastating potential of a quarter-million-dollar, high-tech war machine, eight souls, and two and a half tons of TNT. As Lou's countdown neared its conclusion, Merle and Irv pressed the throttles forward to full power—"war power"—triggering the Fortress to sink slightly into a squat as the tenor of the motors increased. As if on cue, just as Lou's tally came to an end, the glow of the red signal light, shining from the control trailer positioned far ahead alongside the launching path, turned green: the go signal. 653 grunted and shuddered as the pilots eased off her brakes. The ship started to creep forward in a slow, sluggish roll, then a hustle; and, finally, bumping, banging, and shivering down the long, rubber-stained cement lane, she caught her stride. Steadily her pace increased, "40...50...60 miles per hour", relayed Lehere. Accompanying the sensation of the tail wheel lifting off the tarmac, the bomber's noisy dash transformed into a tight, waddling sprint.

Passing ninety miles per hour, the Fortress now moved at a velocity too fast to safely complete an abort and stop before slamming into the hedgerows and thickets sitting just past the end of the strip. "The big thing was getting those planes off the ground. The runways had dips in them and with a full bomb load you always wondered if you'd clear that last tree at the end of the runway," remembered Jim Gegenheimer, who had hunkered down in his crash position in the radio room for takeoff with the other gunners. Leaning forward into the flight deck, Lehere's eyes jerked between the airspeed indicator and the terminus of the runway, the latter seen fast approaching through the windscreen in front of him. "110...115...120..." roared the

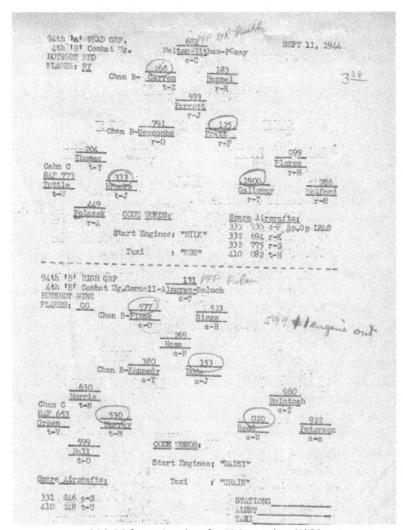

94th BG formation chart for 11 September, NARA

engineer as he braced himself against the force of the four sirens that pulled hard, screaming from the wings. Passing 150 miles per hour, the *Green Hornets* lifted into the air only feet from the end of the runway. Green smoothly drew back his control yoke while Metzger retracted the landing gear and flaps, instantly reducing drag and generating a slight surge in airspeed. Slowly but steadily the *Hornets* persisted to rise, passing over empty fields and pastures crisscrossed with hedgerows and low cobblestone walls. Booming over the rooftops of the village and passing Bury's cathedral tower, she floated on as the pilots set the

151

bomber on a steady climb into the assembly pattern.

That Monday, oil was the target of the day and Bomber Command had summoned the entire 8th Air Force for a deep penetration, maximum effort raid. Atmospheric conditions were estimated to be favorable: "excellent visibility everywhere on the Continent of Europe" projected the "weather guessers." Still, the Group's 333rd Squadron of Pathfinder B-17s, with their ground-imaging radar, would lead the way. The armada, 1,131 bombers arranged in three Air Divisions and accompanied by 440 escort fighters, would insert through a narrow front over Belgium, charge southeast past Bruges and then Brussels, and then enter Nazi airspace. From the German border, the 8th would pivot eastward incrementally, squeezing past Frankfurt and aiming towards Fulda where the three divisions would then divide to assault multiple oil targets in central and eastern Germany.

Assigned with the more complex and far-reaching order of battle, the 3rd Division would drive deep into Southeastern Germany and skirt along the border of Czechoslovakia before breaking into even smaller strike forces. Nine bombardment groups from the Division were given the oil plants at Ruhland, while six others would penetrate Czechoslovakia to wreck a refinery at Brux. The third band of attackers, carrying out the sixth of what would be a total of seven "Frantic" missions, would land in Russian-held territory to regroup and refuel, but not before dismembering an artificial gas refinery at Chemnitz. Finally, Hitler's second-largest synthetic fuel manufacturing facility at Bohlen, just southwest of Leipzig, was allotted to the remaining nine groups, organized in the 4th "A" Wing" and the 4th "B" Wing." The latter drove included the *Green Hornets* and two flights of Rougham boys.

Relegated to the number three position in the low element of "B" flight, the *Green Hornets* would be filling the exposed position at the bottom, rear, and outside of the unit's trailing formation, a place typically reserved mostly for inexperienced, unproven rookie crews. Only the ill-reputed "Tail-End Charlie" slot, today being covered by Lt. Hall's gang of hardened combat fliers, was less desirable. Their experience would be needed as Green's band was largely unproven and one of the bombers with the least amount of defensive coverage from fighter attacks. Additionally, German anti-aircraft gunners were known to acquire sharper fixes on aircraft in the rear of the boxes as they were then able to fine-tune their aim and adjust their shells accordingly.

It was no secret among Allied airmen that the atmosphere above *Bohlenwerks* was exceptionally hazardous to one's health. With the formidable 14th Flak Division's guns covering the expanse of sky above the wedge-shaped Halle-Leipzig-Zeitz defense district and thousands of expert flak cannoneers—roughly 46,000 defense gunners, 6,000 *Luftwaffenhelper* ("flakboys"), 3,000 *Flak Helferinnen* (female auxiliaries), 900 Hungarian and Italian conscripts, 3,600 Soviet POWs, and 3,000 others dug in around the immediate target area—the 94th's planners had devised a flight path that would take them to the far side of the target for their run onto the oil plant. The crusade would test not only the skill but the discipline of the fliers as the route crossed through some of Germany's and the world's most treacherous airspace. The Group would fly the bomb run straight and level down a thirty-mile belt of expert flak gunners, even before the Forts arrived over the target. After dealing their bomb loads, the 94th would swing south from Bohlen and carefully maneuver between the extensive zones of concentrated anti-aircraft batteries, all reinforced by radar, for a speedy breakout. There would be no getting around confrontations with the defensive gunners; but, as the Luftwaffe had proved to be slightly more than a nuisance in the past four months, Intelligence was confident that enemy fighter opposition would be scant.

Somewhere over bitterly-cold English Channel waters and cruising at 150 miles per hour, the gunners plugged their suits into the aircraft's electrical system and prayed that the warmth would come. The heat would be essential as, climbing above 14,000 feet and nearing the still-contested Belgium coast, air temperatures plunged to 15 degrees below freezing. While impressive and innovatively engineered, excluding the revolutionary B-29 "Superfortress" that dominated the Pacific Theater, World War II-era bombers were neither pressurized nor heated. The only warmth to be felt in the aircraft was on the flight deck due to their positioning between the two inboard engines. When the sergeants dressed for battle that morning, they pulled on electrically-heated flight suits over their long underwear, duty shirts, and pants. The individual pieces were linked by a wiring system that, once connected, could be plugged into the aircraft's electrical system during flight. The gear was designed to warm the airmen while shielding them from the freezing conditions that were known to instantaneously freeze exposed skin to metal or bring forth the numbing destruction of frostbite. In actuality, the suits warmed unevenly and were known to provide random, painful electric shocks, though it was not unheard of for the suits to simply fail altogether.

After the heating outfit and duty uniform came heavy-lined leather flying coveralls. Insulated booties were pulled on over a pair of wool socks, followed by large, heavy, lined flying boots. To safeguard the gunner's fingers and hands, thick, lined leather gauntlets were worn over wool mittens. The pilots, however, requiring more dexterity to carry out their tasks and wearing only flight coveralls and leather jackets, only wore thin rayon gloves. Swapping style for practicality, while in flight the officers abandoned their visored USAAF dress hats—the headwear known as the "crush cap" or the "50-mission crusher" that also lent the fliers their iconic look—for leather aviator helmets. The gunners also strapped on similar headgear, the interior lined and fitted with headphones that relayed both vital communication and team chatter. In the clear substratosphere, high above the clouds over the European mainland, goggles were necessary for all, worn to shield the men's eyes from debris, the cold, and the blinding solar rays. A throat microphone and a "Mae West" life preserver were also added to their bulky ensemble. Additionally, each man was issued armor—a steel helmet and a flak vest and apron—which they draped over their torso upon the start of the bomb run as an added final degree of security against the steely rain showers that were known to accumulate over the target area. Adorned in gear that was awkward and ergonomically challenging, most fliers took the risk and elected to only wear their parachute harness and store their chute nearby where they could, hopefully, access it within a moment's notice. Up ahead, in the cockpit, the pilots ordinarily sat on their parachutes or tucked the bundles under their seats.

While still climbing over the Channel, Sid Hatfield, inspecting the sky to the rear of the aircraft over his twin .50 "stingers," observed Lt. Hall's ship, aircraft #599, feather an engine and began to lag behind. Within minutes, the B-17 cut away, turning back for England and Station #468. The trip would be risky enough with four fully operational motors; but, proceeding on three, suffering a substantial loss of power and airspeed from the start, would only be asking for trouble. Over Hitler's Fortress, any maverick Allied bomber, especially a wounded or impaired one, was easy pickings for Nazi gunners and German aerial aces. As a result, the departure of Hall and company opened a void in the back of "B" flights low element. Unnervingly, this was the crew that was to cover the *Green Hornets* six o' clock; but, instead, the neophytes reluctantly assumed the position of "Tail-End Charlie."

In the bow of the plane, Jack wriggled out through the tiny opening in the nose cabin and back and up into the compartment that separated the flight deck and engineer platform and began squeezing his way towards the bomb bay. While incendiary, armor-piercing, and fragmentation ordnance were deployed depending on the target type, today's firepower consisted of ten 500 lbs. general-purpose bombs. To

Cotter pin from the September 11th
mission, Voight Collection

arm his arsenal, the bombardier removed the cotter pins from each bomb's fuse vane. Hung on racks that ran along the interior of the hold, the arsenal was held in place by shackles that would, if not damaged, malfunctioning, or frozen, release their burden the moment the bombardier hit his toggle switch. Upon separating from the shackles, safety wires were yanked free of the fuse vanes, allowing the blades on the tail fuse to pinwheel in the air as the weapon plunged toward its destination. During the wobbly plummet to earth, and with any luck, onto the target, the vanes would unwind in the air stream, aligning the internal fuse with the detonator and ready the bomb for impact. Punching through up to three feet of concrete or ten feet of earth, a pre-programmed internal timing device synchronized the blast, igniting the explosives either on the point of impact or at a slight delay, depending on the type of target and desired effect.

When he returned to his position in the nose, Jack donned his oxygen mask and connected it to the port beside his station. Atmospheric oxygen was steadily becoming a limited resource for the crews who, now rising beyond 10,000 feet, were still far below cruising heights. At five miles above the earth, it would take only moments for a distracted flier, suffering a mask malfunction or tube blocked by saliva, vomit, or blood, to unwittingly slide into unconsciousness. Deprived of oxygen for slightly longer periods, just two or three minutes more, brain cells would begin to die, swiftly followed by fatal consequences if left uncorrected. Now tied into the plane's oxygen system, Jack called for a crew check, the first of many that would occur with regularity every ten minutes to lessen the possibility of succumbing to a silent, suffocating, euphoric death. Hypoxia, after all, was never a glamourous way to meet one's end, if there ever was one.

12
ON TO THE TARGET

Shepherding the colossal machine into its place in the formation and fighting the prop turbulence created by those ships who blazed on in front of them was an utterly grueling undertaking. Unlike the experience of steering through the airspace of the Southern US during training, flying heavy bombers under combat conditions was much more involving and likened by many to handling an old box truck, sans power-steering. The B-17 was a "fly-by-wire" system; that is the

Contrails, NARA

aircraft's surface controls were manipulated by thin steel wires that ran from the flight controls along the interior of the airframe. Therefore, maneuvering the heavy bird was accomplished not through electric or hydraulic systems, but by pilot strength and endurance. Managing engine performance was also a tedious undertaking and it required constant attention. Using too much throttle could result in thrusting out from the element, motor damage or failure, driving the plane into a sister ship, or burning too much fuel. On the contrary, too little throttle and the aircraft could fail to keep pace and altitude with the unit, compromising the integrity of the combat box's protective field of fire. Operating at slower airspeeds also put the ship at greater risk of stalling, whereby the craft loses lift and could plunge uncontrollably from the sky.

Sailing above England, visibility had been unlimited with no undercast, but circumstances had changed as the force penetrated over the beaches of Belgium where atmospheric conditions quickly deteriorated. Worse yet, the Group was suffering the effects of severe turbulence from the prop wash produced by hundreds of aircraft—a consequence of being deployed near the rear of the Wing assembly, which was situated smack dab in the middle of the entire 8th Air Force bomber stream. Two divisions of heavy bombers preceded the 94th and had cut their way across Belgium before working their way into the Reich, leaving a broad, unstable, ruffled carpet of contrails in its wake. Tucked into position in the rear of the 3rd Division, Merle and his comrades watched as the massive fleet, like the fracturing of a giant falling meteor, long white tail and all, fanned out as, one after another, the navigational objectives were reached and then passed without incident. By the time the Group edged wide to the north of Frankfurt, hoping to give the city's lethal ring of flak guns a wide berth, the bulk of the 8th had already departed, hooking off towards targets to the northeast. For a moment it was felt that they had managed to push past the city unnoticed; but, as the bombers swung east—a fascinating display of ground rockets confirmed that, along with the startling appearance of the Luftwaffe whose fighters were holding their position just beyond the range of the heavies' defensive guns—they were being sized-up by eyes both on the ground and in the air.

Over Saalfeld, the 3rd Division, traveling at 22,000 feet, broke off into three forces. Rather than turning north in the direction of key manufacturing infrastructure laying in the heart of Saxony, the

Americans pivoted further southeast, fanning out even more as they neared the edge of Czechoslovakia. At 12:20, the 94th was advancing so close to the Czech border that cannon around Brux lobbed shells at the Group. Luckily, the flak fire cracked short of the formation, but the 94th continued performing "s" maneuvers to thwart the 88s from obtaining a fix. More rockets appeared, including some sent up from the *"Flakstellung"* ("Flak Fortress") around Chemnitz which had been eagerly awaiting the American advance, and cast missiles into the Boeing-filled skies above.

With the smoke trails of missiles still hanging in the atmosphere below them, the Wing, currently composed of around 310 bombers, started a sweeping hook to the left, as intended. What was not anticipated was, as the majority of the division now thrust further northeast, the spacing between groups fell apart. Some of these units found themselves out of position by as much as sixteen miles-four times the standard spacing. At the same time, US weather reconnaissance ships, called "Maypoles," had rushed on ahead to reconnoiter for the attackers. An evaluation of atmospheric conditions determined that attempting a strike on one of the targets was impractical; but, when the scouts attempted to transmit notice back to the main force, radio issues prevented the warning from reaching one of the units–the 100th BG. So as the lead groups now shifted back west, redeployed and enroute to a new target, "the Bloody Hundredth" set off in the opposite direction as scheduled and, in turn, further distanced themselves from the pack. The miscommunication would be disastrous as, at this instant, the Luftwaffe, like sharks sensing blood in the water, took advantage of the error and pounced upon the disorganized, isolated segment. By day's end, following one of the most vicious and largest air battles in history, the German Air Force had arranged a comprehensive thrashing for the 100th. Later to be remembered as "the Battle over the Ore Mountains," the "Century Fliers" lost a third of its fighting force–more than one hundred boys in a little over eight hours.

Moving past the firefight, the 94th BG, on time and on course for their arrival at the IP over Leisnig, ascended to their designated bombing altitude of 25,500 feet. Here, it was a soul-chilling 60 degrees below freezing, but Lts. Green and Metzger sat fixed behind their controls, wrestling the *Green Hornets* through the choppy flight track, clothed in sweat-soaked flight suits. This "exceptionally bad prop wash," as one navigator's logbook noted, had battered the Group since they had reached Belgium, a grueling two and a half hours prior. At 1233 the Forts of the 94th's "A" flight reached the initial point, as confirmed by the sight of a pair of yellow signal flares seen arcing away from the lead ship. The bombers dipped their port wings, sliding into the bomb run about 23 miles east of the target, and 527 long miles from Rougham. "B" Flight fell in behind, falling into trail with the path of the lead elements and lining up their approach to the objective amidst a battering, blinding current of vapor trails and a "great deal of prop wash." The assault was expected to last ten minutes, a reasonably long run, and would be flown straight and level all the way to the oil plant at Bohlen. In "B" Flight, all B-17s would discharge their load on the lead bombardier who, today, was lodged aboard "Hotshot Pink". All the same, Jack made ready his bombsight as the ice-frosted motors in the *Hornets* bomb bay whined, cranking open the doors, and sending angry polar gusts wailing on through the aircraft. With Merle tweaking the throttles and Metzger doing all he could to concentrate on maintaining position on the element's lead Boeing as it swerved and bobbed along in the swells of the buffeted air stream just in front and to the right of the Hornet's nose, the charge to the target was on.

As "Hotshot Pink" led on, a glimmer from up ahead suddenly

A view of the waist gunner's position, Fold3

caught the eye of more than one flier. From a position low and to the right of the 333rd squadron, a lone Me 109 advanced, rushing head-on at closing speeds above four hundred miles per hour. The "Jerry" tore past the first formation of Forts and was nearly on top of the second Flight before most crews even became aware of the challenge. The aggressor, "came in from 1 to 2 o'clock high and went through the formation-200 yards away," reported one of the Group. Lt. Stephen Hoza and company aboard *War Weary Vulture* witnessed the German pass close enough to see details of the pilot as the steely predator rushed through the remainder of the formation. Closing from one o'clock, the hunter ripped by, passing under the starboard wings of Mission Belle and then *Daring Doris* before weaving back, splitting between Lt. Murray's ship and "Reed's Rowdies" on *Gremlin Hotel.*

Behind his twin guns in the ball turret, Sgt. Gegenheimer struggled to get a bead on the killer as it whipped by, bolting off to the southeast. Milliseconds later, Sgt. Hatfield detected a burst of grey shimmer past his window and studied the warrior as he shrunk away, darting off below the horizon and leaving a swaggering trail of smoky

Tail gunner position, Fold3

exhaust. As Sid evaluated his fleeting and seemingly anticlimactic brush with the legendary Luftwaffe, the fighter suddenly rolled off to one side, doubled back, and began quickly closing the distance. Sid reflectively trained his sights on the incoming menace; but, just as the German came within range, he swung away. Amazingly, the fighter had penetrated the entire Group, buzzing past 25 Forts without ever having fired a shot. The only rounds unleashed came from the defense: reactions from a few Fortress gunners who were only able to spray a sudden burst of rounds in the general direction of the bold German warrior. Although no 94th aircraft had been hit, the encounter-sudden, swift, and haphazard, had nonetheless wrecked the crew's nerves as the audacious affront was supposed to be a failed, or possibly deterred, suicidal assault. But the Luftwaffe was not done yet as the appearance of enemy jet vapor trails, scarring the sky above them, only added to the tension.

To compound matters, four minutes after the Rougham fliers had come into line on the bomb run, a large assembly of Allied bombers had been seen off in the distance at their ten o'clock. The men recognized that this unidentified force was not only flying level

Bombardier in his nose position, NARA

with the 94th but looked to be steadily drifting in towards them and closing the expanse with an increasingly alarming pace. Appearing unwilling to concede, the unidentified group of aircraft were, apparently, also on their bomb run, racing on towards their objective with bomb bays gaping. Meanwhile, Merle focused out his frost-rimmed window, taking measure of the inbound danger, now only a matter of seconds away. For a moment he debated redeploying the

aircraft, yanking the *Hornets* out of the element to hurdle the staggered wall of stubborn bombers merging in on his course. They were committed now—they all were, the entire Group; and, despite the many hazards that were gathering and swirling about them, Merle understood that now was not the time to lose one's nerve.

Finding themselves intermixing with a dozen uninvited visitors, the 94th's formation splintered, scrambling like a startled flock of frightened fowl. The Rougham "heavies" dipped, banked, and reeled in a desperate bid to dodge the madness that followed. From his vantage point in the forward compartment, Jack could only hold on and watch as what he must have thought were the last moments of his life before he was to meet a swift, crushing end play out around him.

Hunched in his post behind the convex glass nosepiece, Lt. Williams clenched at the frame of his bombsight and braced himself for the inevitable impact of two giants. Ironically endowed with perhaps the best view of the entire chaotic affair, Williams watched as sixty tons of metal, flesh, and high-explosive ordnance churned past him in a blur only yards ahead. As the wayward B-17 slid into their path, the thrumming of its engines reverberated all through Jack's cabin, causing the *Green Hornets* to shudder violently in the mammoth's wake. Merle pulled hard at his steering column and Metzger, wide-eyed and postured as if he was bracing against a strong gale, followed suit and racked the controls into his sternum. The B-17 lurched upward, gaining a few hundred feet in mere seconds and almost uprooting the entire crew in the process. To the relief of the unharnessed men in the stern, the *Green Hornets* recovered, leveled off, and then settled back into the monotony of the bomb run, leaving the rattled airmen to curse the jumbled mess of "friendlies" as they coasted off to the northwest.

Incredibly, despite the aerial circus, all aircraft of both units managed to avoid what should have been a catastrophic airborne pileup. The men would later recall with wonder how they had narrowly avoided the calamity as two dozen fully-loaded bombers had shuffled "directly through our formation," many plodding past only feet from one another. When the pilots assessed the aftermath, many discovered that they were flying three to five hundred feet above their designated bombing altitude. Moreover, the spacing between and within each element in "B" Flight lacked any resemblance of organization, not to mention an effective defensive arrangement, jeopardizing the bomb pattern and leaving the Group vulnerable to fighter attack. With only minutes before they were to be over the synthetic oil plant and with no time to reorganize the 94th's ranks, the bomb droppers onboard the scattered bunch of Flying Fortresses did their best to gather their nerves and return their attention to the job at hand.

Nearly one mile ahead and several hundred feet below the *Green Hornets*, "A" flight had been completely spared the mayhem endured by their Rougham brothers in the trailing assembly. So far, the 94th had managed to evade a salvo of rockets and a trouncing by mobs of Luftwaffe fighters. They had stared down a reckless, rogue fighter attack and ducked errant bombers; but now, less than one hundred and twenty seconds out from their objective, their luck would be tried once again as blotches of small, inky black clouds began speckling the air directly ahead. Passing through the threshold of the concentration, new puffs unfurled around the bombers, loading the airspace with a dozen more stains of smoke every second. All around them, angry red-orange surges of fire sparked to life and from out of these eruptions from hell, ghoulish clouds of death hung in the aftermath. Most of the time, the men couldn't hear the report of the blasts as the cacophony of the B-17's engines and the rapid pounding of their hearts flooded their ears; but, every so often one of the rounds would crack uncomfortably close as it snarled to life. Some blasts, after ripping into the air, hammered depressions into the airframes. Several protested the presence of the American marauders by spitting their metallic venom of jagged metal shards at their rivals, sending fragments pinging and skipping off the Fortresses' thin hulls. Occasionally, a sliver would cut through a Boeing's alloy shell, opening up a large hole in the skin and exposing the mortal souls within to the odor of its foul breath of burnt trinitrotoluene as it seeped past the men's masks and dominated over the smell of stale rubber. On the ships dashed, slicing through the more menacing smoky apparitions as they coiled and swirled around them before gradually wasting away into the vastness behind them, but with each vanishing menace, a new scattering of bursts emerged. Driving towards Bohlen from the east, the concussed heavies rattled forward, sprinting through the box of flak where the explosions shoved at the planes, bouncing them about the sky.

Floating an eye over his sight's optics, Jack could see no hint of the refinery as the target area; nonetheless, the objective itself was unidentifiable through the thick blanket of clouds that hung below him at 14,000 feet. It was "8/10th" cloud cover—official bomb-aimer jargon explaining that eighty percent of the landscape was shrouded by clouds and, thus, only a small portion of the terrain could actually be visualized. This was far from optimal shooting weather. Equally as desirous to drop his bombs as he was to evade the barrage that continued to boil in the air around him, Lt. Williams scanned out ahead through the pockmarked sky, gaze fixed on the flight leader and softly fiddling with the release toggle while sweating out the signal. From his seat just behind his bombardier, Frank informed the crew that they were over the drop zone, his computations confirmed by the escalating chaos of snapping metal, concussion claps, and flame. Jones, steadying himself against the rocking of the ship, scowled at the face of his watch, willing the small hand onward as it jerked through painfully sluggish intervals. On the flight deck, with loaded backs and constricted muscles, Merle and Irv, battling to reign in their brute, held the *Green Hornets* steady as she pushed through what seemed like a sparking tornado.

Suddenly, between blots of inky smoke, a momentary break in the undercast revealed a grid of bridges, roads, and tracks, many

View of Bohlenwerks Synthetic Oil Refinery after a visit by the USAAF, 1945, Fold3

converging or intersecting like a gigantic steel and concrete arterial system. Multiple rail lines wound through the center of the facility, snaking by several runoff basins before angling away. To the north of the "s" in the rail tracks, a wide road stretched through the complex and off to the left, in the southern section of the refinery, stood two rows of circles—three on one side; four on the other. Visualization of *Bohlenwerks'* seven smokestacks, still partially veiled by clouds and smoke, confirmed that they had, indeed, located their mark.

Tracking over a mile to the rear, Merle and "B" flight watched in fascination as "A" group, aiming by radar, opened the assault. At 1243 hours, from out of the belly of the Group leader fell a series of stubby steel green cylinders. With streams of phosphorous trailing from the first two smoke marker bombs, the remainder of "A" flight shadowed the leader and separated their bomb loads. Three seconds later, "B" Flight replicated the attack and toggled away one hundred sixteen high-explosive bombs, sending them rushing towards the plant's main injector house.

The explosives of the advanced elements of the 94th fell with significant effect within the projected one-thousand-yard mean point of impact, pasting a multiplex of buildings and producing extensive devastation to additional structures laying alongside the pathway of the blasts. With each volcanic-like eruption piping burst, storage vessels ruptured, and concrete, steel, brick, and wood were hurtled into the air, only to tumble back into the scarred, cratered earth. Explosions ignited petroleum stores and the resulting fires began kicking out thick billows of smoke that rose 10,000 feet into the air.

While the official results of the first thirteen Flying Fortresses were deemed "good," the latter attack unleashed by "B" flight was nowhere near as effective. Due to a combination of poor weather conditions, withering anti-aircraft shelling, erratic formation spacing, and, although inadvertent, the deviation from the planned bombing altitude, the bombs fell short and wide of their aim. It hadn't helped matters when the intended method of attack-a PFF assault was swapped for a direct visualization bombing technique while on their approach before being altered once again in the last moments of the bomb run. As such, fifty-eight thousand pounds of explosives toppled nearly one mile southwest of the oil plant, wasting the prime farming real estate of a few unlucky planters.

The shriek of the icy windstorm whistled away as Lt. Williams called out, "bomb bay doors closed." As the men countered the calls of Jack's oxygen check, Frank synched his watch and confirmed his calculations. "Sixty seconds to mark, come upon one-three-zero degrees." The pilots were anticipating the shift, a quick, radical change in heading that would take them off the bomb run and away from the iron-saturated skies above the target. Through the windscreen, up ahead in the distance they could see "A" Flight already initiating their getaway to the Group's rally point near Schmolln. The maneuver proved so drastic that the 120-degree heading change created the impression that the unit's flight path had nearly bent back upon itself. Turning away, the lead element began leaning heavily on their throttles, scurrying off to the south as if treading on hot coals, churning up the thin aerosphere, and kicking out heavy tracks of contrail-trimmed prop wash in the process.

Although the Americans had rid themselves of their deadly haul, the Reich guardians were no less determined to blow the unwelcome guests into extinction. In fact, as if the Group had stirred up a hornet's nest with their explosives, the barrage only intensified. Along with Wing intelligence, Rougham planners had reviewed reconnaissance photographs of AA batteries in the area and, in preparation for the assault on *Bohlenwerks*, carefully plotted the 94th's course of egress. These navigational architects had done their due diligence but had failed to identify recent redeployments of the Leipzig sector's 88mm "*Grossbatterien*" cannons which were, today, augmented with the addition of even larger ordnance, including 105mm guns and rail-mounted, mobile pieces. "Heavy flak after target–[n]ot plotted," recorded one clobbered 94th man. Another noted the fusillade was "tracking, right up there, intense and accurate." Hurrying off the bomb run, *War Weary Vulture, Skinny*, and *Belle of the Brawl II* were walloped by flak and another half-dozen of the 94th's Fortresses had been winged. Plainly, the severity of the pummeling was not anticipated.

Along with shells from the flak boys on the ground whose fire was fixated squarely on the *Green Hornets* and the 94th's trailing formation, Axis aces had been lingering in the glare of the sun, waiting for just the right moment to attack. "Bandits...coming at us!"–The voice was that of Williams, his tenor breaking over the intercom with an urgency that was enough to shock the men into immediate action. Like a well-oiled machine, the Hornets' gunners parried, instantaneously pivoting their barrels towards the menace with heavy-mitted firing fingers primed on their triggers in anticipation of another confrontation with the Luftwaffe. As Pete Riley searched through his tiny portal in the radio room, Sgt. Ostrowski surveyed the broad piece of sky stretching from two o'clock to five o'clock. Further astern, Hatfield flexed his twin Brownings in anticipation, readying to guard against the German in case he found the nerve to circle back around and dare nip at the *Hornets* backside. From his isolated post under the tail of the B-17, which was currently flying in the rear of the formation nearly 26,000 feet above the earth, his circumstances must have given him the impression that he was practically alone and sitting on the edge of the world.

Fitted under the dome of his top turret, Lehere examined his stretch of sky and monitored the drone of the four Wright Cyclone power plants. As flight engineer, Lou was constantly evaluating the mood of the craft-the condition and operability of the array of vital systems that kept the airplane alive, the groans arising from someplace deep in the bowels of the ship, the flaws with her skeleton. Lehere took note of the old heavy's roar; and, as Irv and Merle coaxed the Boeing into the sharp left turn, he stiffened himself against the frame of his tower of plexiglass and iron. The battlement emitted its electrical purr as Lou wheeled about his dual 50s–there was a fighter out there after all–and now was no time to be complacent. Yet, through the muffled purr of the engines and frequent whooshing-pop of flak came a new sound; this one likened to the deafening growl of the *Hornets'* motors but coupled with the intensity of an avalanche. At first, Lou assumed the pilots were trying to find the right balance on the throttles to retain proper airspeed through the bank and hold their position in the formation; but, within moments of detecting the noise, his curiosity turned to concern and then to panic. Although the Flying Fortress was cruising miles above the clouds in the sunny, frozen blue, Lehere noticed a shadow slip over him. Recognizing what was happening, the sergeant went to activate the intercom button on his gun trigger; but, before he could relay the warning, the world around him exploded, heaving him into oblivion.

13

"GET THE HELL OUT OF THE PLANE"

It's hard to explain what happened, but everything was dark. Your inner brain tells you what to do. You know you have to make it out of there.

-Louis Lehere

11 September 1944
1247 hours
26,000+ feet altitude and ascending
Somewhere SW of Bohlen, Saxony, Germany
-25 degrees Fahrenheit

It must have brought back memories of springtime on his father's farm when every so often the storms would roll in, the thunderheads would hang low over the backcountry, and the sky would turn ominously green as an eerie silence took hold of the land. Inevitably, from out of the churning vapors a funnel cloud would begin to materialize, snaking down towards the earth to whip and surge through the fields in a whirling tempest of destruction. It came with the sound of a freight train, one that raked up the spine, sending shockwaves reverberating through one's body, gripping hard at your bones, and leaving no question about the reality around you—something far more powerful, something completely irrepressible was in charge.

That same raging cyclone was with him now, rushing into his face and howling about the cabin. Apart from the peculiar prickly phenomenon bristling on his nose and ears, everything felt numb. His ears attempted to equalize while his body wrestled through a dizzying imbalance as he sensed himself slowly emerging from out of a murky fog that had shrouded his vision. Watching the shadows begin to give way, Merle recognized the weight of his flak helmet as it rested awkwardly awry atop his throbbing head. Beneath the armor, his fleece-lined leather headgear sat twisted, and off to one side of his face

View of a B-17 cockpit, oxygen cylinders, and nose compartment access tunnel (center below) from engineer's platform, Houlihan

dangled his oxygen mask. Reaching up to push back his helmet and reposition his flying goggles, a blistering fire ignited in his hand. The searing pain ripped the lieutenant from the last of the dreaminess, leaving him reeling in agony, confused, and panicking as to why his clumsy hands wouldn't respond. Growling through the pain, Merle's yelps were completely stifled by the wintry gales that swelled around him. He hunched himself low in his seat, finding shelter in a pocket of stable air behind the B-17's ruined, glass-covered, warped instrument panel. Although he was effectively blinded by the scrape of the piercing cold that continued to pummel his face, the lull awarded him a moment to size up the situation. Gaining hold of his panic, Merle quickly studied his gauntlets in search of any indication of injury and was just about convinced that there was nothing remarkable until he focused on his right glove. A sickness washed through him as he realized that what he was inspecting was not his glove at all, but a swarthy, petrified bare right fist. Although his left mitt was still in place, beneath the thin fabric, Green's fingers were completely paralyzed, flash-frozen by the sub-zero windstorm that poured through the windshield and was currently frosting over his instrument dials. The lieutenant, ever the visceral flyer, didn't need to see the gauges, or hear the grinding, shrill wails of the motors, or recognize the severe bank and incline of the aircraft, or feel the tremors vibrating up through the control column to know something was terribly wrong with his *Green Hornets*.

As the cool grip of hypothermia began clawing over him, and an even icier rush of adrenaline surged through his veins, Lt. Green nudged his flight goggles back over his swollen eyes with his inflexible digits. Pressing his forearms against the shivering half-wheel yoke post, he shoved with all his might, leveraging his weight against the controls, trying to win command, but the Boeing rattled on unimpressed, slamming and bounding along through the thinning air. Merle's eyes swept the assortment of over 150 gauges, dials, and levers before him where, behind cracked faces, indicators jerked and shivered, a few giving no hint of life at all. Oil pressures were falling, engine temperatures were rising, and several motor indicators hinted at catastrophic failure. Wisps of brown, pressurized smoke curled around the cockpit and from out of the smog; the odor of burning mechanical fluids and caustic vapors stung at his nose. It was becoming much harder to breathe now and Merle could only manage a series of gasps—deep inhalations that sucked in little more than huffs of wretched gases; and he began to hack uncontrollably, fighting for every breath. A dull, throbbing ache blossomed in his chest and with it, an odd, metallic taste filled his mouth. He coughed again. At first, he only barely noticed the spattering of color that dotted the aircraft's drab control surfaces in front of him; but, choking through more spasms, it was apparent by the shade of the droplets that he was spitting up blood.

Slouched and twisted in his chair, Merle could distinguish that everything above and in front of his instrument panel was demolished. The windscreen had been crushed and lay in shatters, and most of the cabin's side glass was splintered. The overhead windows were completely broken out, and the surrounding airframe was sheered and buckled, leaving a mess of crumpled aluminum fluttering in the fierce slipstream that coursed just above his head. Suddenly a glint of orange flame flared over his shoulder and then slinked away, drawing back into the haze behind him, where just to the rear of his seat sat the oxygen tanks. Alongside the rack of bottles, a network of pressurized air lines and hoses containing flammable hydraulic fluid were fixed along the interior hull of the ship. Glancing to his right, Irv rested lifelessly, head slumped to one side; only his harness restrained his limp frame in his seat. Despite the mayhem, Green recognized that his headset had been absent of any chatter. Merle smashed his paw against the intercom button, keying up his mic only to be met with dead tones, squelches, and static. What had happened was still unclear to the lieutenant, but he could only guess that, due to the extent of the demolition, they had likely suffered a direct hit by flak or possibly had been blasted by an exploding 20mm cannon shell.

During training on B-17s in Florida, Merle had prepared for various common flight emergencies. By that time, he had logged hundreds of hours in military aircraft; but, still, no instruction or experience had prepared him for the magnitude of challenges that were now before him. Multiple engines were faltering–if they hadn't already failed altogether–and the airship was lurching along, climbing above 27,000 feet, and listing heavily to port. Lacking a radio, down a co-pilot, incapable of communicating with his crew, injured, concussed, bleeding, and doing all he could to keep the smoldering plane in the air, Merle was also entirely unable to handle the yoke. He had managed to nuzzle his oxygen mask back onto the bridge of his deadened nose–a small accomplishment nonetheless but one that would help ease the pounding in his head, or so he thought. As his lungs pulled heavily at the lifeline, he recognized that he was gasping stale air, albeit tinged with the raw scent of blood. Merle shifted his attention to the oxygen cylinder pressure gauge beside his seat. While the indicator needle angled drastically to one side, transecting the "0" mark, and below it, the "supply warning" light glowed brightly, it wasn't until his vision blurred that he grasped the significance of the scene. Unbeknownst to Merle, the flight deck's oxygen system had been completely wrecked, resulting in a total loss of the cockpit's supply of breathable air. Venting from the ruptured cylinders, the oxygen did nothing to aid the pilots but, instead, fed a small fire that had lit off behind the flight deck. What was clear to the pilot, however, was that his *Green Hornets*, and perhaps even himself, was almost certainly mortally wounded.

Exhaustion had zapped all but the last of Merle's strength and his body trembled as he labored to hold the rudder pedals firm into the floor. Reaching down beside his seat and the dented fuselage wall, he fumbled with the emergency bell but managed to jab out three short rings, followed by one long blast before locking the buzzer in the open position. Although there had been no signs of life on board his craft, he hoped the crew, if there was any crew left, might hear the signal. As a shadowy veil descended over his

Louis Lehere

eyes, as he felt himself easing away from consciousness; the lieutenant continued to pray that the alert would be echoed at the other alarm bells installed throughout the ship, that the crew would be spurred to action, and that anyone who was alive would get out, and quick.

Lehere

Lou Lehere awoke to not only a painful ringing in his head but to the clanking of the emergency buzzer. Amidst waves of nausea, bleeding from the head, and smarting from a concussion, the flight engineer found himself completely blind. He could sense that he was lying face down, contorted into a position partially straddling the steel footing of his turret's platform and partly wedged in between the cold railing. A furious whirlwind had taken hold of the compartment; and, as he strained to haul his bruised torso free of the turret's pedestal, he sucked deeply at the thin air but was unable to catch his breath. His throat cramped up instantly as the stench of acrid smoke and gasoline filled his nostrils and burnt the back of his mouth. "Fire!" The thought drove a jolt of fear deep through his gut, the desperate reality becoming even more amplified as the Fortress, with her engines whining, convulsed beneath him.

A series of jarring bangs tossed Lehere about his narrow, cramped compartment. Unable to get to his feet, Lou began dragging himself out of the stand and steadily inched through a field of scattered debris that was strewn over the small space between his battle station and the pilot's chairs, situated only a few feet ahead. Between himself and the two aviators, directly in his path and preventing him from advancing any further, was the opening to the tunnel that stretched below the flight deck. Lehere lengthened himself over the cavity where, straddling the hole and balancing precariously, he reached out and started frantically clawing for the pilot's boots. A vigorous current of air sapped his strength, numbing him to the core, and he found he was only able to reach far enough into the pilot's area to, at best, hook a gloved finger onto the iced-over metal seat struts.

Still lost in the blackness, Lou happened upon a bundle of material and recognizing that it was his parachute, Lehere felt for the harness rings and managed to clip the pack to his trappings. At this point, the engineer was quickly becoming overwhelmed by the stifling vapors and smoke, so he skidded down into the tunnel and onto the crawlspace that led to the aircraft's nose. Instead of moving through the small opening that allowed access to the front section where Frank and Jack would be stationed, he felt for and found the handle of the forward hatch door. Giving it a turn, the door failed to respond; so, Lehere, finding that neither his mechanical know-how nor applying the finesse of a flight engineer was sufficient for the situation at hand, decided to employ a slightly more unpolished approach: He began beating his shoulder into the wedged exit hatch. The next few attempts proved just as futile; and, with his heart rate skyrocketing, Lou fought to regulate his gasps and tried to concentrate past the torrent of terrible images of his impending demise that raced through his mind, thoughts that, as it turned out, would be his last before he blacked out.

When Lehere regained his senses and, to his relief, his vision, he discovered that he was tumbling in a turbulent free-fall high above the earth. The realization that he had somehow succeeded in slipping free of the B-17 suddenly became apparent; but, before the airman could count his blessings, the sergeant passed out once again. Moments later and somewhere below the clouds where the atmosphere contained more oxygen, Lehere beat the odds once more and awoke. Having extended his arms to stabilize his ungainly tumble, Lou examined the assortment of green and brown parcels rushing up at him. He hastily caged the "D" ring handle of his parachute and ripped it away from his pack, unleashing a blurred jumble of cables and white fabric. The ensuing violent jerk of the rapid deceleration contorted his body, causing a painful injury to his back. When he recovered his composure, Lou craned his neck towards the earth below him and detected a cluster of buildings swiftly growing larger directly under his boots.

Wagering that he still had time to drift away from the houses below and keen to put some distance between any head-hunting civilians and himself, the gunner decided to perform a skill that he had learned during his time training in the States. More accurately, Lou had not so much practiced the technique but had more observed the process. Outfitted in a harness attached to a scaffolding training prop that dangled the trainer just a few feet above the ground in a marionette-like demonstration, the mentor simply talked the men through the procedure–good enough for government work. By "slipping the chute"–that is manipulating the parachute riser chords to collapse part of the canopy, the instructor explained that an airman could have more control over his path of descent. Naturally, while this risky maneuver could help the jumper avoid undesirable terrain or obstacles, a half-filled chute would cause him to fall more expeditiously.

Seeing that the opportunity was quickly passing, the gunner executed the motions and did, in fact, receive a response. The reply was not what Lou had anticipated, however, and he found himself instantly regretting his attempt. The "slipping" that he had envisioned himself pulling off had turned more of a plummet as not a portion, but the entire parachute collapsed. The speedy approach of hard ground inspired Lou to commit his full, undivided attention to the urgent task of catching air within the folds of his impotent chute. Blessed with another fantastic stroke of luck, the material blossomed once again, leaving the gunner swaying in near silence under the biggest, most beautiful silk canopy that the gunner could have ever imagined. Oscillating only a few hundred feet above the ground and with the details of the land becoming much sharper, Lehere was alarmed to find that he was dropping directly towards a high-voltage wire. Just as he yanked hard on his riser to swing himself wide of the cables, a sharp crack echoed up from below him. The snap arose once more, but this time it was preceded by a lively zipping sound that buzzed through the air not far beyond his chute. And then he could hear another. And another. Having only just dodged the electrical cable, Lou looked up just in time to see a handful of men racing towards him, some of whom pointed rifles at the dangling airman. Unceremoniously reacquainting himself with the ground, Sgt. Lehere rolled into a tangled bundle of paracord, silk, canvas harness, and profanity. Before he could shake off the effects of the impact, a rabble of fuming, gun-wielding townsfolk began tearing at the Pennsylvanian who lay bound in his own web of gear in some annoyed German's garden.

While only the grace of God had allowed the sergeant to escape the wrecked aircraft, delivered him from a hostile world five miles overhead, and spared him from a smashing finale, it was a subtle, soft autumn breeze that serendipitously blew the gunner back over the town of Bohlen, the village immediately adjacent to the bombed-out target zone where the 94th and, ironically, the *Green Hornets* had dumped their vengeance just minutes before. Lehere's good luck continued as local militia soon arrived and wrestled control of the flier from the hooks of the fuming gang. After a rough examination that stripped him of his flight gear, the militia ordered him to gather up his parachute before hauling him away by the collar and shoving him on down the lane. Stumbling further into the hamlet, townsfolk began assembling along the street, posturing and spitting curses and insults at the murderous aerial terrorist. Anticipating any moment to be his last and observing firsthand how the civilians felt about Allied airmen, the sergeant understood that no matter what happened, he had to stay on his feet and keep moving through the corridor of rage. "They didn't have much time for us…," Lehere later recollected about his stroll into the center of town that day, "…and I can't say as I blame them." The authorities prodded their prisoner along until they arrived at a small jail where the mob continued to snarl at the airman even as he was pulled inside the building by his tense captors. The unrest persisted, resonating in the foyer behind him as Lehere was escorted down a long hallway, locked away in a dusky iron-barred enclosure and left to await his fate.

BACK ONBOARD THE *GREEN HORNETS*

George Ostrowski had been standing mid-ship between the *Green Hornets'* two waist guns, bracing against the abrupt turn away from the target when he was unexpectedly propelled forward following a rapid shift in the aircraft's trajectory. He emerged from the tumble, startled, but managed to stagger past the ball turret mechanisms and into the radio compartment where he encountered a bleeding and disoriented

Pete Riley laying slumped on the deck. With the Boeing knocking and trembling violently around him, George moved past the drowsy radio operator and slowed to sidestep along the narrow footbridge that extended through the bomb bay. Negotiating the 8-inch-wide platform in his bulky flying gear while the aircraft bounded along was daunting enough; but, due to the *Hornets'* angle of ascent and severe tilt, George now had to nearly crawl to make any headway to the front of the B-17. Forcing open the door that led to the prow, Ostrowski literally fell into a catastrophe.

Thick billows of smoke streamed past his face, masking much of the shattered enclave and stinging his eyes. As he squinted ahead towards the pilot's compartment, he could only make out tangled bits of crunched metal; although, for a moment, he thought he saw the form of his pilot, folded in his seat and sprawled atop his instruments but was unsure as the view was instantly swallowed up by smoke clouds. When he lunged ahead to investigate the howling vortex, a cluster of auburn fingers of fire licked out from the haze, checking his progress. The surge of heat that followed tickled his face, motivating the sergeant to reconsider any further advance forward. Instead, George ducked into the lower crawlway and slid forward towards the nose cabin in search of Jack and Frank. Clambering along the windswept passageway and sucking in the noxious fumes that curled about the compartment the entire way, the sergeant could only hope that he would find the pair still among the living.

George managed to poke his head through the tiny entryway; but, once inside, was astonished to see nothing but an endless expanse of blue. The entire plexiglass nose cap was missing and most of the surrounding airframe had been crushed, sliced, and shredded, just as if it had been mauled by a vicious, wild animal. The large gaping wound left the compartment completely open to the elements. Through it, a current of air stormed into the ship-the remnants of the fuselage funneling the frosty gale into the interior of the Fort like a mighty arctic wind tunnel. Ostrowski's concern fell upon two masses, both laying just ahead of him and resting among fractured chunks of wood and warped shards of flapping aluminum. He immediately recognized the figures as those of Jack and Frank. Neither moved nor gave any hint of life. Both just laid there, the only motion coming from the fluttering of their frayed flight suits and the erratic jerking of their limp forms rocking in the aircraft's throes. The sight was both tragic and absolutely horrifying. With the force of the hurricane continuing to hammer him, convinced that all of his officers were surely lost, and quickly becoming delirious from the fumes himself, George turned back through the smoke-charged passageway and pulled himself up out of the hole between the two pilot's seats.

Weathering the blistering airstream that penetrated the smashed windscreen, Ostrowski was distracted by movement above him on the flight deck. To George's amazement, he identified the form of Lt. Green, face smeared with blood and wrapped in smoke. Despite being "badly frostbitten and shaken up," George later remembered that Green appeared calm and focused, all the while doggedly working at the controls. When the two made eye contact, Merle could see the sergeant was struggling to make sense of the incredible scene before him. Understanding that the man simply required a little direction, George recalled that the pilot encouraged him to, "Get the hell out of the plane, now!" With that, Ostrowski broke free of his shock and spun back for the rear of the ship. Back he stumbled; but, just as he reached the downed radio operator, George's vision narrowed, then dimmed, as he fought to keep his balance in the spinning cabin. Knowing that time was running out, George whirled around and fell through the compartment's rear door and onto the shell of Sgt. Gegenheimer's ball turret. With all of what remained of his strength, Ostrowski pounded his fists against the hull of the dormant metal sphere where, behind a few inches of steel, he knew his friend reclined. His strikes quickly weakened, glancing off the alloy globe as his body wilted, crumpling onto the dome of the turret before sliding off and spilling onto the floor, coming to rest in a drab, breathless heap.

The last thing that Jim Gegenheimer could recall was a harsh deceleration followed by a tremendous tremor. Now, a pounding resonated from somewhere up and behind his aching head. The thumping continued; and, while he was unsure what had happened, it became apparent to the ball turret gunner that someone inside the plane was trying to get his attention by banging on the hull of his battlement. Shaking off the last traces of the fog in his brain, Jim seized the turret's handles and spun his platform, pointing his guns straight down, taking aim at Germany below. The ball turret needed to be aligned in such a way as to bring its door, a small access hatch located behind the head of the cramped gunner, inside the ship before it could be opened. Only then would the sergeant be able access the interior of

B-17 with bomb bay doors open, Fold3

the bomber. For a moment, a chill of dread rushed through Gegenheimer, as he discovered that the hatch, his only means of egress, wouldn't budge. "The door wouldn't open, but I backed off, and I came up again," reminisced the Louisianan long after the War. Fortunately, the adjustment paid off as the locks disengaged, allowing the tiny panel to give way and swing upward.

As Geg clambered up into the B-17 and fought to gain his balance on the pitching deck, it was evident that something was terribly amiss as "the plane was struggling, and it was climbing." Unknown to him at the time, the *Green Hornets* was, at that moment, clambering above 28,000 feet and still climbing. "It was obvious we were in distress, but the main thing was the bail-out bell was ringing." Geg scrambled to his parachute and prepped for his jump; but, just as he snatched a portable oxygen bottle, he noticed Sgt. Ostrowski lying on the wood planking that lined the floor. George had been separated from his air supply the entire time he was negotiating his way to the front of the B-17 and back; and, after battling on in an environment depleted of oxygen, he had finally fallen unconscious after desperately trying to get a response from his buddy in the ventral turret. As luck would have it, Jim exited his position shortly after the lone waist gunner had fallen into his deadly slumber and, fortuitously, encountered the unresponsive, bluish Ostrowski. Jim managed to fit an oxygen mask onto his friend's face just in time, gradually reversing the lethal progression of hypoxia. As the skin around George's eyes began to pink up, the ball turret operator assessed the surreal scenario before him.

Past the rails of his turret, through the door leading into the radio room, Jim's eyes settled on the leather-clad form of Sgt. Riley. From below his displaced headgear, blood trickled down Pete's face, the red wetness running over his pale skin and drab tones of his flier's kit, collecting in a small red pool on the floor. The aircraft lurched and slammed along as the gunner moved to the radioman's side, dropping himself beside Pete and pressing the man's oxygen mask against his expressionless face, allowing the airflow to wash over his blue lips. To Jim's relief, Riley seemed to be responding just as Ostrowski had; and, after a few minutes of filling his lungs and dousing his blood with oxygen, the radioman was sitting up, propped against the wall, wide-eyed and lapping at the air under his mask. Just as Gegenheimer believed he had made progress with his teammates, winning a moment to gather his thoughts and catch his wind, just over his shoulder, the waist gunner had reassumed a prone position on the floor. In an oxygen-deprived stupor, George had yanked off his facepiece and fell unconscious while Gegenheimer was tending to the radioman. Maddeningly, as Jim hauled himself back to George, Riley, again, passed out. Frustrated and desperately in need of another set of hands, the teenage sergeant pressed his intercom mic and "... called to the tail gunner and got no answer so I worked on the waist gunner and revived him. When he said he was ok, I revived the radioman...."

After what seemed an eternity, Sgt. Hatfield, at last, emerged from out of the cramped tunnel in the rear of the ship. Creeping along on his hands and knees, Sidney pulled himself to his feet, wavered, and began teetering towards Jim who knelt, hovering over a wheezing Ostrowski. Jim watched as Hatfield shuffled past without saying a word, just as if in a trance and, for a moment, Gegenheimer thought he was trying to get to Pete who, stupefied and bleeding, was still struggling to right himself in the radio room. As Hatfield moved past, Jim detected something peculiar about the boy's profile. While Sid had managed to exit his den under the vertical stabilizer, he had also unwittingly wrestled himself out of his fleece-lined helmet and oxygen mask, adding the effect of oxygen starvation to a grotesque head injury.

Jim could see that half of the boy's skull was horribly malformed. Upon reaching the ball turret, Sidney toppled face-first into the open hatch, crashing hard on the steel turret tracks as he fell. Gegenheimer scampered to the tail gunner but couldn't pull the boy's long, heavy frame free of the awkward position.

> *At that point, I had three unconscious men and I knew they couldn't last long and I didn't think I could save all three of them by going one to the other so while I wasn't the pilot, I figured I could at least take the plane down to an altitude to where they wouldn't be in danger.*

The next thing Frank Jones knew, he was lying up against the wall of his cabin and being swept by icy torrents of air. Confusion turned to astonishment as Jones realized that the nose cone and the entire forward portion of his compartment had totally disintegrated. The destruction extended back to the bulbous celestial dome, now hanging shattered in its warped frame overhead, and the ship's nose was now reduced to jagged, aluminum ribbons that flapped wildly in the stormy winds. Jack was slumped out beside him in ruins of crushed metal, panting spasmodically and staring up into the heavens above. There he lay, just feet away from the pulverized beak of the Boeing which, at that moment, was swaying and shuddering over five miles above the earth. Jones slithered through the debris and found that he was unable to put weight on his leg, so he snagged Jack's harness and began heaving the bombardier away from the carnage, pulling the boy back towards the tunnel. Frank squirmed to get out of the rubble but was able to slide through the tiny opening below the flight deck, clutching at Jack the entire time as the ship jostled underneath him. Coming to the end of the crawlway, with swirling rushes of air shrieking down the channel towards him, Jones grabbed hold of the listless bombardier, drove the heels of his boots into the floor, and pushed with all his might. Knowing that the best chance for his friend's survival was out of the artic tornado and up on the next level of the deck, he squatted the full, deadweight of Jack's five-foot-ten, 170 lbs frame, and did so on a busted leg. Boosting the man's limp form up onto the engineer's platform, the act was nothing less than an incredible display of strength and willpower.

Jones propped the lieutenant up against the Fortress' bulkhead and shook the bombardier violently, pleading and shouting in a desperate attempt to awaken his paling companion. Frantically scanning for help, smoke and a tangle of metal obscured the cockpit and Lehere was nowhere to be found. As Frank surveyed his surroundings, he noticed, smeared across the chamber floor below him, a series of crimson striations marked the route he had taken to escape out of the forward compartment. He followed the glistening trail back towards him, quickly tracing the origin of the source to Lt. Williams' tattered trousers. What were once Jack's upper legs were now a ghastly exposed mess of tendon, shredded muscle, and flesh-stripped bone. A spattering of red pulsated from the cleaved tissue; surges of lifeblood that left the bombardier lying in a half-frozen, frosty pool of gore.

Jack Williams, Hoy Collection

At a loss and saturated in his teammate's blood, the Jones sat bewildered by the dreadful scene. He stared at the boy, Carrie Williams' boy, as he rested, sagging against the *Hornet's* wall. Then, after a few moments, Frank slid up beside Jack, wrapped his arms around him, and pulled Williams close. Although drowned out by the B-17's powerplants, Frank spoke to the boy, eager to offer what comfort he could and wishing to, in some way, assure his fated friend that he was not alone. 2nd Lt. Jack Williams bled out on the landing behind the *Green Hornets'* flight deck in the skies somewhere south of Bohlen, Germany. Frank, cradling his friend's body and covered in frosted blood crystals, was left swaying in the oscillations of the broken bomber.

The *Green Hornets* continued to buck and quake as Sgt. Gegenheimer edged his way towards the front of the plane, finally reaching the door that gave access to the engineer's platform and beyond, into the forward compartments. Shoving the door open, the sergeant was met with a gruesome, haunting sight that, 50 years on, would still draw tears to the man's eyes. "When I opened the door where the engineer-gunner stood, there facing me was my bombardier, and from his face I could tell he was dead, and he was blocking the passageway." The ghostly face of Lt. Williams rested against the hull of the craft, his fixed and lifeless eyes, once cheerful and warm but now upsettingly unfamiliar, stared right through the gunner. Along with Williams' flayed remains, contorted metal and cables littered the compartment, blocking all view, not to mention any further progress into the smoke-cloaked flight deck. The destruction in the front of the aircraft was so extensive that Jim, standing just feet away from the navigator, was unable to locate Jones through the smoky clutter. "At that point, I figured the rest of them were gone," regretfully recalled the ball turret gunner. Fearing that the burning ship could blow up at any second, Jim hurried back to the rear of the bomber, dead set on getting the others out. As he neared the sleepy non-coms, however, it was now the ball turret gunner who, exhausted and oxygen-starved himself, edged away into unconsciousness.

With the rest of the crew wavering at death's door in the rear of the aircraft, on the flight deck, Merle, miraculously, emerged from out of his stupor. Beside him, he discovered Lt. Metzger alive but struggling to gather his bearings. As was the case with himself, Green was startled to find Irv's hands were both completely exposed. Absent the thin layer of silk; fabric that even if donned correctly would have been completely inadequate to effectively shield the skin underneath from the starkness of the atmosphere, the co-pilot's hands had also been instantaneously exposed to temperatures nearly 60 degrees below freezing after the windscreen had disintegrated. Following only seconds of exposure to such temperatures; a situation made worse by the hellaciously frigid 100-plus mile per hour slipstream that barraged their faces, microscopic ice crystals had formed within the pilots' tissues, destroying cells, clotting blood flow, and cutting into the walls of their vasculature. Their exposed skin soured into a deep bluish-grey color and the flesh had become solid to the touch, but still, the trauma progressed even further. The cold penetrated the underlying muscle,

183

icing-over tendons, solidifying ligaments, nipping at nerve cells, and creating wounds severe enough for bone to suffer its sharp bite with irreversible and debilitating effects. Ironically, while their injuries were

induced by the sudden and unexpected torrent of subzero temperatures, the lieutenants' wounds were comparable, in some senses, to damage seen in severe, full-thickness thermal burns. As a result, all of Metzger's fingers and both of his thumbs were horribly frost-bitten and crumpled frozen into a solid, contracted muddle of digits that he guarded against his heaving chest.

Shooting a glance to his left, Merle discovered why the #1 and #2 engine indicators inset in the cracked instrument panel in front of him showed to be so unruly. Both props were missing from the head of each motor, the cowlings were stripped, and what remained of the engine blocks appeared to be crushed and

Irving Metzger, Metzger Collection

dented. Looking practically vertical towards the opposite wing due to the aircraft's bank, just feet beyond Metzger's fragmented right window, engine #3 was belching out thick, black smoke while orange flames flared out from underneath the cowling, flicking back along the nacelle. Inches to the left of the engine gauges, the altimeter told of a steady increase in altitude; the meter now rolling past 30,000 feet. Accompanying the stupefied ascent, troublingly, was a distressing reduction of airspeed. Under his quivering boots he could feel the rudder pedals becoming sloppy and noted the increased amount of slack in the control column: all indications that the Fortress was nearing the point of a stall. Merle knew immediately that if they were unable to break away from the ascent soon it would be only a matter of moments before the still-functioning engines of the fading B-17 would lose their ability to maintain lift, at which point, the plane would then simply keel over and plunge earthward in a potentially unrecoverable, spiraling death-dive. As if the endeavor wasn't harrowing enough, the pilot recognized that he had to bring the craft down to a much lower elevation that was not only better suited to manage the damaged vessel but, most importantly, richer in oxygen to support life. Seeing that the optimal environment was miles below him, the task was not to be an easy one, and time was running short.

The Boeing continued her climb into the blue ether as the lieutenant stiffened his forearms against his steering wheel, rekindling the terrible burn that, once again, ripped through his fingers as he strained to stabilize the aircraft. Beside the pilot, Metzger had recovered enough to follow suit, positioning both of his arms across the face of his control column. Together, both wearied men pressed hard, doing their best to drive their yokes forward but failing to gain much influence over their floundering, banking ascent. Merle bumped back the throttles, bringing the lamenting motors to a purring idle. A few flashes of stubbornness followed before the heavyweight relented and, grudgingly, eased down her broken snout. It was just the opportunity Merle had been waiting for. The lieutenant instantly elbowed the stick forward and without a moment's delay, the old bird pitched downward in acceptance of the dare and set off hurtling towards the layer of cumulous far below. The aviators slid forward in their seats, their safety belts catching them before they could topple onto the face of the broken instrument panel where, behind cracked screens, the arms of the altimeter now rapidly unwound.

Bolting towards the earth, the ship moaned and then skidded obliquely, hinting at entering into a spiral, all the while shuddering violently as if to protest the mad recklessness of its drivers. With his boots smashed against the pedals, practically standing on the rudder controls, Merle shifted all his weight to counter her urge to rotate. Hanging on for dear life in the waist section of the bucking B-17, Sgt. Ostrowski recollected that Merle "...brought it down so fast it's a wonder that the wings didn't come off." Rushing on, the Fortress drowned in a whiteout of clouds as turbulent ripples spasmed through the fuselage. The bomber's immense, outstretched wings wobbled as the plane plunged through the choppy, billowy layers until, finally, the *Hornets* punched free of the last wisps of white vapor. Rising up at them with alarming speed, an irregular checkerboard of fields and meadows spanned out below them, stretching all the way to the hazy horizon.

On a good day, bomber pilots were known to return from their lengthy forays stricken with, among other aches and pains, worn-out biceps, cramped forearms and knotted backs; the price of being a handler of a heavy bomber. But today, maimed and disoriented, the *Hornets'* flight officers were now facing a nearly impossible task of recovering a ruined airship from a dive. As Irv harnessed and wrenched back his column, Merle bumped forward the starboard engine's throttle handles, pouring on the coals and picking up the velocity needed to "drive" the ship out of the dive. Greasy smoke spewed from the engine just beside Metzger as it hiccupped and burped but to Merle's surprise, it, along with the undamaged outboard #4 motor, proved it still had some fight left. The duo flexed back their control sticks, heaving against the crushing compressive force of air rushing over the bomber's airfoils while the peculiar pull-of-gravity sensation blossomed low in their guts. To their astonishment, the aircraft slowly, begrudgingly began abandoning her determined descent. She continued on through a long swooping glide and, with the fliers nearly depleted, reared up level just as the arc of the horizon came into line with the *Hornets'* bobbing wingtips. Panting and with arms still folded around their yokes, the officers leveled off the bomber just as the revolutions of the altimeter needle slowed, paused, and then held at the 5,000-foot indication mark.

14
KAPUT

11 September 1944
Approximately 1300 hours
1,500 feet altitude
Position: Unknown, somewhere south-southwest of Leipzig

The faces of Pete and George were above him now and he could feel the pair shaking him vigorously, trying to churn the last of the listlessness from his sluggish body. The world came back to Jim with sharpened intensity. Gone was the stinging cold, as was the thumping of flak; only the dulled howl of a lone Cyclone engine could be detected now. A faint stream of smoke whipped past the right waist window, introducing the smell of gasoline and burning electrical systems into his oxygen mask. Beyond the smoke, golden and emerald fields and forest slipped past not far below, as did the occasional charming Bavarian village. At another time, the view would have been a stunning, completely breathtaking glimpse of some of the most magnificent and spectacularly remarkable landscapes in all of God's creation but now, despite the heavenly panorama, it was what the airmen did not see that was overwhelming. Troublingly, their Group, and with it, the protective fields of fire, was nowhere to be seen. Cruising at no more than 1,500 feet above the middle of Nazi Germany, the bomber boys felt very alone.

Just then, a racket of broken chatter scratched to life over Jim's headset and through the faint, fragmented transmission came a sound. Winded and unsteady, the voice was unmistakably recognizable as that of Lt. Green, and he was hollering to the men to abandon the aircraft. Sergeants Riley and Ostrowski had, at last, extricated Hatfield from the ball turret, but as the youngster was rolled onto his back, the group was dismayed by the sight of the senseless tail gunner. Hauling Hatfield to the side access hatch, Jim and George jettisoned the door and held the boy halfway outside the aircraft hoping "…to force air into him", but it became clear that Hatfield's condition was only worsening. Confronted with a harsh reality, out of time and options, and with friendly territory still hours away, the men recognized the gravity of the grim choice and heartbreaking decision that was now before them. "So we decided that two of us would throw out the tail gunner who we thought was dead", said Gegenheimer with a pause, many years afterward. "We'd throw him and one would hold his ripcord and I would go out second." Riley had decided to stay on, hoping, in some way, to assist the pilots. Fully aware that, while the plane was in extremis and his jump cushion was being squandered by the second, Riley understood that by staying on he was resigning his fate to that of the *Green Hornets* and Lt. Green.

Holding Sidney's frame in the opening of the door, the pair couldn't help but hesitate. Each battled the voices in their head that shamed them for coming to such a sad decision; one that continued to scream at them not to abandon their friend even as his body dangled in the doorway. Sid, like every non-com on the crew, had earned his spot, first among airmen, then as an aerial gunner in the US Army Air Forces, and finally as a valued, beloved teammate on Green's squad. He had shared in the same epidemic of homesickness that ran rampant through the team during their muggy, hot mosquito-filled summer at Drew, and was always heard jabbering on about the current pendant race. When he and the boys visited the bars and nightspots of Tampa, Sid had provided motivation to his soused associates who, now inspired by Hatfield's pep talk, deployed charge after charge against the defenses of the unsuspecting young Florida belles. When the wannabe lotharios were beaten back, their waited Sidney with more liquid reinforcements. At night's end, with gangs of military police on the hunt along the boardwalk and backstreets for overly-inebriated GIs, Sidney and the band would dodge the patrols, their calculated evasion techniques inevitably devolving into a mad-dash scramble back to the safety of their hotel. Back on base, with the day's training complete, Hatfield was famous for herding his dog-tired associates to a patch of grass to toss around the baseball. When he had had his fill propelling rockets into the gloves of his associates, he would drape a long arm around the shoulder of one of the other lads and yank the flier about like an overgrown, excited schoolboy as the group retired to their barracks for the evening. Now, somewhere over Germany, Sidney's arm was wrapped around the fabric of his silk parachute which had been unpacked and gathered there by two of those same lads. Above woodlands and patches of grazing fields, with the aircraft swaying gently and as the world around him slowed, George lessened his grip on Hatfield, felt the boy's weight spill back through the exit door, and then "...finally let him go."

RUSSDORF, GERMANY

Stirred from their homes by the drumming of motors, residents of Russdorf spotted a large, four-engine aircraft bearing white stars and curious markings gliding over the pastures and grassland east of the village's crossroads. They instantly identified the plane as one of the terrifying American bombing machines, but as it grunted past, they could see that the giant had been severely damaged. Its muzzle was cleaved and hacked open, and ripples of smoke spewed from both wings. Captivated locals watched, from out of its murky wake, a parachute unfurl and snap open. Seconds later, a second sheet could be seen streaming from out of the bomber's flightpath, thrashing through the air until it too caught and swelled just above the distant woods, leaving its cargo swinging beneath like a pendulum. As a third fluttered to life off in the distance further south, a crowd of men, women, and children began racing toward the nearest of the three chutes. Dangling from the canopy, a spiritless figure could be seen, rocking back and forth. His arms hung loosely at his sides, and he made no attempt to reach overhead to handle the risers to try and control his descent. The airman crumpled hard into the dirt, the thud from the impact unsettled the peace of the yet-unspoiled countryside. Surprisingly, as the crowd came upon the site, the airman remained still. He didn't hurry to his feet or attempt to scurry off into the thicket but lay motionless in a field on Willy Keller's farm.

Remarkably, the American had practically landed in the lap of not one, but two doctors. One, Dr. Strachura, just happened to be calling on a friend and fellow physician nearby when the Allied bombing attacks delayed his return home. When the commotion of a large aircraft was heard just after one that afternoon, the men stepped outside just in time to see parachutes sinking out of the sky. Soon after, Strachura found himself kneeling over a fresh-faced, unresponsive American boy. Palpating along the side of the flier's neck, the doctor was unable to detect a pulse, but what he did feel was an undulation in the back of the boy's skull where a sizable depression suggested multiple fractures. Although those in attendance were disturbed by the airman's blue skin, all watched curiously as Strachura conducted his assessment of the boy who fell out of the sky.

To avoid detainment, interrogation and harassment by the investigating authorities who had yet to arrive, locals left the sergeant's body to lie in the field where he had come to rest. When no one came to take charge of the airman by sundown, residents brought the American to a nearby house and laid him in the front room. There he remained until early on the morning of the 13th when, at the oversight of a Luftwaffe Major, the young flier was stripped of his uniform and buried in the Russdorf cemetery, adjacent to the chapel. A cross was fixed at the head of the grave with the inscription, *"Hier ruht ein amerikanischer Flieger"*-"Here rests an American flier."

Almost immediately after Sidney's body toppled from the B-17, Sgt. Gegenheimer dove out into the blue and was instantly flung downward by the prop wash of the giant airship. Taking note of the whine of the bomber's motors quickly fading away, Jim found himself staring up at the sky, feeling as if he were floating in another world, far removed from the havoc that had dominated him while onboard the aircraft. When he flipped over, however, he found that in basking in the calm of his new setting, he had made a crucial miscalculation. "I realized I shouldn't have been free-falling and I pulled my ripcord. I only made about three swings and hit the ground and sprained my ankle but thank God I landed in a plowed field." Upon touching down, smarting foot and all, no more than twenty minutes had passed since the sergeant had emerged from his ball turret.

After collapsing his chute and hiding the billowing fabric deep in the undergrowth of a nearby thicket, Gegenheimer proceeded to plod further into the woods, all the while skimming the land for any sign of his waist gunner and determined to put as much distance between his landing site and himself as fast as was possible. After some time pushing through the forest, the sergeant opted to rest his aching foot and assess his bearings but within moments, a commotion was heard fast approaching from along a narrow fire trail that cut through the forest. Jim flattened himself on the ground as best he could, hiding low amongst the fallen leaves, willing himself to conform to the slightest depression in the earth. The sound of boots pounding against the ground intensified and as he tried to control his breathing, the noise from the footfalls merged with the fierce thumping in his chest. Then came new sounds, voices of men fanning out into the timber around him. Within minutes, a handful of men, dressed in civilian clothes and armed with what he thought to be "blunderbusses," converged on the prostrate gunner. Surrounded and recognizing that the game was up, Jim cautiously rose to his feet, extended his arms above his head, and surrendered to a jubilant bunch of captors.

The posse led their prisoner back down the trail, all the way prodding and swiping at the hobbling American with sticks just as if they were driving livestock to a pen. The chattering assembly soon emerged from the forest and joined with another group of armed civilians; this one composed of roughly equal amounts of agitated menfolk and inquisitive teenage boys. As Gegenheimer was ushered towards the lot, a few of the captors were seen standing over a figure that he instantly recognized as that of his waist gunner. Jostled to the ground, Geg was relieved to see a familiar face, as was George who was equally as comforted by the unexpected reunion. There was no sign of Sidney, however. George skimmed the faces of the men in the crowd, most of whom appeared hotly engaged with others from the group, but Ostrowski searched on, finally making eye contact with one of the youngsters in attendance. The waist gunner motioned to the boy who, apparently pleased by being solely solicited by the nefarious company, gleefully approached the capitulated couple. Betting that the ward understood some English, Ostrowski asked the young German about a third prisoner. The boy glanced around apprehensively, shook his head, and quietly responded, "kaput."

The rabble, thought by the two Americans to be something of a local militia, looked to be squabbling amongst each other and, after a few tense minutes of heated deliberation, one amongst them strode towards the bomber boys, pistol in hand. "The first thing they did, one spoke a little English, they offered us a pistol to shoot ourselves," Jim remembered. As enticing of an offer as it was, both sergeants promptly

191

declined. "So I said 'no, I don't want to shoot myself," smirked Gegenheimer, recounting the incredible interaction many decades later. Irritated and out of patience, the captors tugged their airmen to their feet and marched them off in the direction of a nearby town.

Under guard, the gunners trudged into the village, later to be understood as Zwickau, where the locals were in the process of returning to their daily duties after having sought shelter when the air raid sirens had first whined earlier that day around noon. Some in the crowd strode out from the growing mass of locals and into the street, trailing behind the procession as it advanced down the lane and hollering their displeasure at the "*terrorfliegers*". The addition of the new welcome party was every bit the motivation Jim needed to straighten his hitch and quicken his pace, as did George who was timidly eyeing the assemblage of visibly enraged hostiles that shadowed them along the streets, gripping at clubs and ropes.

Coming to the town center, the Americans were pressed into a "stone enclosure" roughly the size of a city block and fenced in by eight-foot-high walls. Gegenheimer described what transpired next:

> *They got the command of the town square and all the people came around. They put my waist gunner and I in and they turned us around and the head man gave some orders and he had some riflemen out there aiming at us. About that time, I said my prayers real quick because I didn't know how fast you died from a bullet to the back of the head.*

A few paces behind him, the militia honed their aim on the American villains. George, feigning an abdominal wound and pretending not to understand what was desired of him by the armed gang, rallied all the swagger and mettle a man could muster while literally under the gun and attempted a smooth transition out of the line of fire. Confusion turned to agitation as the firing squad recovered their senses, swatted Ostrowski back downrange, and refixed their aim. Jim Gegenheimer continued:

> *When he gave the order to fire, neither the waist gunner nor I attempted to run or do anything, so the townspeople actually cheered when we didn't flinch. It wasn't the fact that we weren't scared to death, there was just nothing you could do about it. It*

was just the situation you were in.

Apparently unamused, many of the riflemen responded to the audience's sudden change of heart by chambering a round in their rifles, but just as they were aligning their sights on the airmen for a second, and presumably, last time, a military truck squealed to a stop in front of the courtyard's gate. *Wehrmacht* troops piled out of the back and, with weapons at the ready, rushed into the center of the enclosure. The soldiers shouted at the riflemen and leveled their guns at the would-be executioners who, now covered by a larger force, fit with greater firepower, appeared just as dumbfounded as the sergeants. With the riflemen coolly slinking away into the crowd, stone-faced soldiers snatched the pair of smirking yet flabbergasted Americans and led them off to the local prison.

15

THE ESCAPE

Having muscled himself up between the pilot's seats, Sgt. Riley was shocked to find the embattled flight team alive, though maimed, and working at their instruments. Pete reported in, shouting over the gale to relay that he had drummed out an emergency transmission via Morse code; standard operating procedure in case of a crisis, but had not received confirmation from the Group. But there was more unwelcome news: George and Geg had both been hurt. Both had "hit the silk", as had Sidney, although Hatfield didn't look good, and Jack...Lt. Williams was dead. The words stung Lt. Green hard. All of his boys were injured in one way or another, but Merle couldn't help but be fixated on his departed friend, his best pal, whose body lay resting in a thawing pool of blood against the bulwark just behind him. Alongside the lifeless bombardier, Frank cradled his own injured paw, also frostbitten and, as was apparent for everyone else on board, was clearly in desperate need of medical attention.

For the time being, the B-17 remained airworthy, although, now powered on by the might of only one good engine, the Boeing had been reduced to a staggering, screeching shadow of the once magnificent airship she had once been. Both port engines were annihilated and although the fire that had threatened to take over the inboard #3 engine before torching into the wing's fuel tanks had been extinguished, the motor was all but dead. Its propellor windmilled feebly in the slipstream, creating more of a hinderance due to the increased drag, so Green feathered the blades. The pilots now coerced the ship on not through finesse or skill but by sheer muscle and bullheadedness. Knowing that the bomber was fading and that time and altitude were running short, Merle debated on having the others bailout. Both Frank's and Jack's parachutes had been swept from the aircraft when the nose compartment had fragmented, leaving three parachutes between the four survivors; in essence, stranding at least one of the crew to the plane. Although he was barely able to retain control as it was, Merle believed that he could hold the bomber steady just long enough for the others to leap clear. Before he could finish verbalizing the plan, however, Jones, Riley, and Metzger, unwilling to entertain the thought of deserting their "skipper", scoffed at the proposal, immediately and forever dismissing the thought. He would just have to come up with another plan.

A Flying Fortress with heavy damage, Fold3

The most practical option before them, Merle realized, was to find an impromptu landing site; a level field or meadow where they could get the crippled Fortress on the ground, and fast. Supposing they were successful in setting down, surviving the impact, and assuming that the plane didn't blow up in the process, the men, checked by the extent of their injuries, would have to hike quite a distance through unfamiliar and hostile land before reaching friendly territory. The getaway would also require them to evade hundreds of German troops who would be explicitly committed to hunting them down, that is if a bomb-shocked civilian lynch-mob bent on settling a score did not get to them first. There would be no hiding, no resources, no cavalry coming to help. Capture, it would seem, was practically inevitable.

As the bomber limped on, treading air, Merle found that the damage to his hands and face was more severe than he initially thought. He continued to choke down swallows of blood, his body ached, and the pain: fierce even when masked by the numbing biological mechanisms of shock, only continued to intensify. Worse still, due to their raw, inflexible hands, neither he, nor Metzger could effectively retain control of their yokes for longer than a few excruciatingly tortuous seconds before the agony forced them to relinquish the controls to the other; a continuous process that was becoming old, very quick. Deprived of a fit co-pilot, fielding a decimated crew, and fighting for every second to keep the smoking 17 from tumbling out of the sky, Merle realized that despite his determination it would only be a matter of time before his strength, their luck, and possibly any remaining hope, would finally give out. So much for the glamor of the Air Corps! Retightening his latch on his control column, Merle recognized that there was only one thing that he could do; he began to pray. But then, unexpectedly, with defeat looming, something peculiar happened.

Amidst the blaring engine noise and surges of wind that rushed into the cockpit around him, Merle noticed the chaos suddenly quiet. Also quelled were the stifling feelings of doubt and confusion and fear and pain that twisted wildly around his brain; the turmoil now replaced by an odd tranquility and a sense of peace. A voice arose out of the calmness, absurdly out of place but somehow familiar, unwavering, and comforting. Instantly the voice was recognizable as that of his wife, Rose, and she was urging him on, spurring him to keep going, to not give up the fight.

Months before, while families meandered around the assortment of Army flying machines that sat on display across the tarmac at Hendricks Air Field following the conclusion of the promotion ceremony for B-17 transition training, one slim graduate was seen ushering off a pretty brunette in the direction of one of the school's parked bombers. Floating around the aircraft with his gal in tow, Merle rambled on about the machine's amazing capabilities and nuances. He pointed out its cavernous bomb hold and the plane's incredible arsenal of machine guns which seemed to jut out in all directions. With a whiff of braggadocio and unable to bridle his boyish delight, the lieutenant gestured towards the Fortress' cockpit and gave a rundown of the plethora of flight equipment; technology far more advanced than his father's glue, wood, and canvas bi-wing that Rose had flown in back on the farm. He had fallen in love with the B-17 and it was clear he was proud to pilot the machine but one significant innovation that he had described to his wife, one that he had been trained on and pressed to utilize, annoyed Green.

A predecessor of the present-day automatic piloting system, US heavy bombers of World War II were fitted with a rudimentary electromechanical system that relied on an arrangement of interconnected gyroscopic compasses. This system, called the Automatic Flight Control Equipment, or AFCE, instantaneously adjusted the aircraft's elevators, ailerons, and rudder to compensate for deviations detected in the plane's flight. This granted the aircraft the ability to maintain a relatively straight and level course when employed, effectually allowing the pilots to fly "hands-free", without having to operate the control yoke. Directional changes could also be accomplished with precision by manipulating the dials and switches engineered to regulate the bomber's degree of bank. All things considered, Merle loathed the thought of having to employ this killjoy "autopilot." He adored flying, after all, and he had enlisted to be an Army aviator, not to relinquish control to a robot. Rose, however, knew her willful husband: a flier concerned more, at times, with passion than proficiency, but despite being a novice herself, Rose could see the value in the equipment. "Merle," she had asserted to her headstrong partner that day at Hendricks, "if you need it, use the autopilot."

Tucked low behind his controls on the flight deck of the *Green Hornets*, Rose's voice echoed in the lieutenant's head once again, but this time it ringed with enlightenment. "Merle, use the autopilot," directed the voice with a calm matter-of-factness. With that peculiar encounter, Merle became convinced that with the AFCE engaged, by balancing engine rpms, tweaking the pitch of the propellers, and fine-tuning the aircraft with the foot pedals when needed, the *Green Hornets* could stagger on for a little while longer. Even so, every bit of luck would be welcomed along the way, but, as the birdman saw it, it was entirely possible.

A degree of relief washed over the crew as upon actuating the autopilot master switch and adjusting the flight surface control knobs, they felt the bomber steady herself, awarding the frazzled aviators a few moments of much-needed reprieve. Breathless and trembling, Lts.

Metzger and Green soon realized that despite having averted further immediate misfortune, they were far from deliverance. Taking measure of their prospects, it was clear that returning to England was to be ruled out as the Anglo-isle lay at least three hours away, closer to four on one good engine, thus making the likelihood of completing the quest highly improbable. The other option, the only remaining option, was far more daunting.

During the second week in September, Group intelligence officers informed the aircrews that "friendly lines" had been established adjacent to the western border of Germany proper. Fortunately, prior to take-off on the morning of the 11th, Lt. Green

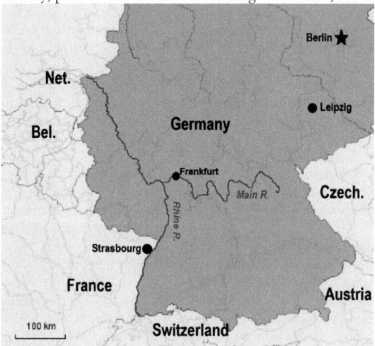

and his officers had carefully studied their maps, taking note of, among many other details, the arrangement of Allied front lines. The beautiful Alsatian town of Strasbourg, just across the German border in occupied France, was still tightly in enemy control but US ground troops and armor units had pushed within fifty miles west of the city. This bulge of recently secured territory created an enticing refuge for any battle-weary bomber traversing southern Germany and in need of an emergency landing field.

An alternative harbor for roughed-up aircrews was

Switzerland, positioned further up the Rhine from Strasbourg. For those beaten-but-not-bested Allied aircrews who could survive and make their way to Strasbourg in the middle of September of 1944, the Swiss border, and the American entrenchments west of town, were virtually identical distances. The only other alternative was to proceed northwest, moving through the lethal Rhine valley defenses and the northern sector of the Siegfried line, made worse by the especially treacherous airspace that could be saturated with the Luftwaffe's best within minutes.

It was somewhere over Western Thuringia that Merle made the decision to make a run for Allied lines around Strasbourg. Despite the difficulties, statements collected from the crew afterward note that not only was Lt. Green determined to avoid capture, but he was resolved to "bring the plane home." Surrender, after all, just didn't have the ring to it. Fed by hydraulic fluid and oxygen-rich pressurized air venting from severed hoses that ran around the crumpled flight deck, the flare-up in the *Green Hornets* had left much of the interior of the cabin scorched. Remnants continued to smolder but visibility on the flight deck had improved dramatically since the fire had burnt through most of the flammable material-another stroke of good fortune for the men behind the controls. However, to make it to France, and the safety of Allied lines, it was clear that they would need more than luck and a pilot's stubbornness.

Together, the men began effecting their escape. The tools of a navigator: charts, maps, slide ruler, stopwatch, route planning documents, sextant, astrocompass, astrograph, drift meter, and radio, were either all smashed or had been blown out of the airplane. What they did have available to guide them out of the bowels of the Third Reich was a compass, a few wristwatches, and an airspeed reading; the most rudimentary instruments of an aviator. Although he found himself deprived of his plot tables and navigational maps, Frank recognized that the key to their withdrawal was to use the river system as their guide. He had made sure to commit the prominent topographical features to his memory while at briefing that morning and amidst the dozens of minute details presented, two notable rivers stood out. First, far off to the west lay the River Rhine; the large, meandering course of water that poured south to north through the fertile region that bore its name and delineated the southwestern portion of the border between France and Germany. The other equally conspicuous waterway in the area, the Main River, wound along from Bamberg in the east and swept west through Frankfurt before dissolving into the Rhine just beyond Mainz. In essence, the Main split the Fatherland in half while the Rhine bisected the western territories.

Frank knew, in theory at least, that by following any of the streams and creeks in the area, they could progress up the system of waterways and eventually stumble upon the Main. Then, mirroring the river's flow west, they would inevitably reach the River Rhine. Once the Rhine was located, the crew could follow the waters south until they hit Strasbourg where, just a short distance further lay Allied-controlled territory. For Merle, an aviator who matured his abilities as a teenager by steering on the rivers, back lanes, and train tracks while piloting over the prairies and woodlands of central Illinois, the task was not inconceivable. The true test would be in keeping the plane aloft for the two-plus hour trip as they crept through the fields of flak batteries that pockmarked most of Western Germany, including those poised ahead in their path in great numbers encircling Frankfurt. After all, any slow, low-flying American aircraft would make an easy target for the crack shot gunners. Furthermore, with the loss of the non-coms, and in turn the ability to parry any Luftwaffe attack, the *Green Hornets* was practically a sitting duck.

Coasting at just over one thousand feet altitude above rolling pastures, foothills shrouded in impenetrable forest, and fertile expanses of grassland, the flight was as picturesque as it was treacherous. Herds of milch cows could be seen grazing lazily, scattered upon gentle sloping hillsides, and vast basins converted to rugged highlands upon which sprouted clusters of thick, lush vegetation. Occasionally the ruins of a castle, once splendid and imposing but now long abandoned and in decay, were spied, perched atop stony outcrops. Sleepy, pristine hamlets, unchanged for hundreds of years, sat cradled within the depressions of the land, straddling the shady banks of cool, meandering tributaries and rippling streams that toppled over steep, rocky faces, and terminated into hidden forest pools. While beautiful, the land was charged with mystery, harboring innumerable secrets within a labyrinth-like wilderness of primeval, haunted forests, some of which provided inspiration for the Brothers Grimm. For generations, legends of witches, specters, devils, and cave-dwelling ghouls had been passed on to persuade local children to keep far from the shadowy woodlands and close to home: testimony that even the locals knew the forests to be unsafe. Outsiders were even more intimidated.

A century before Christ, the Romans had warily advanced into these timberlands and established a series of outposts. The garrisons allowed the centurions: invaders too, to safely hunker down behind reinforced entrenchments and thick palisade walls between their expeditions into the eerie terrain of the supernatural where hostile and exceptionally formidable tribes of "barbarians" lurked. In the end, the Germanians had rid their lands of Caesars' legions not by pushing out the aggressors but by luring them to their slaughter. Nearly two thousand years later, the inhabitants were determined to rectify a new affront and repeat the affair, but this time they would handle Brits and Yankees.

By 1400 hours, the *Green Hornets* was holding at an altitude at just over three hundred feet above the undulating countryside. She had gradually been shedding elevation as the single hot, overburdened powerhouse pulled with barely enough strength to keep her in the air. To complicate matters, the AFCE was not performing properly, forcing Merle to, once again, adapt his flying techniques. Like most aircraft, trim tabs were engineered into the trailing edge of the B-17's elevators and rudder. These small, manually adjustable flaps were essential to compensate for changes in the aircraft's center of gravity, the loss of an engine, or the torque of a motor. A behemoth like the Flying Fortress was never meant to be flown by the trim tabs alone, just fine-tuned as needed. Yet, by continuously evaluating the plane's flight path and making nearly constant corrections by rolling the trim control wheels with the palm of his muddled hand, Lt. Green was piloting the bomber almost entirely by these accessory flight controls.

Despite the precariousness of their situation, with the anxiety came optimism. As the tally of miles between them and Bohlen increased, so too did the crew's belief that the *Hornets* was actually going to make it to the security of Allied lines. Along with their hopes, the run of water they had been tracking had swelled and was now the size of a rambling river, the Kinzig, and as it washed from out of the hills, the country abruptly opened into a broad valley. Dropping into the depression, the Fortress swooped over a scattering of cottages and white-walled, wooden-framed houses lining the outskirts of another pleasant, unmolested German community that rested peacefully along the winding watercourse. Out Metzger's splintered window, the spires of a medieval Romanesque-Gothic church towered over the center of the village, and up ahead in the distance, a long, sloping range of mountains could be spied, hunkering in their path.

By now, the B-17 had attracted the attention of the locals, some of whom were not so keen at the arrival of the Americans and had already began readying a welcome for the trespassers. With Frank scrutinizing the horizon and the lieutenants ushering the noisy, smoking airship along the Kinzig not high above the village rooftops, small orbs of green and red light flared up from out of the patchwork of grass fields directly up ahead, just beyond the bounds of the hamlet. Merle studied the phenomenon, following the strange, yet mesmerizing sequence of tiny colored spheres as they rose from the field and surged up at him. More glowing beads of light followed, spurting out from multiple sites across the wide, flat meadow, all accelerating and converging toward the B-17 with fantastic speed. Without warning, the sky around the aircraft transformed into a turbulent firestorm of sparks. Torrents of blazing bolts of light ripped through the air just outside of the cockpit, hissing as they rocketed past in phosphorescent blurs. The illuminated salvo of bolts flickered around them, many bursting as they thumped and pounded into the *Hornet's* aluminum skin, showering the cockpit with splintered metal, and enveloping the fliers in a twirling cascade of lightening and embers.

16
FRIENDS AND ENEMIES

Secretly I thought, how do the Americans manage to let such colossuses operate daily in such large numbers over Germany? That can not go on like this. Then all our cities will fall to ruins over time. And that's how it happened.

-Heinrich Goy

11 September 1944
1400 hours
Leipziger Strasse
Lieblos, Germany

The air raid siren had sounded just before noon, being replaced quickly after by the haunting howl of massive aircraft. The sight of the great American bomber force, scoring broad swathes of contrails through the sky as they inched past overhead, fascinated many of the local boys, including Heinrich Goy. Earlier that day, the adventurous 14-year-old had snubbed the alert to shelter and, instead, joined his friends on the outskirts of town to investigate the airfield where legends of the Luftwaffe would frequently seek haven. Just beside lay the community of Lieblos; a name taken by some as meaning "loveless." In fact, the village's agrarian forefathers had bestowed the splendid, fertile, peaceful land with a name paying tribute to the area's "good ground".

American planes had been using the Kinzig Valley as a highway to breach into the heart of Germany for some time, and by 1944, the daily appearance of US aircraft over Lieblos provided entertainment for the schoolboys and had become so routine that residents could set their watches to it. Heinrich had become so well versed with each of the unique airframes that he could identify the aircraft, friend, or opposition, simply by the whine of its motor. The youths had, many times, imagined themselves piloting the fighters, the "hunters" as they were known, and setting off into the blue where they would, like the Teutonic Knights of old, valiantly engage the invaders in battle, striking them from the heavens. But those days were still a few years off, and for now, Heinrich and his pals would have to wait.

By early afternoon on the 11th, with the signal of "all clear" still yet to be heard, Heinrich pedaled his way down Leipziger Strasse, heading towards the hamlet of Roth after leaving his band in the fields outside of neighboring Gelnhausen. "I had no fear, but it was a queasy feeling," he remembered as he continued along the lanes with "eyes and ears wide open." He had just wheeled into the center of town and stepped off his bicycle when, from out of the east, the grumbling of motors captured his attention. As the growling reverberated down the cobblestone streets, a massive airplane suddenly screeched into view, roaring just above the rooftops and soaring directly towards Heinrich. He, like most locals, had never seen an American bomber at such close distance but immediately recognized the airship as a B-17. Feeling the vibrations of the motors in his bones, the teenager abandoned his bicycle and took cover behind a nearby house. The vessel soared by so close that Heinrich " ... could see the pulpit, machine gun stands, [and] the rear guns under the huge rudder," even identifying that "[t]he big American license plate was clearly visible". Smoke trailed out of one of the engines, and the ship's nose was annihilated and looked to be "pushed in". "'Oh dear God,' I thought, 'they are flattening the airbase now'", recalled Goy.

From behind him, came a staccato of hammering. The racket deflected off the buildings and echoed along the stony streets as golden bolts of light whizzed by, sizzling just feet above his head. The surges slammed into the aircraft, each crunch cutting free sparking chunks of metal from the monster's body. Like a startled fowl, the bomber reacted dramatically to the surprise and dumped a wing, triggering the aircraft to veer off to the northeast in a rapid descent. When the B-17 passed behind the pitched roofs of the village, Heinrich jumped on his bicycle and chased after, guiding on the trail of smoke.

At Leipziger Strasse 15, Gustav Wiedenbeck was minding his garden when the four-motored bomber screamed by directly overhead, nearly clipping the ridge of his roof in the process and causing the entire world around him to shudder and tremble. With his house rattling on its foundation, he was mesmerized by the display of tracer rounds streaming over his flower garden and lighting up the Boeing. Breaking free of the captivating spectacle and standing so close to the path of fire that the shockwave of each projectile could be felt as it cut through the air around him, Wiedenbeck recovered his wits and "fell on the floor to keep from getting wounded".

Nearby, 15-year-old Gerhard Solzer was near the Kinzig Mill on the southern fringes of Lieblos when,

> ...*a huge low flying aircraft suddenly flew over me. I knew immediately that it was an American Flying Fortress. One of the engines was smoking badly and the aircraft was losing altitude. The aircraft disappeared from my field of vision and a short time later its motors were no longer to be heard.*

Just after two o'clock, the *Green Hornets* had unknowingly wandered directly into the defense system that ringed Gelnhausen Air Field. The site had been strafed by American fighter planes twice in the past week but today, the Germans were ready and lay in wait. When, from out of the hills motored a lone Allied bomber plane, the field's anti-aircraft gunners trained their sights on the beast and tracked the boisterous, low-flying aircraft as it drew closer. Sputtering within 700 yards of their barrels, the defenders opened fire on the lame giant with medium flak guns and pummeled the Fortress with volleys that cut holes through their easy game. Recognizing the ambush at the last moment, Merle put the *Hornets* into a violent bank, frantically attempting to avoid the German's snare. Green's evasive maneuver caused the ship to pitch sharply out of the kill zone but, in turn, depleted the aircraft's ability to maintain lift. Traveling below three hundred feet, altitude was in short supply. Powered by one taxed motor and squandering the meager cushion of air that they sailed upon, the B-17 no longer had the ability to keep itself in the air.

The Fortress set down with a bone-jarring jolt, tremoring as it ground its way through the soft dirt. With a succession of metallic shrieks, the *Green Hornets* wobbled onward, cutting a deep gash through the earth and churning up a track of dust as it slid on with wild abandon. One of her wingtips caught soil, causing the outer portion of the wing to shear apart between ribs and tear away as fragments of metal and an aileron broke free and fluttered through the air. She recoiled from the dislocation only to bury the leading edge of the opposite wing into the ground, slightly ebbing the skidding bomber. The Boeing burrowed forward and struck a lone apple tree that stood in the middle of the acre, severing the wing at the root and carving open a long gouge in the left flank of the fuselage. There, the dented remains of #653, the *Green Hornets*, came to a spinning conclusion in Karl Koch's cornfield.

Lt. Irving 'Irv' Metzger, Tampa, 1944

With only seconds to act, Lt. Green had directed the sinking aircraft towards an open strip of land just beyond the village and set the plane down on its belly. "Believe it or not," said Lehere in an interview, "the pilot belly-landed that plane just by using the automatic pilot. He controlled it with these little knobs and toggle switches because he couldn't use his fingers. Now that shows you what kind of flier he was."

After slamming to a halt, Green and Metzger rapidly cut off the engine, choked off the fuel, and flipped off the battery and master switches. They forced the cockpit's fissured side windows out of the way and as Irv pulled himself out through the opening with his elbows,

Merle assisted the Flight Officer by pushing him through the cockpit. Jones lurched past the pilot and as clouds of smoke began overrunning the flight deck, Frank rushed for the window, shouting that he couldn't pull Williams' body free. Irv toppled out of the cockpit, landing hard onto the ground nearly eight feet below and Frank followed suit, spilling out of the window, and collapsing into the soil. The impact knocked the wind out of Jones in the process, but the navigator managed to shuffle away. Up above in the cockpit, Merle caught a glimpse of the young bombardier through the billows of smog. Jack still rested quietly behind the pilots' seats, wedged between the turret beams and pinned under debris that had worked loose in the rough landing. With flames curling out of the tunnel below him, Green took one last look at his friend, turned, dove to his window, hauled himself out of the opening, and tumbled free of the aircraft.

Glancing off his table during the tumultuous landing, Pete was thrown onto the deck of the radio room compartment. It was the second time that day that he had been unexpectedly and violently hurled forward while toiling at the radios in his cabin behind the bomb bay and again, for the second time, he managed to get back to his feet. To his wonder, the ship hadn't exploded, so he sprung up, propped a boot up on his desk, and wrenched himself up through the large hatch in the ceiling of his cubicle. Hoisting his frame out of the compartment while wearing his heavy, bulky flight gear proved quite the undertaking but the blood-stained sergeant managed to roll out of the hatch and onto the ship's spine, sliding down onto the wing and finally dropping the last few feet into the raked dirt. The radioman trudged to the front of the B-17 expecting to help his injured comrades away from the unstable, smoking, gas-filled bomber but, instead, Riley noticed a man, dressed in civilian clothes, duck low and step through the gaping, smoldering wound in the front of the aircraft. Pete followed and hopped up into the mutilated nose compartment where he found himself surrounded by several small fires and entirely enveloped by smoke. Choking on the fumes and now being licked by mechanical fluid-fueled flames that were melting the aircraft's thin aluminum skin off its alloy skeleton, Sergeant Riley snatched onto the man and yanked him free of the cabin. Unknown to Riley, the man he had snatched out of the B-17 was the local cemetery caretaker, Friedrich Griessman. "Fritz", as his friends knew him, described the event to American investigators in 1946:

After the plane had landed I went from my house to the plane because I was in the Red Cross, thought I could help, if anyone was wounded. I was in the plane but an American man from the plane put me out because the plane was going to burn.

Dipping out of the Boeing, the two men beat a hasty retreat away from the bomber. As the unlikely duo tromped through the dirt, Riley spotted a figure, another civilian, standing at the crest of the adjacent railway embankment. The man waved, beckoning the flier to follow him as he turned and then moved off slowly, glancing back over his shoulder every few steps. After warily scaling the incline, Pete came face to face with the man who, looking the flier over, studied the blood trickling from the American's head. Motioning to a nearby gatehouse, the man helped haul the shaken airman towards the structure where a woman had emerged and stood clutching dressings and several rolls of cloth. The man settled Pete down against the well as the woman stepped forward and began cleaning the cascade of blood that continued to dribble from the gunner's forehead. The man knelt alongside and pressed the bundle of bandages to the wound, holding it in place as the doting frau wrapped the radioman's head with gauze. When satisfied with her work, the woman strode over to her well, retrieved some water, and returned to the sergeant's side, passing him the cup of

Gerhard Solzer, 1954, Geschichtsverein Grundau

cool liquid, which the Riley guzzled down ravenously. While the American couldn't understand what the couple was saying, Pete could tell by the way they attended to his injury, the manner in which they spoke to him with relaxed tones, the way they looked at him with concern and sympathy, that these people were not the enemy.

Before the dust had settled after the Fortress had come to a rest on Koch's land, a sizable crowd of locals had begun to gather at the crash site. The group stood along the edge of the field, examining the Boeing from afar, gawking at the Americans and watching a fire that glowed in the front of the slain machine. Gerhard Solzer, a teenager from Lieblos, had been one of the first on the scene and had watched when from "[o]ut of the smoking aircraft climbed 4 or 5 American flyers in fur jackets and big boots." Upon witnessing the "heavy" being shot up by the guns at the airfield, Karl Ost, another Lieblos resident, pedaled his bicycle to the rail crossing. Like many others, Ost hurried to the gatehouse for a chance to see one of the so-called "*terrorfliegers*" up close. When arrived, he merged with the curious group who stood nearby to watch as the wounded American, more boy than monster, was swathed with compresses.

Suddenly aware of his growing popularity, Riley recognized that it was probably in his best interest to get back to his crewmates. The flier gestured appreciation to his hosts and turned towards the cornfield where a thick plume of greasy smoke was billowing into the sky and hurried back down the slope. Stumbling to the base of the embankment, a large group of armed German soldiers; troops stationed just down the road at the airbase- the same airbase that had shot apart the *Green Hornets* with their flak guns, encircled him amidst a flurry of shouts. Walled in by the frenzy, Pete lifted his hands above his bandaged head, half-expecting to be shot through. To his relief, he was only searched and then escorted over to where his three fellows reclined by the side of the field. Upon rejoining his crewmates, other soldiers hustled past, fanning out into the crowd of onlookers to scribble down the names of those in attendance, taking particular interest in the those who were thought or seen to have had contact with the Americans. As the drama produced by the colliding of two worlds subsided, the soldiers seemed to relax as they realized that their four prisoners-a disheveled, shocked, and bloodied gang, were in no state to offer any resistance. The troops studied their captives, looking for sidearms, exploring their pockets and cumbersome flight clothing, and snatching away their escape kits before stepping back to gawk at their conquered rivals.

Battling to get to his feet, Lt. Green spat out a few mouthfuls of blood, stood tall through the dizziness that swirled in his head, and requested to speak with the unit's commander. One soldier, a non-commissioned officer, stepped forward and presented himself to the American. Green informed the man that he had wounded men and asked that they be given the bandages from their survival kits to treat their wounds. The German shot a glance at the lieutenant's hands, both still feebly held up beside his head in a sign of capitulation, while just behind the wavering pilot, Metzger and Jones lay sprawled out on the ground, occasionally conceding a grunt or anguished moan. Unphased by the appearance of the American's shaky, stiff hands, the sergeant declared that medical care would come later. Then, without another word, the man stepped past. Merle sensed a fit of anger simmer inside of him, but before he could get his dander up, he was mid-stride, stumbling through the grass and flanked by a pair of captors who prodded him in the back, steering him towards the convoy of military trucks that sat reverberating along the road.

With their adversaries secured, much of the soldier's interest had shifted to dousing the fire in the Fortress in hopes of recovering any articles or equipment for intelligence purposes. Nothing of significant importance was to be found as the blaze intensified, first cooking the nose section and then engulfing the flight deck. Flames had also lapped into the upper turret compartment where, snared in the bent wreckage, the body of Lt. Williams still lay entangled. In the process of the shootdown, the Norden bombsight had dislodged and fallen out of the plane. The device was discovered by a few locals who, seeing the strange contraption and fearing punishment for investigating any further, backed away. They promptly alerted authorities, leading the soldiers directly to the pasture where the device lay just as they had found it. Seeing that only four Americans had been rounded up at the crash site, a patrol was dispatched to comb the area and ordered to expeditiously hunt down any other members of the crew who may be in hiding or attempting to evade. When questioned about the status of his men, Green stared back at his charred aircraft and grimly reported that there was only one other airman with them, that he was still inside of the bomber, and that the man was dead.

After the Americans were taken away by the soldiers, Gerhard Solzer pounced on the opportunity to explore the B-17; one of thousands like her that the people living in Lieblos had seen streaming miles above them on an ever-increasing basis and in more significant numbers. Before leaving the wreck, Gerhard collected a souvenir, taking "the opportunity to unscrew both hand-grips from one of the side machine guns. They served as the handlebars on my bicycle for a long time." Also unwilling to let the sensational opportunity to look over the aircraft pass him by was Heinrich Goy. The teen got more than he bargained for, though, later describing the awfulness he would see when he ventured up to the flight deck. In an interview with author and local historian, Eckard Sauer, author of *Abstrutz Im Kinzigtal*, Goy recalled the scene:

> *The wings were broken off and the cockpit was completely burned out and destroyed. One of the two pilots was still sitting dead in his seat. He had been badly injured. Beneath his knees, the bones of his lower legs protruded and his head was deformed. A terrible sight that I can not forget until today.*

Lieblos local boys Goy, Horr, Thienhaus in US Army dingy, 1945, Goy Collection

The boy then slipped back to the tail gunner's station under the large rudder. "I could not resist…," he explained, "…and sat on the

seat, [and] grabbed the handles of the machine gun in my hands."
Where, just hours before, Sgt. Hatfield had spent the last few moments
of his life, Goy, only a handful of years younger, "imagined the
situation of the gunner when you were shot at by fighter planes at a
height of ten thousand meters." The teenager finished his examination
and then returned home.

The "pilot" that Goy was referring to was actually bombardier
Jack Williams. In the days to follow, the soldiers trusted with securing
the site lost interest in the ruins, providing more opportunities for
locals to sneak off souvenirs from the fascinating American warbird.
One woman from the village came away with a chunk of the plexiglass
nose, or what was left of it, while another lucky youngster emerged
from the hull satisfied with his excavation and brandishing the aircraft's
emergency survival axe as spoils. The remnants of the *Green Hornets*
would lay on Koch's acres for almost a month before authorities cut
the bomber apart, cannibalizing her salvageable remains, which were
then dispersed to salvage yards to be repurposed as scrap for the Third
Reich.

With devastating strategic bombing raids being conducted by
the Allies on the German homeland with regularity and seeing the
opportunity to capitalize on the collateral damage, the highly
persuasive Nazi propaganda organization began portraying Allied
airmen as little more than flying murderers: "*Mordfliegern*". Although SS
commander Heinrich Himmler had previously issued directives
encouraging civilian violence on captured Allied fliers, it was
Propaganda Minister Joseph Goebbels who was instrumental in
dehumanizing the "airborne mobsters" unleashed from fields across
the Channel. Combined with the frustrations of continuous bombing
raids and stirred on by Goebbels' deceptive indoctrination endeavors
promoting "*lynchjustiz*", an immeasurable number of episodes of
civilian-led violent crimes transpired against downed English and US
fliers over the course of the War. Nearly three-fourths of a century
past, the total sum of civilian aggression towards downed Allied Air
Forces personnel still remains undetermined. Despite much anecdotal
evidence, as well as an abundance of official documentation detailing
the events, such violent behavior was far from being a uniquely
German trait. More cases of "*lynchjustiz*" were recorded in Austria and
Hungary, where grounded Allied fliers were scolded by the public as
being terror "cowboys", than in any other nation. Alternatively, there

are several examples of encounters where blitzed Britains took matters into their own hands when Luftwaffe pilots had been shot down over English soil.

For every similar desperate and callous act of violence that transpired during the conflict, there were innumerable acts of

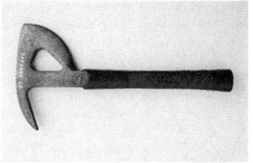

Green Hornets' emergency axe, Sauer Collection

humanity, sympathy, respect, and love. In conducting post-War interviews with residents of Lieblos and neighboring Gelnhausen, the US War department documented numerous examples of the extraordinary compassion shown for the Americans whose fate just happened to have crossed paths with their own on that day in September. "The crew was treated well after landing," says Eckard Sauer, whose research included discussions with eyewitnesses present at the event in 1944.

> *In the Kinzig Valley area, no Allied airman had been beaten or killed. The inhabitants were fed up with the war in late 1944[,] they longed for peace. When American troops arrived at the end of March 1945, they were considered by many to be liberators.*

Perhaps no Allied flier downed in the region had been on the receiving end of civilian vigilante vengeance, but this did not change the fact that the locals were no strangers to the horrors of the War. Targets in Frankfurt and its suburbs, lying just twenty miles distant, had been bombed by US and British planes for quite some time. Mainz, just slightly further west, Schweinfurt, not far south, and Fulda to the northeast, just to name a few; all had been on the Allied hit list for years at this point. The smoke from such attacks would have been clearly visible from where the *Green Hornets* crashed, not to mention

213

that the villagers had witnessed the havoc released on the Gelnhausen airfield by strafing US fighters, just days before. For years now, Nazi broadcasts had been transmitted into their homes and horrifying stories of wide-spread bombings had arrived on the backs of their displaced family, friends, and countrymen. Loyalist, party member or not, it was clear the effect these bomber boys were having on their nation. All the same, the residents opted to help the four Americans who made a sudden, unexpected visit on the afternoon of the 11th of September.

Phillip Solzer (second from right), Geschichtsverein Grundau

Those who assembled at the thrilling scene in "Koch's Acre" knew very well that by assisting the Americans in any way, they would be in defiance of State law. They were conscious that as treasonous "defeatist provocateurs", as Hitler branded those who dared defy the State, they, at the very least, would face interrogation, with imprisonment and torture being a very real consequence. In one of the series of interviews conducted by Sauer, Gerhard Solzer further detailed the events of that memorable afternoon but also explained the fallout that the family faced thereafter. "One of the young soldiers was bleeding badly from his head. My mother brought bandaging material from our nearby house and my father Phillip administered first aid." As a reward for his kindness, Gerhard's father "...had to report for questioning the next day at the barracks in Gelnhausen." The interrogation was surely nerve-racking, but, as the junior Solzer conceded, "Luckily my father was not arrested."

Regardless of the potential repercussions of being deemed a nemesis of the Reich, the men, women, and children who demonstrated concern for the aircrew; treating their injuries and comforting as much as they could, exhibited a bravery to be admired. When, in their hands lay their wounded, defeated "enemy", they chose mercy over cruelty, compassion over apathy, and forgiveness for their fellow man. In fact, fully aware that his crew had crashed within the Reich's border and had fallen short of both friendly lines and a populace loyal to the Allies, Metzger, a Jewish-American bomber pilot, was convinced that those who came to aid and comfort him and his fellows in the barren cornfield, were kind, empathetic Germans, going so far as to describe them as "partisans".

Disgusted with the treatment of Jack Williams' body, which had been pulled from the bomber's wreckage and buried in a hastily dug pit alongside the field by a few put-out soldiers, Fritz Griessman returned to the scene two days later. Accompanied by some more-than-willing volunteers, Griessman organized the careful recovery of

Friedrich 'Fritz' Griessman (on ground), Geschechtsverein Grundau

the corpse. He tendered the mess of remains back to the cemetery and cleaned the body as best he could. After wrapping the officer in fresh sheets, the caretaker arranged what was left of the body in a simple wooden casket, a container that he had constructed specifically for the flier. On the 14th, the coffin containing Lt. Williams was hauled to the northern end of the cemetery and gently settled into a new plot where he could rest in the shade of the trees, overlooking the beautiful, rolling meadows and pastures encircling the village. The Germans marked the location of the outsider with a simple wooden cross bearing the inscription, *"Hier ruht ein unbekannter amerikanischer soldat"*- "an unknown American soldier rests here". In attendance of the burial and wishing to pay their respects to the stranger were many of the townspeople who had assembled to see the young flier laid to rest among their own departed loved ones in, as the founders had christened ages before, "good ground." Despite falling short of Allied-

215

controlled territory by less than an hour more of flight time, Jack Williams had, in fact, in some way, reached the safe harbor of "friendly lines."

17
SNAKE PIT

12 September 1944
Oberursel, Hesse, Germany

Dulag Luft from guard tower, Camp King Archive

Merle, Irv, Frank, and Pete had spent a fitful, pain-filled night in the confines of a drab, "local jail in a small town"; more than likely Gelnhausen. The morning following the crash, the airmen were loaded into a military truck and set off opposite the rising sun. Entering the city of Frankfurt not long after, the fliers couldn't help but notice that their German guards seemed to clutch at their rifles a little more tightly,

217

paying little attention to their cargo and seeming more preoccupied with the goings-on outside. Before departing, the canvas flap had been closed snuggly around the bed of the truck. At first, the crew assumed the effort was to prevent them from gaining their bearings but now, bumping through the bomb-cratered streets of Frankfurt, breathing in the smoke from fires that flickered among the rubble, and alerted to the guttural shouts of outraged and despairing residents, the airmen comprehended it was they who were being concealed. Beyond the flap, the suburbs of Frankfurt and neighboring outskirts were burning, set aflame by RAF airships the night before.

Smoke from the fires in the south of the city continued to billow into the sky as the truck squealed to a stop in front of a sign that read, "*Kupferhammer*". Sentinels directed the frazzled crew into the street and ruled them into line amidst a sizable conglomeration of demoralized English and American AAF detainees who, in dirty olive flight suits and torn blue blouses, had been gathering nearby at a trolley stop. Soon after, the group began filing up the road. Progress was agonizingly slow as many within the Allied amalgamation had difficulty walking, but other wards, armed with machine guns and huffing, perky-eared canines, brought up the rear of the column and pressed the group along. The assembly plodded past brick and timber-framed, white-walled buildings including one that resembled an American gas station, decked out in Coca-Cola posters. Aside from the nostalgic advertisements, it was the structure's water spigot that drew the most consideration from the parched flock, many of whom were readily chased off by the *hausfrau* who apparently had become quite accustomed, and irritated, with the routine of the continuous flow of these unwelcomed visitors.

Not long after, the fliers hobbled up to the gates of a compound where two parallel twelve-foot-high fences, each capped with razor wire, stretched out before them. Overhead, expressionless figures carrying machine pistols and rifles stood beside spotlights and glared down upon the muster of men from within the shadows of their towers that flanked the prickly portal. All along the perimeter, more similarly manned fortifications stood menacing along the wire as additional sentries, tethering more large canines, paced around the camp's acreage. Inside the fence was a complex of bleak wooden structures, an administration block, and a guard house.

218

Dulag Luft, Camp King Archive

The facility was called *Auswertestelle West* by the Germans and was the Luftwaffe's primary intelligence gathering, evaluation, and processing center for AAF airmen who had fallen into capture. In American and British circles, the center was more notoriously recognized as "Dulag Luft", a contraction of "*Durchgangslager der Luftwaffe*," meaning "Transit Camp of the Air Force". For virtually all wing-clipped Allied fliers, this was the first stop in their journey before being sent to one of the dozens of prisoner of war (POW) camps dispersed throughout the Fatherland and German-controlled Austria and Poland. The influx of captured British and American combat crewmen had swelled during the summer of 1944, and by the time Merle stepped through the gates of Dulag Luft, nearly 2,000 other Allied airmen were passing through the complex for processing every month; consequences of an era of "good hunting" on behalf of the defenders.

Long before Allied airmen were lined up at in-processing, sometimes even before the detainees had arrived at the facility, the staff was hard at work covertly observing and carefully assessing every inch of each man's character. It was not unheard of for the Germans to slip one of their disguised interrogation officers into the tram cars loaded with bruised and battered Americans and Englishmen before reaching the camp in a commonly effective ploy to gain intelligence. Even the men's flight gear and uniforms told much about the prisoner. The perceptive staff could commonly identify where an airman was based through subtle, tell-tale signs, including stitching patterns and uniform manufacturing tags. Even the pencil markings on laundry slips and identification cards were enough to determine if the man had operated out of Thorpe Abbots, Rattlesden, Great Ashfield, Knettishall, or one of the hundreds of other Allied aerodromes in East Anglia, including

The view for thousands of Allied airmen upon their approach to the interrogation center, Dulag Luft, USAF Academy

Rougham. Other interrogators presented themselves as helpful administrative clerks, and covertly collected details about habits, likes, dislikes, mood, emotional and mental state, and any sign of psychological weakness during seemingly unostentatious interactions. The Luftwaffe workforce at the interview center was specially chosen for their ability to speak fluent English and familiarity with and knowledge of American culture. Behind the scenes, as US and British fliers were being studied, the intelligence corps consigned each man to a specific interrogator who specialized in questioning bomber crews or fighter pilots, as well as the man's specific personality type.

While there was, undeniably, a calculated method to the procedure of processing, evaluating, and disarming their targets, Dulag Luft evaluators routinely employed additional techniques to harvest material. Their tactics included bribery, bullying, deceit, isolation, displays of empathy, sensory deprivation, controlling the interview location and ambient room temperatures, direct and indirect questioning, starvation, and even the threat of physical punishment or execution. Threats of being handed over to the SS or Gestapo, whose personnel could regularly be seen moving about the German Air Force-run complex, were also common. When fallen fliers refused to respond to inquiries, German staff habitually informed them that they already had all of the facts and merely desired that the man confirm or admit to knowledge that they already had. Many who called their captor's bluff were entirely flabbergasted when the interrogator retrieved a file from their records and began reciting the names of their folks back home, identified the grammar school that they graduated from as a kid, and even recited the names of girls they had dated before entering the service. While not fully realized at the time, the German intelligence machine was extensive, counting on contributions and the research efforts from Nazi-sympathizers and assets based in the continental US. Agents accessed local newspapers and school yearbooks and, on the rare occasion, even befriended an airman's family or boyhood chums. The coded material was then passed on through channels, eventually arriving on the desk of an interrogator at Dulag Luft. While elaborate and complex, the practice proved to be incredibly effective for German intelligence purposes.

Although most evidence supports that the staff at Dulag Luft, in contrast to the Gestapo, rejected utilizing torture and abstained from administering executions, numerous incidences of the physical abuse of Allied airmen have been documented. Even those fliers familiar with the protection afforded to them under the Articles of War remained in a constant state of uncertainty as the perception of such possibilities was omnipresent as was the design. On occasion, prisoners could hear the struggling of an unidentified and, presumably, uncooperative fellow captive on his way to a waiting firing squad. Many of these events climaxed with the cries of the offender and culminated with rifle shots and finally silence. Whether or not executions were actually committed is not likely, however, as such a sentence was in blatant disregard for the rules outlined in the Geneva Convention. More than likely, the act was no more than an unnerving morbid charade, one of the countless scare tactics devised by the staff to intimidate the prisoner into cooperation. Be that as it may, such incidents, or rumors thereof; one of the many unique happenstances at the interrogation center that supported the idea that "no amount of depression, privation and psychological blackmail was considered excessive" within the complex's confines, did have a disturbing effect on the witnesses. In the end, all was calculated at Dulag Luft with nothing being overlooked, left to chance, or considered too inconsequential.

Pete helped Frank hobble onward from the main gate while Irv and Merle followed close behind, guarding their mutilated hands.

Reaching a courtyard and framed in by series of long, wooden structures that squatted on drab, brick foundations and bore steel-barred windows, the column was halted, reformed into something resembling a military formation, and ordered to keep quiet. Ushered inside the reception building, uniformed camp personnel snarled for order, demanding that any officers step forward and identify their charge. It was a simple, yet crafty technique to organize and, more importantly, collect intelligence on the overwhelmed, distressed herd. From here, the Germans separated the non-coms from the rest and led the latter off to the next room where Merle and the officers were ordered to strip naked and face the wall while a squad of guards inspected the men's uniforms and examined their bodies. The first of many apprehensions with the intake process arose as the inspection finished and the officers were told to snag a pair of trousers and a course, quasi-military blouse from the camp's stockpile as a replacement for their Army-issued flightdress.

Green was then shown to a nearby table where a man in a suit explained, in broken English, that he was there on behalf of the International Red Cross (IRC). He was commissioned, so went the story, to collect basic details that would help assist in the lieutenant's processing; an entirely routine procedure, he assured the wearied aviator. Translating from a pile of papers that he had introduced to Merle as "Red Cross forms", he read:

Date of Birth?" Where born? Profession? Religion? Married? How many Children? Home address? Next of Kin? What was your payment during the war? When shot down? Where taken prisoner? Squadron? Group? Command? Station No.? Letters and Aircraft Number? Type of Aircraft? How is your health?

"Second Lieutenant Merle Green, 0-820000" was the response to the torrent of queries. The man countered by expressing his concerns over the officer's lack of cooperation and, without hesitation, repeated his questions. Green, skeptically eyeing the papers, once again recited "Second Lieutenant Merle Green, 0-820000." With this, the now seemingly inconvenienced "Red Cross" representative looked the American up and down and scratched in his identifying characteristics: "Figure: slim. Head shape: oval. Face shape: round. Weight: 77. Hair: brown. Eyes: blue. Nose: long".

A furious stream of commands then prompted Merle to guide down a long hallway where a guard motioned him into one of the offices. Inside, behind a large wooden desk loaded with folders and reports, sat a slender, dark-haired, dapper Luftwaffe officer. Following military etiquette, Merle straightened to the position of attention and brought his right paw to the corner of his eyebrow in salute. In perfect English, the German cordially welcomed the lieutenant, informing Green that he was attached to the "interrogation branch" and requested that he take a seat. Easing himself down into the chair, the bomber pilot held back a series of congested convulsions that erupted from his lungs and raced up his throat. Doing his best to veil the agony that washed over his clammy face, the presence of fresh blood on his lips betrayed him. The German opened the parley by expressing his sympathies for the clearly suffering American flier and, as a condolence, an offering of cigarettes, chocolate, and whiskey were presented to the lieutenant, all of which Green sharply declined. Instead, Merle informed the man that he and his team only required medical treatment; aid that he had been promised to receive nearly twenty-four hours before, he pointed out. In a momentary fit of irritation that unmasked his feigned courtship, the interrogator exploded and flippantly advised the American that medical care would come later.

Recovering his suave persona, the German ensured Merle that it was only a matter of time before he would be taken to a hospital to receive care for his injuries. There he would enjoy hot meals and rest. He could shave and would also have the opportunity to bathe and wash away the stench of gasoline, smoke, and sweat and the accumulation of dirt, oil, and blood that caked his body. He would be treated by the best medical personnel available, he was assured, and in addition, efforts would be taken to properly inform his family of his status, surely easing their worries. In fact, the transfer documents were right there in front of him. If only his paperwork could be finalized, the process would move forward. The delay, regrettably, was due to his incomplete in-processing documents and the lieutenant's unfortunate lack of assistance-a misunderstanding that he assumed the young American was keen to rectify.

Merle didn't bite. Suddenly, the pilot felt the same familiar blast of fury that had washed over him while he stood swaying in the cornfield where he had set down his B-17 the day before. The German, meanwhile, focused his eyes back onto the forms that lay on the table in front of him, pencil cocked at the ready. Green held his composure as the officer continued his maneuvers. Finding the man more interested in matters far surpassing "name, rank and serial number- the only information the wounded aviator was willing to concede to his increasingly disgusted and impatient captor, Merle sat silent. Green absorbed a sermon that the man had obviously rehearsed before; a speech, he surmised, that had been presented to countless other airmen who had previously occupied his uncomfortable chair.

'The Cooler' building, Dulag Luft, Camp King Archive

At the conclusion of the rant, Merle planted his discolored, ossified hands onto the man's desk. No details beyond name, rank, and serial number would be given, he professed, no unit information revealed. Nothing more would be gained by his trickery and deception. Instead, the lieutenant responded by repeating his request for medical attention, noting that his men were all in dire need of the care that they had been convinced of receiving. This second appeal for help was dismissed even faster than the original but this time, the German, seeing that his mark was proving to be far too inflexible, appeared to suddenly lose interest in the pilot. Closing the folder on his desk, he fired a glance over Merle's shoulder. With a flick of his fingers, a guard entered from the hallway, putting an end, at least temporarily, to the dialog.

The majority of airmen passing through Dulag Luft were

prodded into cells arranged into one of two structures positioned just opposite the reception building and known as "the cooler". Some fliers arriving during the fall of '44, found themselves corralled into a fairly sizable room with a few members of their crew or other Allied Air Forces personnel. Most, however, were shut away in much more cramped and uncomfortable accommodations. Many of these lodgings were found to be already occupied by unusual tenants whose tiny claws could be heard scratching around the rooms on their eternal search for a discarded morsel of food that was rarely ever to be found. Informed that they could be held in these quarters for up to thirty days, per the Geneva Convention, the space was eight feet high, six feet wide, and twelve feet long. It boasted one iron-framed bed, a small table, one chair, and a "slop jar" to eat from. Laying mangled on top of the cot, a straw-filled bag served as a cushion. High up on one wall of the room, a small single window had been covered up, shutting the unfortunate occupant off from the world and leaving him to linger in a dark silence. To discourage any "unpermitted leave", as the guards facetiously called escape attempts, Merle's boots were snatched away; just one more tactic used to unnerve the fliers by stripping them of their self-identity and comfort. The heating system: the same system that was inoperable in the sweltering heat of the summer, was now, strangely enough, said to be "broken." This, all at a time, when, oddly, the cells were beginning to feel the chilly approach of winter.

At Dulag Luft, downed fliers were given a portion of bread and some jam each morning. A broth, boiled with carrots, potatoes, or if lucky, a mixture, was doled out mid-day and, reappearing in the evening was another bread and jam ration. Less frequently, prisoners were provided a cup of coffee or given a bowl of something resembling watered-down soup. Most days, the guards would pass a rusty mug or dirty bowl of water into each cell, normally splashing some of the precious liquid onto the floor in the process and leaving an ever so subtle departing slight for the parched boarder. Excluding the occasional bribe by an interrogator, prisoners were denied cigarettes, as well as toilet paper and contact with any other prisoner.

When men needed to answer the call of nature, the guards routinely delayed fulfilling requests, some even ignored altogether. If a watchman was secured, the prisoner was led to a foul straddle latrine at the end of the long hallway where the entire process was performed under the watchful eye of their keeper. Business having been completed, the guards were sure to inspect the toilet. Besides leaving notes for other captured fliers to come across, detainees had been known to discard paperwork, intelligence, and other items that they had snuck past screeners in the filth, and staff had eventually caught on. Rightly paranoid about listening devices placed in their walls, word had spread among the captives warning of "stool pigeons". These were German agents, portraying themselves as sympathetic captured Allied airmen who were eager to strike up a friendly conversation with any newly arriving disoriented, homesick, terrified, or otherwise vulnerable, loose-lipped flier.

As unpleasant as confinement in "the cooler" was, Merle was hauled down the stairs of an adjacent structure and placed into a cold, desolate chamber. Utilized in times of overcrowding and sometimes employed on the more insufferable of visitors, numerous fliers make reference to this despicable construction, referred to as the "snake pit" due to the grimy, reprehensible conditions of the small chambers that locked away the unfortunate lodger in complete seclusion. Green's inflexibility had earned him a hasty exit from the interview but now, stashed away in this vault, he also found himself tormented by a wound worse than his injured hands. The interrogator had injected him with a sense of hope; a horrible punishment for any forlorn, damaged prisoner to suffer. For now, Merle was forced to idle in isolation, ever awaiting the promise of medical care that always seemed to be on its way but never arrived. Closed off inside his cell and assaulted by bouts of intolerable pain- misery that was only compounded by the accumulation of the psychological strain of the past day, Merle fell onto the filthy cot and passed out.

It was the groan of the heavy cell door that next provoked the lieutenant back into the nightmarish reality. A man, dressed in civilian attire and clutching a bundle of cloth, stepped in from the light of the hallway and approached the groggy pilot. Behind him, a sentry moved up and stood in the doorway, machine pistol slung over one shoulder and both unsympathetic eyes fixated on the American. The man sat down next to Merle and without saying a word seized one of his wrists and began inspecting the lieutenant's wounds. Green winced at the jolts of pain that bristled through his hand as the inspection continued but the man held firm and continued to rotate Merle's palm, poking and thumbing at the hardened digits. Both hands had been badly damaged-"frozen", as Merle would describe, but it was his lame right hand that was cause for most concern. His nails had turned grey but most worrying, each of the four fingers on his right hand were now entirely numb and inflamed. Bulbous sores had erupted on the back of both of his hands, and from the blisters, dribbles of discharge oozed steadily. Convinced by his assessment, the man reached into the bundle of fabric that he had brought in, retrieved an object from its folds and, after firmly regripping the lieutenant's left wrist for leverage, drew the object along the backside of his hand. A deluge of watery liquid trickled

Merle D. Green, POW intake photographs

from the incision and spilled onto his soiled bedding. Realizing that the man was opening the blisters with what he hoped was a surgical blade but shocked that he felt no pain, Green relinquished control of his other arm. Seeing that only the superficial layer of his left hand had been flash-frozen over Bohlen, sparing the nerve channels lying underneath, the procedure was not so enjoyable the second time. When the German finished milking away the last of the discharge from Merle's scored, raw hands, the man went about splitting open the pustules that had broken out along the tips of his frost-nipped ears. The civilian surveyed Green's worn face, taking no notice of the tearing that inundated his patient's eyes, but instead, focused on his irritated nose. The artic-like gales that had roared into the *Green Hornets'* flight deck the day before had scraped at the skin around Merle's swollen eyes and gnawed open the bridge of his nose. After bandaging the American's ears and wrapping both of his throbbing hands with dressings, the visitor settled the flier's wrist in a makeshift sling. Then,

227

just as unceremoniously as he had arrived, the civilian withdrew and disappeared back on the other side of the cell door. Merle collapsed against the wall of his chamber, gasping and drenched with sweat, as the emotionless sentinel pushed the heavy door back into place, casting the disheveled lieutenant back into his hole.

The following day, Lt. Green was summoned to the interrogator's office for what would be another equally productive and fruitful interview. This time, however, the interaction would be far more disturbing. The German officer, now absent of all of his previous day's charm and patience, explained the futility of delaying his collaboration as all matters related to his mission and combat team were already known. All that was needed was for the lieutenant to simply clarify intelligence that they already possessed. Merle was made aware that all of his men had been speedily rounded up by the German defense forces and, lamentably, at least one was dead; the news relayed with a brazen smugness. He was also reminded of the consequences of withholding information and failing to participate in the administration process. The interrogator continued by reciting mission specifics from his file but Merle, finally breaking free of the faces of each of his crewmates that poured through his mind, looked at the man, straightened slightly, and reported, "Second Lieutenant Merle Green, 0-820000".

Sifting through a folder that he had retrieved from one of the cabinets behind him, the German studied a few of the pages, removed one of the sheets and then slid it towards the flier. Merle instantly recognized the sheet. It was the same "Red Cross" form that the in-take staff had endeavored to have him complete during his reception at the camp. Green was astonished to see that the document had been updated with additional, and fully accurate, personal details to include, among other things, his religious denomination and occupation before the War. Merle's eye's skimmed on, slowing on a sequence of numbers, the arrangement seeming oddly familiar: "1212 E. Brown Str." His stomach sank. It was his wife's home address in Springfield. Before he could make sense of the apparent invasion into his private life, Green was hauled to his feet and spun out of the room. Hands pressed Merle along the corridor and marshaled him up to a table where more camp personnel awaited.

After being assigned a prisoner number; Merle's was #52800, a staff member fished out the lieutenant's left thumb, pressed it into the ink pad, and stamped it on his prisoner of war card. With the ink still wet on his thumb, an annoyed fellow in Luftwaffe garb positioned behind a camera on one side of the room snarled, summoning Merle to step forward to a worn line that had been painted on the floor. With his hand tucked into the crude sling, the lieutenant staggered to the mark, straightened his bruised, trembling frame, pulled back his shoulders, and raised his swollen face to the man. As Green stood there, posed in a position reminiscent of the "brace" he had so loathed years before during his early days of flight school as a "dodo", he glared back at his captor. Infuriated but played out, the pilot stared ahead and winced at the flare of the camera's flash bulb.

The civilian who had visited Merle's cell and opened the blisters on his hands and ears the day before had also attended to Frank Jones and Irv Metzger. They too, had the fluid drained from the abscesses that shrouded their hands which were then dressed in cloth bandages. After three days, having failed to extract any material and seeing no further use for them, the intelligence staff transferred Frank and Irv to *Klinik Hohemark*, the camp's infirmary for severely injured prisoners. Here the dirty, pus-stained bandages covering the men's hands were removed, allowing the staff of English, German, and American medical personnel and orderlies to begin treating their injuries. Both cases were deemed severe and for the next few weeks, they would remain at Hohemark awaiting transfer to a more suitable facility. To their relief, Sgt. Riley, still feeling the effects of the severe head injury that he had sustained while in flight over *Bohlenwerks*, was also being treated at *Hohemark*. Luftwaffe staff were closely monitoring the radioman's condition, however, and upon showing the first signs of improvement, Pete was shipped to a permanent prison camp. Alarmingly, the whereabouts and condition of Lt. Green were unknown.

Seeing the need for more advanced, specialized care, Frank and Irv were transferred to Reserve Lazarett at Obermassfeld, Germany. Nearly all of the Allied personnel that were staged here awaited advanced operative care, and when the co-pilot and navigator arrived, a considerable backlog of cases were waiting to be treated. For the time being, the two would just have to wait it out and be on the lookout for any distraction that would help to transport them far beyond the confines of the concertina wire which, no matter how improved their condition may become, bound them to this reviled, foreign land for a disturbingly indefinite period of time.

A three-story, former agricultural college-turned-Hitler-Youth-facility, Reserve Lazarett at Stalag IX-C had been procured by the Luftwaffe in 1940. Designated as an orthopedic hospital, it had gained a surprising reputation for carrying out specialized treatments and achieving astonishing results. The acclaim was rightly won despite inadequate resources, poor sterile conditions, and a consistent lack of a sufficient supply of water, all of which would continue to hamper the overcrowded facility until War's end. The lazarett's medical staff comprised of English, Canadian, and New Zealand nurses, orderlies, and doctors who had been collected up by the Germans following a series of successful offensives in France and Africa earlier in the conflict. Articles of War dictated that, being medical staff and not combat personnel, these prisoners be eligible for repatriation. Admirably, all had elected to stay on as detainees so that they could continue to care for the constant stream of broken and marred Allied warriors. As it turned out, 2nd Lt. Merle D. Green, with his putrefying hand, was one such case.

One day, in the middle of October, Metzger and Jones were amazed to recognize their pilot among the dozens in the new lot of disfigured and incapacitated combatants arriving at Obermassfeld. Seeing their friend worn and listless, Frank and Irv were alarmed by Green's physical state. Luckily, the Lazarett's medical team was informed to the lieutenant's condition and quickly took measure of the man's injuries. Scabbing had begun to replace the blisters and sores on his ears and nose, but the condition of Merle's mangled, now blackened right hand, was disturbing. With the fear of further tissue death and bone loss imminent, the doctors saw no other option available. Merle was hurried to the operation room where, deprived of the benefit of proper anesthesia and nearing senselessness, a British Army surgeon went about slicing into the necrotized, foul, pus-inflamed tissue and whittled out the infected bones of what had been the boy's right hand.

18

KRIEGIES

September 1944
Zwickau, Saxony, Germany

After three days of interrogation in the Zwickau jail, Jim Gegenheimer and George Ostrowski were transferred to Frankfurt by railcar. The trip was made even more unpleasant as the civilian commuters sharing the carriage quickly identified the pair of *"terrorfliegers."* None dare approach as the duo was attended to by a set of armed soldiers, but it didn't stop the riders from hissing and scowling at them as if to imply, "If it weren't for your guards...". The RAF had again paid visit to Frankfurt the previous night, and now several districts lay aflame. Allied bombs had ruined nearly 90 percent of the magnificent, old city, reducing much of the metropolis to immense piles of fractured cement, shattered brick, and ash. Many of the rail lines had been knocked out in the violence, and passage through the town by train was impossible. These circumstances forced the four unnerved men-two Americans and their two German escorts, to dismount the train and finish the venture along the flame-lit, troubled streets on foot.

The scene was like something out of *Dante's Inferno* as mayhem ensued all about the town. Trolley cars lay overturned alongside rail tracks stacked in twisted piles and "rolled up like pretzels". The haze of smoke wafted along the boulevards where apartment buildings and shops once stood but now, nearly every structure had been cracked open, many reduced to nothing more than a heap of debris, set aglow by countless spot fires. Everywhere, civilians scrambled about, some pushing baby carriages along animal-like game trails tramped out through the dust ruins, while others carried briefcases packed with clothing or wheeled along wooden carts loaded with what little remained of their lives. People could be seen sitting along the streets, many in tears, most defeated in some way, but all bewildered, dismayed or enraged by the demolition. Blessed with English-speaking guards, the gunners were cautioned to "Keep your mouths shut or they'll get you." It was apparent that the advice was not an unfounded cautionary tale.

Bomb damage in Frankfurt, 1945, Fold3

As Ostrowski and Gegenheimer crept on along the streets in the dark under the skeletons of bomb and fire-gutted buildings, a crowd of townspeople, recognizing the uniform of the *Wehrmacht*, confronted their guards. The Americans stealthily shrunk into the shadows as the small mob cornered the two young soldiers, inquiring about the location of any prisoners. After a few tense moments and some clever talk on the part of their chauffeurs-turned bodyguards, the sergeants breathed a sigh of relief as the posse moved on, annoyed but satisfied with the soldier's explanation.

Somehow unscathed, the four young men reached the gates of Dulag Luft where the Americans were welcomed just like thousands of other Allied airmen before them. As their in-processing commenced, the gunners were stripped to their underwear, systematically searched, and then moved along through the machine. "They knew pretty well that they weren't gonna get any real information out of a gunner," Jim remembered. "We never really even knew where we were going." This didn't discourage Dulag Luft staff from practicing their art. Prodded for intelligence, thoroughly searched, fingerprinted, photographed, sized-up, and questioned some more, Sgt. Ostrowski and Sgt. Gegenheimer were then directed to their cells in "the cooler". "You could stretch your arms out and touch both walls," Jim recalled, "and you had a wooden bench; that's all you slept on at night."

Berlin may have given oversight of the interrogation center to the Luftwaffe but that did not stop High Command from placing SS and Gestapo personnel inside the complex to surveil day-to-day pursuits. It was understood that while Heinrich Himmler's security organization and the secret police would not interfere with the staff's productive enterprises, an uneasy agreement had been established allowing representatives of the SS and Gestapo agents to be fed the occasional Allied airman who was then interrogated as they saw fit. Unfortunately, it was the SS who claimed Ostrowski.

During his stay at Dulag Luft, George was frequently summoned to the office of an SS Major where, in the blur of the following days, he was "questioned almost continuously". At the onset of each meeting, the Nazi would drop a large file, stocked full of papers riddled with intelligence, on the desk in front of the stoic American airman. "He knew more about our flight than our base knew", admitted George years later. The gunner's obstinacy did little to impress the German whose standard means of questioning was to beat Ostrowski repeatedly with a rubber hose before returning him to the seclusion of his room, walloped and bloodied. After days of this routine, some overly zealous guards enthusiastically assisted the pulverized sergeant to new lodgings. The room resembled his previous dwellings, decked out in the same minimalist décor: bleak-colored flaking wall paint, concrete flooring, a solitary water pot, timeworn blanket, rustic ornamental heating pipes, and single wood-shuddered windows, all graced with the same vermin, rodents, and gloominess that seemed to take hold of the entire dismal complex. The only exception was that this slightly larger, yet equally grimy chamber boasted not one, but a pair of straw-covered cots.

In the night to follow, George was startled awake as the door to his cell flew open. In stormed two guards towing a limp figure which they heaved onto the empty bunk beside the panicked *Hornets* waist gunner. The Germans turned and left, slamming shut the door and sealing Ostrowski into the now all-too-familiar black stillness. George remained motionless, crouched in a corner, waiting, listening for a sign. In the dark, it was nearly impossible for George to detect much or make out any features of the room. Finally, after what felt like an eternity, he gathered his courage, crept to the other cot, and gently placed his hand on what he felt to be a man's chest. There was no response. Sensing the slow, labored rise and fall of the man's respirations, the sergeant jerked back his hand and felt wetness covering his fingers. Ostrowski spent the remainder of the night on his mat, curled up against the wall, listening to the weak pants of his fellow occupant, emanating softly in the darkness. At daybreak the next morning, George found his new roommate, a 2nd lieutenant-bombardier in a blood-soaked flight jacket, lying on the cot beside him. The man's gasping had stopped sometime in the night, and now no signs of life could be detected. In spite of the sergeant's pleas for assistance, the body was left to lie in Ostrowski's company for the rest of the day.

With their sojourn at the interrogation center finished, Luftwaffe personnel led Ostrowski and Gegenheimer from the facility to the center's transit camp where they began a journey that would take them nearly 400 miles east by rail. Escaping multiple near-strafings by Allied planes outside Frankfurt, the train clattered on, pulling further east until the wail of air raid sirens greeted the riders as they entered the Nazi capital. When a bomb from a British Mosquito bomber blew up nearby, shaking the rail cars, coating the riders in dust, and summoning out repair teams to fix the tracks, Gegenheimer, no stranger to cramped conditions, hopped up into the overhead luggage rack to wait out the ensuing delay. The break was a much-needed momentary escape from the dramatic reality before him as it was the 17th of September, his nineteenth birthday.

Somewhere in the eastern territory of the Reich, George and Jim were pressed into "cattle cars" and locked in among a mauled clutter of similarly conditioned Allied aviators. These transport cars were unheated, windowless boxcars designed to accommodate forty men or eight head of cattle, hence their name "forty-and eight." The freight carriages, many almost certainly among those allocated to carry Jews to the concentration and "death camps" in the preceding grim years, were loaded far above capacity, and most were forced to ride out the trek standing upright. Conditions inside the cars were barely suitable for livestock. Over the Oder they rolled, passing into what had been Polish territory but was presently German-Pomerania, and finally drawing up to the secluded, tiny rail station at Kiefheide, just outside of Gross Tychow. Ironically, George Ostrowski's grandfather had been born less than eighty miles away before he immigrated to the US at the beginning of the twentieth century.

Arrived at their terminus, scores of soiled Allied men leapt down from the foul-smelling boxcars and, under the eyes of unamused guards, were gathered into one large group, parallel the tracks. The Germans encircled the mass and set off shackling together pairs of fliers. When all sets had been established, the guards stepped back to savor the anticipated scene soon to unfold. The escorts could be seen smirking, some even doubled over in laughter or coolly enjoying a cigarette as German sentries alerted their dogs on the prisoners. They then proceeded to rile up their vicious canines who snarled and snapped their fangs in frenzied excitement. Just as the anxieties reached its peak, the soldiers released the mongrels upon the huddled, completely defenseless collection of prisoners, only to call off the drooling beasts at the last moment.

Although the rattled fliers didn't know it at the time, a similar but much more brutal event had occurred just a few months prior. Known as the "Heydekrug Run", one new group of Allied prisoners had also been chained together upon their arrival at the rail station but were then forced to sprint down a forest-enclosed trail. On the run, German guards jabbed the "*schweinhundes*" with their bayonets and bludgeoned them with the butts of their rifles. Guard dogs tore chunks of flesh from the slower sprinters and those unfortunates who had been thumped to the ground. Fortunately, the chaotic jumble of prisoners remained on the path as machine gunners hid in the adjacent forest, waiting to gun down any "escapees." The group eventually arrived at the camp, although winded, bloodied, and traumatized. Adding insult to injury, when the injured trudged to the camp's doctors in their tattered and torn uniforms, the German physician ignored the ailments and dismissed the shredded and pierced prisoners. The doctor was not above documenting the contacts, however, and officially diagnosed "200 dog and bayonet wounds as 'sunstroke'". Gegenheimer could not forget meeting two of the "Heydekrug Sergeants at the camp. The boys, both survivors of the inhumane episode, had been nicknamed "Big Beat Up" and "Little Beat Up", the monikers owing to the permanent scars adorning the prisoner's bodies. Both men would forever bear reminders of "The Run" on their legs, buttocks, and backs; their lingering cases of "sunstroke" oddly resembling the scars of bayonet punctures and canine fangs.

Hustled away from Kiefheide rail station, the line of Allied airmen, Jim and George among them, trudged along an unassuming dirt road that penetrated an endless stretch of thick, secluded pine forest. After a two-mile march through the wilderness, the vegetation opened up, revealing an enormous, 300-plus acre clearing where a complex of long, wooden structures sat sprawled out before them. A series of guard towers, each outfitted with a menacing combination of machine guns and spotlights, had been installed in interval around the camp. Each tower hovered over a pair of parallel concertina-wire fences; the outside fence being electrically charged. As further discouragement, the Germans had laid a hedge of rolled barbed wire between the fences. Fifty feet inside the thorny barrier, a twelve-inch-high wooden rail lined the entire perimeter. This was the visual reminder, erected by the Germans for the benefit of the deplorables within, to refrain from crossing over into the ground between it and the fence. Once past the railing, trigger-happy sentinels would eagerly dispatch any who approached the wire, whether in an act of despair, a show of defiance, or even to retrieve an errant baseball.

It was common knowledge that, to discourage escape attempts, the Germans had adopted a "shoot-to-kill" policy. Still, acts of disobedience and escape attempts were not the only time the captors chose to flex their muscle. In June, a man had been killed by rifle fire without warning after exiting his crowded hut via the window. Several despondent boys would be shot when they willfully approached the warning wire, and, on another incident, six English airmen were unexpectedly machine-gunned while they rested in their barracks. The offense: having failed to extinguish their interior lights during an air raid drill. Furthermore, numerous examples tell of instances where guards randomly fired bursts of machine-guns into the compound to, as one American lad would later write, "...remind us of who was in charge." Thus was Jim and George's introduction to *Stammlager der*

Luftwaffe IV; Stalag Luft IV.

Entering the camp, the airmen were funneled into a large barn-like structure, the reception center, and greeted by their new hosts. "When we got to the camp…," says Gegenheimer, "this was really the first time we got roughed up. They made you strip and searched you and everything, and they had a red-headed captain there who lost his wife and children in a bombing raid." Thumped and pounded through the processing line, Jim and his companions were given two worn horsehair blankets, a toothbrush, toothpaste, a set of aluminum utensils, a bowl, and a change of clothes before they were relocated to the compound yard. The complex was divided into four large, rectangular sectors, or "lagers," each separated by more razor wire fences. The administration building, infirmary, storerooms, and guard's barracks, all "verboten" to the prisoners unless accompanied by a guard, were located in a fifth sector, the "vorlager." Lagers A, B, and C held most of the camp's American population with D Lager, kidded as being the "Limey Lager," held a mixture of additional US airmen and British fliers. Though Stalag Luft IV was also a temporary home to men from France, Canada, Australia, New Zealand, South Africa, Poland, Norway, and Czechoslovakia, it was the camp's Russian captives that received the worst of things and were treated with open disdain by the Germans.

American POWs with the rank of staff sergeant or higher were disqualified from having to perform manual labor but Russian soldiers, whose leadership had declined to sign on to the stipulations laid out in the Geneva Convention, were recognized as fair game no matter their rank. The most abhorrent, demeaning, and back-breaking of chores, described by many US detainees as nothing less than cruel slave labor, were appropriated to the Red Army prisoners, including cleaning the overflowing latrines; a repulsive work detail accomplished with inadequate and broken equipment. Reports of beatings and even the execution of Soviet soldiers at Stalag Luft IV were not unheard of either. To the Germans, these were the *"Untermensch"*-the subhuman peoples of the East who perpetuated the plague of Marxism. Perhaps the most favored way to torment Stalin's communist vermin, not only at the camp outside Gross-Tychow but throughout the entire Stammlager organization, was by the process of slow starvation. As such, desperation followed. At one point, after snaring, skinning, and devouring a feral dog, a gang of starving, emaciated Soviets was briskly led outside of the camp wire and shot.

To discourage digging, the barracks buildings, called "blocks," were constructed on posts, creating an open, two-foot-high void beneath each building. "It was really an escape-proof camp. It was up on pillars, and you could look under the house and you could see a matchstick," recounts Gegenheimer, "so there was no possibility, like Stalag XVII, of escape." Inside each "block," ten small rooms branched off from a center hallway. Each room featured a single window that provided limited ventilation and light until four in the afternoon when the openings were boarded up, shutting the men up until the following morning. Once the buildings were locked up for the night, the prisoners were forbidden to venture outside, even to attempt a visit to the stinking slit-trench toilet. Though the men had been warned upon their arrival that, if discovered outside of their hut after hours they would be shot, none attempted to test the threat. In each room hung a single lightbulb, suspended above a wooden table flanked by a few chairs and bordered by eight two-tiered bunks; accommodations only a fraction of the men slotted to the room were able to use. The remainder slept crammed together on the filthy, wood-plank floors. When the *Green Hornets* gunners entered their assigned block, they noted:

> *They were supposed to have 16 men per room in double bunks. Our room was like 20 by 20. Well we had about 24 per room and there were no bunks, and they just gave us this material to put excelsior in and we slept on the floor. That was just like stacking up bodies right next to each other.*

Some men scraped together piles of sawdust to lie on, while other, more fortunate boys acquired bug-ridden sacks packed with strips of excelsior bedding. At one time, two-hundred and forty men were consolidated into one "block", accommodating for fifty percent more occupancy than that for which the simple structures were constructed. All buildings lacked running water and had only one toilet, although two outdoor latrines had been built within each lager. In having to accommodate over two thousand men, the trenches would consistently reek and habitually overflow. No bathing facilities were available, and fleas, scabies, and lice were epidemic among the inhabitants. When enough of a rationed stock of coal could be

A typical 'block' barracks for Allied POWs in Germany, USAF Academy

gathered, a single pot-bellied stove labored to warm each drafty, leaky hut.

As if the scene was not startling enough, the overly aggressive guard dogs were left to roam the camp freely after hours. With only thin wooden planks between them and the hounds, the prisoners could hear the beasts growl and pant in the night, chomping at the men at any opportunity and primed to maul any foolhardy unfortunate who ventured from their shelter or left a finger to dangle between the planks. Unsurprisingly, Stalag Luft IV was deemed deplorable by an International Red Cross (IRC) committee dispatched to the camp in October of '44 after having failed in all regards including shelter suitability, food quality and abundance, medical care, religious opportunities, and bathing and toilet facilities. Further prisoner's rights violations were revealed in the visit but in considering the dire circumstances that existed throughout the Reich and compared to the conditions at the other Allied POW camps, the site was deemed acceptable.

Newcomers to the camp, now known as "kriegies", slang for "*kriegsgefangene*"- "prisoners of war" in German, quickly grasped that there were two types of guards at Stalag Luft IV. The first breed was primarily composed of older wounded German soldiers, many of whom had been scarred in clashes with Stalin's forces on the Eastern front. It was found that many of these guards had worked or received some education in the United States and, as a result, spoke reasonably good English. As new airmen arrived at the camp, some guards could be heard asking, "Anybody here from Boston? Anyone from Chicago?" Between the two species of German watchmen, these were the more humane staff. Some downed airmen found that many of the men who stood post over them were, comparably, friendly individuals, although the Germans were careful to conceal their compassion from their peers.

The other, more nefarious, vile corps of guards were the "goons". These were the Germans who sat eyeing the kriegies from their elevated "goon boxes" where they enjoyed any opportunity to fire shots within the ranks of prisoners, or stroll around Stalag grounds, looking to cause turmoil or dole out a beating. On random nights, they would switch on the lights and burst into the barracks with their "goon squad" companions, conducting sweeps of the "blocks" in search of contraband, weapons, and radios. Meanwhile, the prisoners were hurried outside to stand at attention, sometimes for hours at a time, in rain or snow, and many times, dressed inadequately, waiting for the investigation to conclude. In some instances when the defenseless occupants were allowed to remain inside while the hunt was occurring, prisoners were frequently throttled, thrown over furniture, or shoved against the wall in the process. The raids usually ended when all tables had been upturned, bedding had been ripped from the bunks, and all personal possessions were strewn across the floor. The "goons " often departed the blocks with nothing more than the prisoner's personal effects, cigarettes, and any other spoils that caught their fancy.

To counter the surprise inspections, prisoners known as "stooges" were recruited to act as lookouts, and alerts of "goon up" could be heard preceding the hooligans as they approached the blocks. While many of the Germans were not so subtle in their efforts and chose to simply meander amongst the populace, some guards, dubbed "ferrets", resorted to sneaking under the barracks or clambering up into the attic space to eavesdrop on kriegie conversations. Generally, the presence of these Germans was little more than a nuisance to the perceptive inmates. To pass the time, the "crazy Yankees", as the guards dubbed the prisoners, found pleasure in antagonizing their watchkeepers; called "Jerry-baiting". At "appell"-morning roll call, the men were known, on occasion, to cause confusion in the ranks of the annoyed lot of overseers by purposefully muddying up the German's count. Not to be outdone, on other days the captors feigned displeasure with the numbers and invented inconsistencies with their tally to drag out the routine, sometimes for hours, while the formations of tired, shivering, and aggravated detainees were forced to stand by.

Stalag Luft IV became "a byword for brutality" amongst the Allied fliers. It was a den of many rotten Nazi captors, including Camp Commandant and ardent Party member Oberstleutnant Aribert Bombach. Another man recognized for his savagery was Hauptmann Walther Pickhardt, better remembered as "the Mad Captain" and the "Beast of Berlin". This was the red-headed officer that Jim and his comrades encountered upon their entry to the Luft camp. Standing just over five feet tall, Pickhardt was seen as being as "nutty as a fruitcake" and so smartly outfitted that you could "cut your finger on the creases of his immaculate breeches and shave in the shiny reflection of his highly-polished black jackboots." A remarkably "brave soldier if you weren't armed", Pickhardt presented the textbook specimen of the villainous Nazi officer. He relished the arrival of new detainees whom he routinely welcomed by mounting the platform at the train station to scream like a maniac while waving his Luger wildly above his head. Along with his cronies, the Hauptmann took delight in pillaging the prisoner's belongings and dealing out excessive physical abuse to any hapless person caught in his path. When, to the amusement of the detainees, a German worker was killed in an electrical mishap at the camp, Pickhardt was seen rushing towards the amused bunch of kriegies, pointing his Luger at the chuckling, hastily scattering, congregation and popping off rounds in their direction. Even some of the Hauptmann's subordinates were uneasy with his morbid candidness concerning the handling of the prisoners. His fiendishness was exemplified in numerous instances, including promoting his strategy to cure the food shortage dilemma by executing prisoners. When the "Mad Captain" called for all Jewish detainees to make themselves known and detach from the rest of the population, the airmen recognized a dangerous moment fast approaching. In the end, the camp's senior American officers ordered the men to ignore the order, undoubtedly circumventing a calamity that could have ended with dire, and far grimmer consequences.

The kriegies also assigned nicknames to many of those who were consigned with standing guard over them. To them, they were

"Snaggletooth", "Hollywood", "Medals", "Trigger Happy", "Crowbar Pete", "Rigor Mortise", "Snake Eyes", "Fritz", "Rifle Butt", "Dirty Gus," "the Three Stooges", "Dopey" and "the Spider", to name a few. Still, one guard stood heads above the rest, literally and metaphorically, in brutality. Decades after the conflict ended, survivors still recoiled at the thought of this sadistic guard, Hans Schmidt. The man-some would debate if there was actually any humanity in the bastard, was called "Big Stoop" due to having to bow his six-foot nine-inch, 280 lbs. frame to pass through the barrack's door. Among his means of masochism, the beast was famous for delving out thrashings with a belt fitted with a large heavy metal buckle. Some of his assaults ended only when his unfortunate victim's head was smashed open. Without warning or provocation, others found themselves under the fiend's boot, being stomped ruthlessly until Schmidt had his fill, regained his composure, and then moved on past the startled crowd of onlookers as if on a stroll through the countryside. Schmidt's preferred move, however, was to sneak up on unsuspecting kriegies and slap his massive brutish mitts over the victim's ears, rupturing eardrums in the process.

Unknown to the others who had believed him to be lost, Lou Lehere had reached Dulag Luft in late September. After spending time in solitary confinement and resisting all interrogation attempts at Oberursel, Lou was sent to the camp at Gross Tychow. Following an enthusiastic reunion, Sgts Gegenheimer and Ostrowski led Lehere around the complex to introduce him to *Stammlager Luft IV*. Adding to the joyous surprise and on the heels of the engineer's arrival, Pete Riley was also welcomed to the prisoner camp. "We thought they were all dead," recalled Gegenheimer with delight. Collectively, the sergeants began piecing together the details leading up to the mysterious and devastating happenings over Bohlen. It quickly became evident that it was not anti-aircraft fire or fighter planes that was responsible for the unfortunate turn of events, but something equally as devastating and exponentially more heartbreaking. Another B-17 from the 94th, they concluded, had collided with their own Fortress and delivered a fatal blow that not only knocked out the *Green Hornets* but the friendly ship as well. Though numbed by the enlightenment, there was one triumph for the gunners to be savored. Like little boys sitting around a fire, attending to their grandfather as he told tale of a marvelous adventure, Jim, George, and Lou listened in awe as Riley gave his account of the daring escape attempt, being shot up by flak gunners, the crash landing, the crew's capture, and the days that followed. Most compelling, however, was the account of how "the Chief" had somehow kept the plane airborne over enemy territory without use of his hands. It was only after they were shot out of the sky, Riley added, that the CO had been coerced to submit. Glowing with pride; a small but much-needed win, the boys were amazed by the feats of their leader, yet not surprised at all.

Each morning, as a part of their food allotment, the kriegies were given loaves of hard, repulsive bread. This staple of the Stalag was the much-revolted ersatz loaf, manufactured with 50% rye grain, 20% sugar beets, 10% minced leaves and straw, and 20% "tree flour". The son of a Gretna baker, Gegenheimer reminisced, "When you got there, you actually gave it away-that's how bad it was." After a few days of enduring the misery brought on by an empty stomach, even the most revolted of prisoners, including Jim, happily consumed every crumb of the potato starch and sawdust-packed *"ersatzbrot"*. Geg later explained the delicate process of doling out bread shares:

> *You had to cut it into twenty-four slices, the deal went like this: It's your turn to slice the bread for everybody and you get the last piece. Well, you talk about an operation! It looked like surgeons working so that there'd be a piece left for you in the cut.*

One of the most popular meals to grace the kriegie's gastronomic palate was their rendition of steak: roasted patties of spam, meat referred to by the GIs as "ham that failed the physical." But phony beef would not be the only compromised eats served at Stalag Luft IV. One day, as one POW stood beside the food wagon, surveying the haul, the man couldn't help but notice something peculiar about the ration. The flier carefully studied the cut of meat, glanced at the pull horse, then back to the slab, and then back to the horse as a look of realization washed over the man's face. Enlightened of the day's culinary carte-du-jour, the airman returned to his block and announced to his fellows that horsemeat stew was on the menu for the evening meal.

Three potatoes and a serving of water was passed off as soup, the most common meal served in the camp, with some meager portion of tough, barely edible, dehydrated vegetables rounding off the men's daily allotment of food. Other recipes included hot water garnished with "grass, roots, and leaves"-"whispering green death", as the fliers dubbed it, a purple cabbage soup, called "Purple Death", and a revolting chow designated, "green hell", also known as dehydrated spinach. All too frequently, the men discovered that they were also sharing their rations with teams of tiny, white worms. During the first few instances the sight was off-putting, but as a consistent caloric deficit took a toll on the men, the addition of these squirming dinner guests eventually proved to be a welcomed staple in the kriegie diet. It was no wonder that the prisoners delighted in the arrival of Red Cross packages, even if they were allotted only a mere one-quarter to one-half box per week.

Upon being dismissed from morning roll call, the men were left to "kriegie time" where they could pursue activities and hobbies. With virtually endless time on their hands, some inhabitants chose to walk laps around the camp perimeter while others tallied up the number of barbs on the wire fences. Many tended to small gardens or attempted to lose themselves in one of the books from the camp library. Miniature sailboats, fabricated from odds and ends collected from around the compound, were constructed and set loose in the Stalag's water pit- a cement depression filled with filthy water to be used in case of fire. The prisoner-published newspaper, *Kriegie Kronikles*, provided comic relief to a vast audience within the camp, and a considerable number of young men even attended college-level classes administered by qualified fellow internees. A few of the compounds even offered courses in English literature, French conversation, Italian, physiology, and science.

America's favorite past-time followed the men across the ocean as well. Baseball teams were formed, and squads challenged other lagers, providing some temporary, yet sentimental, deliverance from the confines of "Kriegieland". After service on Sundays, football was the event of the day. So serious was the business that, to help the participants muster all the strength they could for the game, it was not uncommon for lagers to donate food to their athletes. The contests, a series that culminated with the "Kriegie Bowl", were greatly appreciated by the American boys, although the English lads seemed indifferent, but curious. In contrast, the "Jerry guards", watching from afar and thinking the players were scuffling, seemed slightly paranoid.

The more innovative prisoners at Stalag Luft IV collected

cigarette packs, deconstructed the boxes, and converted them into playing cards. Being that he did not smoke, George Ostrowski traded his valuable allotment of cigarettes for the vitamins that were packaged within other kriegie's RC parcels and kept a diary of camp life and the goings-on on the pack's wrappers. For most, however, the long, dull monotony would be spent warding off depression and despondency, avoiding "wire happy" disease, and dodging the guards. If receiving a letter from home was a welcomed treat during their days training in the States and while they were stationed in England, being the recipient of a note while confined within the Stalag system was an indescribable joy. Not wanting to be left out of the democratic process that was presently culminating back home, on November 7th the camp held a "straw vote" for the Presidency of the United States. Per *the Kriegie Kronicles*, mirroring the results collected 4,000 miles distant, the count at Stalag Luft IV showed, "...that the now President Franklin D. Roosevelt carried the pseudo vote by a veritable landslide." "Well, cheer up gang," assured the post, "maybe we'll be home in time for 1948's voting. Who knows?"

Next to securing food, the pursuit for entertainment, and thereby distraction, was a ubiquitous priority. On one memorable occasion, the bomber boys and fighter jocks were drawn to the sound of a sputtering Luftwaffe fighter passing nearby. When it stalled, sinking behind a wall of trees and converting into a fireball, the "Yanks" applauded and jumped up and down, just as if they were back in the States cheering on their high school football squad to victory, all the while to the annoyance of the home team. The poor sports responded to the uproar by firing bursts from their machine guns just above the heads of the Allied fliers. With the dirt around the airmen jumping in spurts from the impacting rounds, the crowd scattered and took cover behind their huts as the celebration was rapidly smothered out.

In one of the blocks, a combine had scavenged parts to construct a radio and covertly fed the masses current goings-on and happenings, broadcasted by the BBC. The winter campaign in Western Europe was now in full swing, and the POWs kept their ears to the airwaves. They followed developments of a setback caused by a strong German counteroffensive in the Ardennes where battered American ground pounders, crouched low in their foxholes, engaged in the "Battle of the Bulge". As Christmas of '44 neared, the blocks decorated pine branches with tinsel from cigarette cartons, tin can lid ornaments, and dyed cardboard stars. To their surprise, a special midnight Christmas mass had been approved and notwithstanding the freezing temperatures, the entire population gathered on the assembly grounds. With the beams of searchlights panning across the starry sky overhead, the chorus club treated both Germans and POWs alike to carol after carol. For the finale, thousands of boys, all hailing from every corner of the US but, at present, transplanted far from home, stood and to the astonishment of their noticeably captivated guards, sang "God Bless America" as one. When the refrain concluded and the echoes faded off into the night, the teary-eyed crowd paused for a moment and then melted away, all returning quietly to their barracks. For many, the season's festivities were a sentimental affair as the celebrations did much to rekindle the joyous memories of their boyhood holiday merriments with family, friends, decorations, presents, and, of course, food.

In late January 1945, upon the chilly sea breezes came thunderclaps like that of a distant, colossal storm. As the sounds rolled in from the east throughout the day, at night, pulses of light could be detected with the booming in the sky far beyond the trees. Night after night, the brilliant shows of illumination intensified and men on both sides of the wire began to realize that something big was looming on the horizon. Whether or not it was their impending liberation or imminent destruction that was near, was yet to be determined.

19
"HOW VERY GOOD GOD IS TO US"

Lt. Merle D. Green, husband of Rose Marie Green, 1212 East Brown Street, and the son of Mr. and Mrs. Otto Green of Pleasant Plains, has been reported missing in action over Germany since Sept. 11. He was serving as pilot of a Flying Fortress and in his last letter to relatives here, dated Sept. 10, said the Sept. 11 mission was to be his third.

News that their eldest son had been lost on a mission over Europe reached the "Red Top farm" by telegram on September 26th. Bob grew flustered when he learned that his idol and older brother was missing, and Hattie became so distraught that she confined herself to her room for days. The report was frustratingly vague and gave little detail as to whether their boy was hurt, killed, or captured, and as the "ETO", the European Theater of Operations, essentially covered the entire continent, his whereabouts were anyone's guess. Word always spread quickly in a small town and on September 29th, news of the local boy's disappearance debuted in the Springfield paper. For the next few days, readers continued to scan the columns hoping for further developments, anticipating details regarding the pilot. Although they held out hope, many knew Merle was flying with the 8th which, at that time, still held the reputation of being as glamorous as it was dangerous.

Understandably, Rose was beside herself with worry. Hoping to ease her anxieties, Rose's aunt wrote a letter hoping to lessen her fears:

My dear Rose Marie,

My prayers and sympathy are with you and Merle's dear parents. He has been in my prayers and I've been asking the Blessed Mother to take care of him. He may be a prisoner. It will be about three months before you find out so keep on praying for him. He has such a good face. I know he was a good boy…and Rose if the dear boy has paid the supreme sacrifice, that Heaven may be his reward.

Rose Green

Where others would be overcome by grief and despair, Rose seemed to become more resolute, if not tenacious. She hunted down addresses of officials in the War Department, sending off a torrent of inquiries to Washington DC, Maxwell Field-practically anywhere Merle had been with the Army, always pressing for more insight. She also penned notes to the wives and mothers of the crew, hoping to share news and exchange information, but above all else, doing what she could to help support the other families. In fact, Rose's most valuable service to each of the crew's kin was in her ability to help strengthen their faith and reassure them to hold confidence in His plan. She offered the following to one concerned individual, Agnes Gegenheimer, mother of the missing ball turret gunner:

All we can do is pray and trust in God. I feel as you do, that they are safe and it might be a while before we hear from them. But we can wait knowing how they must feel about us. Again I am thankful that James and they were with Merle. We, too, are all praying and asking God to keep them safe.

Rose and Agnes found comfort in a mutual understanding that, by God's plan, their loved one would be delivered through the ordeal and, if designed, would one day be returned home to them.

In response to her relentless letter-writing campaign and doggedness that bordered harassment, the War Department assured Mrs. Green that there was no other news to be passed along. She was advised that she should expect a delay of up to three months, ninety agonizing days, without the benefit of additional details concerning her husband and the crew. Discontented and not to be pushed aside, Rose pursued other options. A friend of the Green's had recently returned to Springfield after completing his tour in England and when Rose learned of the man's visit, she chased down the prospect. First, she convinced the veteran to reveal the restricted location of Merle's airfield: Station #468. Then, armed with the

Rose

knowledge of her husband's assignment, she tracked down a contact through a network of mutual acquaintances, well-wishers, and strangers, finally coming to the name of an intelligence officer currently stationed at Rougham. Hastily, "Mrs. Lt. Merle Green" dispatched another letter to England. When it reached the aerodrome, following a bit of investigation, the message was passed on to the 410th Bomb Squadron and, from there, handed off to Lt. Basil Pullar. While not on the mission on the 11th, Pullar felt inclined to help the troubled wife of his former hut mate. Rose sent word back to Gretna as promised, and in spite of being totally oblivious of the events following the collision and the forced landing, her note proved incredibly accurate:

Dear Mrs. Gegenheimer,

I just received a letter from one of the fellows who lived in the same barracks as Merle. He, Lt. Basil Pullar, wrote, 'The fellows that saw Merle leave the formation said his plane was not badly out of control and was not on fire as there is a good chance he made it to some neutral country or at least he could have bailed out or made a crash landing, in which case he and his crew would either be in hiding or a 'prisoner of war'.

In late October, amidst a blur of long, restless days filled with uncertainty; a purgatory in of itself, a small card arrived in the mail at the Denny residence, addressed to Rose. English censorship markings had been stamped on one side of the letter, and alongside were other unrecognizable marks and the words, "*Bis Nord Amerika*". Upon turning over the note, she read the following type-printed message:

SepT 15, 1944
Dulag-Luft Germany

I have been taken prisoner of war in Germany. I am in good health/slightly wounded. (cancel accordingly). We will be transported from here to another Camp within the next few days. Please don't write until I give new address.

Kindest regards

Flipping the card over, Rose noticed that "MERLE D. GREEN, LT ASN 0-820000 AAF" had been filled in above a small typewritten line that read "No further details". Unbeknownst to Rose, in the days following his arrival at Dulag Luft, Merle had slowly scratched in what little details he could on the card with his less disabled, non-dominant hand-his graceful penmanship abilities now reduced to deliberate, simple linear marks. To spare his wife any further trouble, he had made sure to scratch out the "slightly wounded" option. The note was soothing to Rose as it gave comfort that her husband was, at the very least, alive.

Around the same time, a second telegram, issued from the War Department, was sent to the Green farm in Pleasant Plains. The cable confirmed that their eldest son was, in fact, a prisoner of the Reich, confirmed by the International Red Cross. A second article soon appeared in the State Journal-Register:

LT. MERLE GREEN.

State Journal-Register

Lt. Merle Dean Green
Prisoner of War
Mr. and Mrs. Otto Green have received
word through the Red Cross that their son,
Lt. Merle Green, who was reported missing
in action, is a prisoner of the German army,
and that more information would follow this
telegram.

A new note did indeed follow, made out to Rose, and adorned with stamps similar to the Dulag Luft card. *"Kriegsgefangenenpost. "Mit Luftpost par Avion"*. *"GEPRUFT 89"*. *"Geburenfrell"*. Although she was unable to decipher the words, Rose was optimistic, tore open the letter and began skimming across the large, messy script. Unlike the flat, matter-of-fact message on the pre-printed POW card that she had received formerly, this letter was handwritten and more spirited, even slightly playful, hinting of the charismatic man that she was agonizing over to have back in her arms. In this, his second communication in just over two months, the pilot began by conveying his adoration for his lovely wife and then express regret for being away and causing her worry. Most of all, he was apologetic for being otherwise engaged on their second wedding anniversary. Without elaboration, Green revealed that he had hurt his hand during a mission but assured his wife that the injury was nothing to be concerned with, concluding with, "Rest of crew O.K." Of course, all of this was just a white lie.

Despite knowing a plethora of particulars concerning the crew's whereabouts and condition, the Germans at the interrogation center had refused to give Merle any word of his men's condition. If the report that Pete Riley had provided him with while aboard the *Green Hornets* on the 11th of September was correct, and he hoped he was mistaken, Sidney was most likely dead. Furthermore, whether Merle was unwilling or incapable of acknowledging the loss, Lt. Williams was also gone. Knowing how Rose felt about Jack, Merle deliberately failed to mention the bombardier.

In another letter, sent from Rose to Agnes after receiving news that her husband was alive, Mrs. Green wrote:

> *…So you see Mrs. Gegenheimer, the news gets better all the time. One of these days, it won't be too long, you too will get good news. I feel even more sure of this since I heard about Merle's safety. Being that he was the pilot, he couldn't leave the ship until they had all left it. I sort of feel that he might have made the boys bail out and that he crash-landed the plane. In such a case the boys would not be together and it would take longer to hear about them. It's wonderful that all this time has passed and you haven't had any news. They tell me that a death is reported much faster than a capture. I feel about James and the other boys as if they are my brothers. I never knew any fellows that I admired and liked so much as they. They were so eager to make good, to have the best crew and to do their job. Every day that I waited to hear about Merle I offered it up to Our Sorrowful Mother. Every day still I pray that she will let you and the other mothers of the boys know soon. We are praying and having masses for the boys. I hope you hear very soon.*

Regrettably, fortunes would, again, change for the CO's wife as, without warning, Rose's mother, Frances, began experiencing severe chest pains and was admitted to the hospital. Upon visiting her in the recovery ward, Rose's aunt, burdened with grief, suffered a stroke and passed away a few days later. Sadly, Frances Denny would follow, both sisters dying suddenly and at the same hospital within four hours of each other. The loss was devastating for the Denny family but especially for Rose, who, besides losing her mother and fretting over her husband, had a brother and sister away in the service and was left to take care of her younger siblings and brokenhearted father.

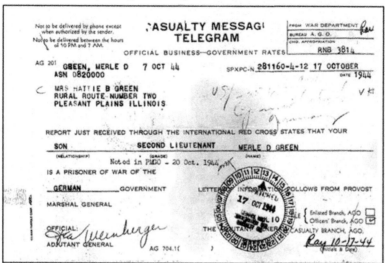

Times were no better for the Hatfield family. Orville Hatfield, unaware that his little brother was at that moment lying in a small rural cemetery in central Germany, was tormented day and night by an unrelenting barrage of disturbing unknowns. Sid had been missing for weeks and the only notice had come from a battle casualty report issued from the War Department, coolly advising the family that the gunner had not returned from a combat flight over the Reich. Also in limbo, the sergeant's father, Theodore, could do nothing but fret over his missing boy. The widower's worst fears would soon be realized when, in the last days of October, his 19-year-old son was declared "Killed-in-Action" via Western Union telegram. A picture of the young gunner appeared in the Huntington Herald-Dispatch on November 14th, accompanied by the gloomy announcement:

SERGEANT HATFIELD KILLED OVER REICH
Sergeant Sidney, I. Hatfield, son of Theodore F. Hatfield, 410
½ Bridge Street who had been missing since September 11, is
now listed as killed, the War Department has notified his father.

In Alabama, Frank Jones' people were the recipient of multiple letters from the War Department regarding the missing navigator. Initially, the Army had told them that Frank's plane had collided with

Rose (left) with friend

another B-17 from the Group and that airmen had been seen parachuting out of the carnage, though it wasn't clear from which aircraft the chutes came. Naturally, much confusion remained but considering that a "KIA" notification had yet to darken the threshold of the Jones home, it was assumed, and hoped, that the flight officer had been among the jumpers and was captured and put in a prisoner camp. All of this had come in late October. By November, Frank's father, Edward, was writing the War Department to clarify an unusual report sent to him by AAF officials in England. Allied intelligence had intercepted a German broadcast boasting about the capture of, among many other downed fliers, a "Flight Officer Frank M. Jones of Montgomery." No specifics were to be had but the report, along with IRC records and later confirmed by the Air Forces, helped reinforce the belief that his son was safe and still alive.

In the flight engineer's hometown, neighbors of the Leheres opened the Butler Eagle on Thursday morning, the 28th of September, to the unsettling news of losing another one of their local sons. Under the headline "Bomber Down", readers were troubled to learn that the local steel mill worker had gone missing over Germany. Jane Lehere had been eagerly anticipating a letter from her husband whose status, at that point, was still uncertain. She too struck up a friendship with Mrs. Green, and in the following correspondence sent between Butler and Springfield, the two young wives found they had much in common.

Dear Rose Marie,

You don't mind if I call you 'Rose Marie' do you? It's such a pretty name and 'Mrs. Green' and 'Mrs. Lehere' does sound so formal, don't you think so? It's nice hearing from you since you and your husband knew Louis so well. You mentioned how he wished I could have been with him-well you don't know how much I wished the same thing! But the way things were it was just impossible, that's all. Yes, Louis and I had our first anniversary... It's not so nice to meet such an occasion alone-we were so sure we'd be together our first anniversary-but I guess fate decided differently.

Three months after the assault on *Bohlenwerks*, Jane and her mother-in-law were still devoted to their writing crusade and were busy dispatching messages to anyone who could assist them in locating the Butler gunner. By the turn of the new year, the only acknowledgment that Jane had received was a *"Postkarte"* similar to the one that Merle had sent Rose from Dulag Luft. Like Lt. Green, Lou marked that he was in good health and unhurt although he too had been injured in the accident. To prevent placing undue stress on their devoted, loving companions, both men had chosen to withhold revealing their injuries. Be it intuition or something else, Jane felt something wasn't right with her husband. She added to the letter to Rose:

I was very sorry to hear that your husband's hand was injured. I'm worried because the first (and only) card I had from Louis was in his handwriting and perhaps he was wounded too. It said he was in good health but I'm worried. Was your card already printed too? I wonder why I haven't received Louis' address yet-I am so anxious-I meet the mailman every morning! Something that puzzles me-why would Merle say 'Rest of crew O.K.' whenever Lt. Williams is still missing and I don't know about Sgt. Riley or Frank Jones. I wrote to their folks but haven't heard anything from them yet. I hope they are alright. Perhaps he doesn't know about Lt. Williams. I sure feel sorry about him and also Irving. They weren't so fortunate as Louis and Merle, were they? Although maybe Louis is wounded, too. Anyways I'd rather they be German prisoners than Japanese-how about you?

It was nearly two months after Jim Gegenheimer had vanished somewhere over the Nazi homeland that his mother received an  official announcement of her son's capture, but the news did not just trickle in from the War Department. Newly reassigned to the 99th Bomb Group in Tortorella, Italy, Paul Klekot became distraught when he learned from a source at Rougham that his former crew, his nine brothers, had been involved in some sort of trouble and had failed to come back from a mission just days after his departure. For weeks, rumors were still filtering back to the 94th regarding the crew, but it was suspected that there were many casualties. One of the lot that was confirmed dead was Paul's old bombardier, Lt. Williams. Klekot was

Rose Green

devastated by the grim discovery. He immediately wrote to the mother of his dear friend, Jim, offering what little particulars he had and passing along some words of support to ease her worries. Finally enlightened, or perhaps more fittingly, hampered with the knowledge of Jack's demise, Agnes forwarded Klekot's message to Rose and asked for advice on handling the grief-stricken Mrs. Williams. Rose had herself become all too familiar with how to cope with the crushing weight that accompanies death and loss, and although the demise of Jack Williams cut deep, she forced herself to carry out the duties entrusted to her as the crew's home front leader. She offered Agnes the following:

Mrs. Gegenheimer,

About this letter from Klekot; Do you think Mrs. Williams should read it? If you do would you send it on to her? I wanted to let her read it and I dread being the one to give her such news as this. I know the mothers of the boys would be happy to know it happened as it did and not as I'm sure we all imagined. If Jack was the one who made the sacrifice, I know he would have wanted it that way, for every one of the boys would have done the same for him. They were like that. I don't suppose why we will ever know why some are taken and others like ours are spared. How very good God is to us.

Jane Lehere had been corresponding with the Metzgers, but when she became aware of the bombardier's death, she struggled to find the nerve to relay the terrible news to Jack's mother. Like the other wives, Jane didn't have the heart to tell Mrs. Williams that her son had been killed.

Before the War, George Ostrowski was regularly mentioned in the local paper due to his exploits on the gridiron and ice rink but in the fall of '44, Lorraine Ostrowski's boy was back in the local headlines but this time, regrettably, his feature was listed under the local "POW" section. The Philadelphia Inquirer alerted its readers to the status of one of their own; Peter Riley, who was described with no other elaboration than being, "held by the Germans" and the ball turret gunner received similar press in his town of Gretna that same month. Although Agnes Gegenheimer had heard rumors that her son had surfaced within the prisoner system, the Army had finally confirmed through German authorities, that Jim was indeed, confined in one of the Stalags.

In the months to follow: the climactic epoch leading to the finale of the War, every member of the *Green Hornets* team would come close to their breaking point. All would be put through even more deprivation, and the misfortunes to come would be cause for each man to question whether they would survive to see themselves returning to their homes and loved ones.

20
"TELL EVERYONE 'HELLO' FOR ME"

Late Fall 1944
Reserve Lazarett
Obermassfeld, Germany

Dear Rose:

They had to take the fingers off my right hand due to the frostbite that I got at the time of the crash. I am O.K. otherwise and expect to be home before long. I am getting good care here and have plenty of company. I am looking forward to my first letter from you. I expect it to be a long newsy one about everyone but more than that I want to know what you do all day every day. As for myself I have been making plans for our chickens, pigs and kids-hope you like them. Things as a whole look much brighter and with a little help from St. Joe we will soon be back to normal. I can only write three times a month so don't expect too many letters. Tell everyone "hello" for me. All my love.

-Merle

While Lt. Green recovered from his amputation, his navigator and co-pilot were recuperating from their own procedures. The English doctor who had taken off Merle's fingers had performed Metzger's challenging amputations and wrote to his parents "…to forewarn them and prepare them for the shock of Irving's disability." Like Merle's procedure, Irv's surgery was just as necessary but required him to relinquish all his fingers and both thumbs. The condition of Frank's hand had also worsened and began to fester. After a thorough evaluation, camp physicians determined that none of the digits could be saved, and all five fingers of Jones' left hand were surgically removed. Doctors also evaluated and reset his aching leg, which had been nagging him for nearly two months.

On October 14th, 1944, Frank, Irv, and Merle were among dozens transferred by bus to the nearby rehabilitation facility at Meiningen. The hospital was far beyond capacity when the officers arrived, with nearly five hundred wounded and convalescing prisoners, representing half a dozen countries, crammed into a few large wards. The clinic at Meiningen had been specifically established to care for the most extreme of cases and a wide variety of wounds and

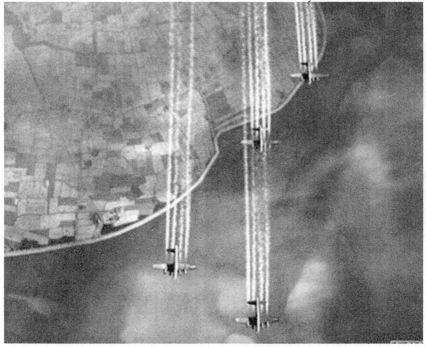

The contrails of a flight of B-17s scoring the European sky, Fold3

disabilities. One of the most prized additions to the clinic, the facility boasted a sizeable gym stocked with makeshift and fabricated weight equipment. The staff had scrounged up some gear, but most items had been fabricated by the more ingenious prisoners, with "no help from the Germans." It was operated by a staff of captured American medical personnel who stretched the men's aching joints and helped exercise their weakened frames while burn victims received specialized attention in the improvised burn ward and benefitted from rudimentary skin grafting procedures and therapy massages.

In between appointments, the detainees bartered items from their RC parcels with the guards, pursued various hobbies, read, or scribbled in their journals, compliments of the Red Cross. Some of the most anticipated events at the Meiningen lazarett were the dramatic stage performances; promoted, organized, cast, and executed by the prisoners themselves. The colorful plays and skits were cast by an assembly of committed amateur thespians, many of whom portrayed classic characters in their true-to-life form, sans limbs, tormented by the memory of slain friends, and brandishing actual scars. Despite struggling to decipher the dialogue delivered in the heavy brogue of the Scottish kriegies, these amateur performances were a huge draw.

While at Meiningen, Merle roomed with another 8th AAF pilot by the name of Lloyd Carter. On the 19th of October, Carter's bomber had been shot out of the sky over Mainz. One of seven survivors from his aircrew, Lloyd parachuted from his B-24 Liberator and plunged in the River Main near Griesheim. Carter was still encumbered by his parachute harness as he inched up the muddy bank where a local, Karl Stoll, came face to face with the spent pilot. The German, later identified by his neighbors as an ardent "Gestapo Agent", said nothing but raised his Luger toward the flier and pulled the trigger. The bullet blasted into Carter's face above the left side of his nose and exited just below his right ear, passing clean through his mouth but missing all vital structures and arteries by mere fractions of an inch. The lieutenant then sank to the ground at Stoll's feet, bleeding and unconscious. Having witnessed the event, villagers rushed the American to authorities in Frankfurt where doctors spent seven days stabilizing the bomber pilot in a community hospital before they transferred him to *Hohemark*. Carter spent the following weeks recovering on the second floor of the *Klinik* and, like Jones and Metzger before him, was trucked to Obermassfeld. Not yet fully mended, Carter was again relocated, this time to Reserve Lazarett at Meiningen, where he met his new bunkmate, a weak, gaunt young man from central Illinois. The pair, Carter with half of his face wrapped in dressing and Green with his bulky, bandaged hands, struck up a friendship. In the long hours spent alongside one another in recuperation, each shared stories of their youth, mused over their loved ones, and reminisced on their life before the War. Carter would later be moved to the prisoner camp at Moosburg, positioned not far from Munich.

Every now and then, the men could hear a familiar murmur swelling from beyond the distant hills. It was soon accompanied by the sight of the American Air Forces-the 8th from the north and west and the 15th from the south, clawing across the heavens on their way to level the targets of the day. Rushing outside to watch the great show, it was not lost on the men who had themselves manned the gun stations and charting tables and tweaked the bombsights or handled the control columns of similar machines that some of those passing overhead were their close friends. As the current of aluminum overcast passed beyond the trees to slug away at the Germans, the men couldn't help but wonder if they had been forgotten.

Dear Mom,

No word from home yet. My hand is nearly well and I feel fine. Sure wish I could have had Thanksgiving dinner with you. Tell Bob he may have to do my Spring work for me. I'll do the rest. See you soon.

Love,

Merle

A delegation of the Swiss Welfare Committee toured the lazarett late in November, authorized with investigating cases for approval of repatriation. Merle was advised that due to the severity of his injuries and deteriorated physical and mental state, he, along with Lt. Metzger, was slotted to be sent home in the upcoming American-German prisoner exchange. As the Germans saw it, absent fingers able to manipulate gun triggers, these rivals were effectively neutralized. Word of the transfer was poignant as the pilots learned that Frank, still dealing with the discomfort of his finger amputation surgery and irritated by a tender leg, somehow did not qualify to be included in the trade. Recalling the neglect and the denial of timely and adequate medical care that he undergone after the crash and while at Dulag Luft, Green was beyond incensed by the decision and confronted the staff. Seeing that his CO was only drawing unwanted attention, Frank assured his friend that he too would be returning to the States soon, as Allied victory was only a matter of time. Whether it be chance, fate, or just bad luck, as Merle and Irv counted down the days to their homecoming, Frank was being readied to be processed into the German prisoner camp system.

Anxious for his time as a POW to draw to a close but still without a departure date in sight, Green wrote another message to his wife:

Dear Rose,

With Christmas drawing near I find myself not only thinking of you all day, but dreaming of you at night. I want to thank you for so many wonderful memories. I'm sorry I didn't get to tell St. Nick what I wanted you to have for Christmas. I'll make it up to you on your birthday-in person. My hand is getting along just fine although I have had three operations. I am gaining back some of the weight I lost. By the way don't send any parcels. It takes too long for them to get here and I should be home by then. I hope this finds everyone in the best of health and you are getting along O.K. I am wondering what plans you have for our future but I'll bet they'll be O.K.

All my love
Merle

As 1945 broke, Lt. Green and Lt. Metzger were, at last, presented with transfer documents. Leaving Meiningen, the train wound its way east, grinding along portions of the *Reichsbahn* that had yet to be wrecked by Allied incendiaries. Sitting out the War behind the walls and wire of their hospital camps, Irv and Merle had grown to all but ignore the daily air raid sirens that wailed at the forthcoming arrival of the largest aerial fleets ever to be deployed; that of the US Army Air Forces. Regularly, they could hear the pounding of bombs echoing down the valley, some emitting concussion waves that rattled the windows of their building. Hearing and feeling the explosions was one thing but observing the aftermath rushing past just outside their carriage window was something that neither man had anticipated. The scene was that of the systematic destruction of Germany, and they were witnessing it firsthand and up close. There was little doubt in the minds and hearts of all who viewed the apocalyptic scene, that the old Germany was forever ruined.

A pillar of smoke rising behind a group of Flying Fortresses, Fold3

After journeying to Annaburg, Irv, Merle, and 493 other American POWs then proceeded south by rail on the 14th of January. The journey was agonizing at times as the men sweated out one strafing attack by American planes on scavenge and another near-miss. When progress along the tracks was made, it was at a painfully slow rate. As a consequence of effective and extensive Allied fighter and bomber strikes, the train had to be re-routed around bombed-out marshaling yards and shuffled in among other rail traffic, troop transports, and freight cars. Five days after departing Annaburg, the locomotive reached the German-Swiss border at Konstanz. There, the wounded were relocated across the border.

The official exchange was carried out opposite of Konstanz at Kreuzlingen, Switzerland where nearly five thousand Allied and Axis prisoners waited, eager to complete the transfer process. Like the handful before, the swap was conducted under the supervision of the IRC, with collaboration between German, Swiss, English, and American authorities. From Kreuzlingen, Irv, Merle, and their group proceeded southwest, crossing the Alps, and rolling into France. When the train stopped alongside a US Army field kitchen, the riders enthusiastically disembarked the coaches to enjoy their first real food in months but many of the depleted couldn't manage the fare and became sick. Nevertheless, the men managed to remount the carriages and continued their journey, finally terminating at the port of Marseille.

Debriefings followed, and the men received additional medical care, food, and access to bathing facilities aboard a pair of military hospital ships that lay in dock. With final preparations being arranged, the pilots quartered aboard the US Algonquin. After viewing a few films and reading up on the progress of the War; an entirely contradictory description than what had been disseminated to the pair while in German detention, Lt. Green and Lt. Metzger transferred to the luxury liner-turned-"mercy ship", *SS Gripsholm*.

With five months of captivity behind him, on February 8th, Merle slid into the indigo waters of the Mediterranean. The vessel squeezed through the Strait of Gibraltar and into open ocean, coasting west over the Atlantic. Eight days later the Illinois State Journal ran the following:

2 Local Men, Held By Nazis, To Return On Gripsholm
Lt. Merle Green Among 463 Soldiers Due to Arrive Next Week

Two Springfield soldiers are among 463 army officers and enlisted men, former prisoners of Germany, who the War Department announced yesterday, are being returned home on the Swedish exchange ship Gripsholm. Also aboard the Gripsholm are 665 US civilians and 78 Canadian personnel. The Swedish ship is due to arrive in the United States next week. All of the soldiers are sick or wounded and were exchanged in Switzerland for German prisoners of war. Lt. Green, pilot of a B-17 bomber, was reported a prisoner of the Germans on Oct. 18. Previously he had been listed as missing over Germany since Sept. 11.

After thirteen days at sea, passengers flooded the decks of the ocean liner, pressed up against the ship's railing, and squinted far out ahead, eager to be among the first to catch sight of the hazy coast of the United States.

GRIPSHOLM DUE TODAY
Exchange Liner Bringing 1,206 Repatriates to the United States

-New York Times February 21, 1945

As "*Diplomat Gripsholm Sverige*" sat in mooring at Jersey City's Pier, the wounded hobbled down the gangways in long lines before being trucked by a fleet of ambulances to Halloran General Hospital on Staten Island. A steak dinner trimmed with all the fixings greeted the returnees that evening. The following day, the men attended an award ceremony in the hospital's auditorium. One hundred-forty of the 463 men had earned decorations, and then were released to a small army of reporters who mobbed the servicemen, seeking interviews and popping photographs with the "[w]ounded American boys,

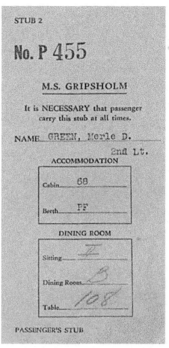

so broken in body...". Days prior, as the *Gripsholm* was still cutting west through Atlantic waters, Rose, waiting in Springfield, received a Red Cross telegram advising her that she would not be permitted to meet her husband at the docks upon the ship's arrival. Instead, she, along with the families of the other servicemen, would be able to receive the returnees at a designated reception center. As expected, Rose, determined to meet her husband on the pier if not the boat itself, planned to ignore the "advisement" but ultimately conceded. So it was that on February 23rd, standing among a mass of damaged and disfigured soldiers and airmen gathered on Lexington Avenue, Rose embraced a worn, rail-thin version of her husband for the first time in seven long, trying, dreadful months.

Over the next few days, the lieutenant was shuffled through the Army's re-processing protocols established by the government for newly returned personnel. In between appointments, the Greens enjoyed a few moments where they were able to continue to reacquaint themselves. Rose would return to Springfield as, for the time being, Merle was to remain at Halloran for additional treatment of his still-unhealed battle scars, as would Lt. Metzger who had returned with

Merle on the *Gripsholm* and was also currently rehabilitating. With all signs pointing towards the approaching resolution of the War in Europe, Merle believed that, with God's grace and although a little worse for wear, all of his "boys" would be home again soon…all except for Sidney and Jack. Little did the CO know that as he sat, reporting his knowledge concerning Frank and his non-coms to Army intelligence, Pete, George, Jim, and Lou were enduring an unbelievably arduous, remarkable, and frequently, inhumane experience.

21

DEATH MARCH TO FREEDOM

Late January 1945
Stalag Luft IV
Gross Tychow, German-controlled Pomerania

The bellowing of heavy artillery could be heard echoing from the east, now with continuous effect. It seemed that the once unstoppable Nazi colossus, so successful in earlier campaigns in numerous theaters, had disintegrated in the face of the advancing Soviet juggernaut. Consequently, for the kriegie overseers, avoiding the calamity of falling into the hands of the Russians, who were known for doling out severe reprisals on German soldiers and the populace alike, was paramount. As fear of comeuppance took hold of the German contingent, whispers of the impending execution of Allied POWs spread between the lagers like wildfire, leaving many to speculate over the recent excavation of a sizable "potato pit", dug adjacent to the camp. Undoubtedly, death and uncertainty hung on the mind of all during those final days in January 1945.

Apprehensions peaked and finally boiled over when, at the end of the month, the airmen were told to make ready for a three-day march. Unbeknownst to the kriegies, with the Soviets gnarling in from the east, German High Command had reluctantly ordered the prisoner of war camps in Poland and Czechoslovakia be abandoned, and the populations relocated. The prisoners were being shunted back into the core of the Reich homeland, placing further distance between them and liberation. Stalag Luft IV's evacuation plan called for all columns, a total of approximately 6,800 men, to withdraw west along separate but parallel routes in order to aid their speed of travel and lighten the burden on the local farms which were expected to supplement the prisoner's food supply while on the move. As an added advantage for the Germans, in the event of a rebellion, the spacing would keep the uprising insulated and more manageable.

In the early hours on February 6th, 1945, with the Russians a mere forty-five miles distant, the inhabitants of Stalag Luft IV, including Lou Lehere, Jim Gegenheimer, Pete Riley, and George Ostrowski, were roused awake by their German guards and ordered to ready themselves to leave camp. Bedding was frantically deconstructed and packed within the men's makeshift knapsacks, along with a change of clothes, miscellaneous items, and what foodstuffs they were able to scrounge up. Wriggling into their heavy wool overcoats to help keep the hint of the glacial breath of the approaching winter at bay, they pulled on knitted stocking caps and swaddled themselves deep in their scarfs.

Following their capture, the health of the *Green Hornets'* gunners had diminished drastically, leaving them, like most of the camp's population, weak, frail, and malnourished. To this day, some speculation exists as to whether conscious efforts were taken by the German command to slowly starve the prisoners to death. "At the time we were getting a daily intake of 700 calories," reports Lehere, "and we were really in no shape to begin a long march." Aside from their enfeebled state, most at Stalag Luft IV, including the captors themselves, believed that it was not only futile to abandon the camp to reposition the detainees as it was widely accepted at that point by both sides that the War was all but lost for the Germans, but the move was seen as highly irrational. Regardless, at dawn, in a wind-chill of 10 degrees below zero and with over a foot of newly settled snow sitting on the ground, the first assembly of three hundred or so scrawny kriegies stepped away from the Stalag, turned northwest, and set their shoulders into the chilly breezes whipping into them from off the Baltic. The remaining prisoners were likewise divided into similarly conditioned groups of approximately two to three hundred boys. At various intervals throughout the next two days, these assemblies slid out onto the snowy road and set off on their hike. Passing beyond the stockade's fences, huddled in Army greatcoats and wrapped in blankets and layers of any clothing they could get their hands on, the men couldn't help but wonder if Hitler was now trying to eradicate them through exposure.

So began their exodus from Pomerania and what would be known as the infamous "Black March," "the Death March", or "the Shoe Leather Express". For most it would be remembered simply as "the March" and it commenced in what was the harshest winter in recent European history. On average, each kriegie would lose approximately one-third of his body weight during his traipse through Germany in 1945. Walking an average of eighteen miles per day, Gegenheimer remembered, "that three-day march turned into a three-month march...".

Kriegies on the March, 1945, USAF Academy

While filing out of the Stalag early on the morning of 6 February, the guards made point to steer the prisoners by the camp's stockhouse. Despite the alleged Allied strafing raids that had targeted the camp's food supply convoys, preventing the delivery of much-needed food stuffs, large stockpiles of RC parcels had been amassed inside the shed. The boney, frail, and now much irritated kriegies quickly set about snatching up the bounty as they were instructed to grab whatever they wanted from the cache. "[T]hey told us to take whatever we wanted. A lot of the guys took two parcels", recalled the *Green Hornets'* engineer-gunner but noticed that "after the first day of hard marching, they threw the extra parcel away." Once on the march: one that they were told would require no more than a few days of hard treading, the prisoners found themselves weighed down by the excess supply of food. Scores of encumbered trekkers began to rid themselves of much of their load and left a trail of discarded goods to litter the frosty paths in their wake. By day two of the march, the camp's residents, seventy percent of whom were considered stricken with physical ailments or chronic illness even before leaving the *Stammlager*, were entirely exhausted, and men began to drop out of the column. Some were gathered up by their peers, many of whom were barely capable of keeping upright themselves, but a number of others, unable to walk on blistered or numbed feet or too weak to stand, were left to an unknown fate. With the Russians hot on their tail, the Germans weren't about to let up the pace. Dozens more would follow on February 8th as the long lines of freezing men plodded past Stolzenburg.

Just days into the march, the men found themselves in increasingly desperate times, walking on with hollow pockets, barren knapsacks, and empty stomachs. An outbreak of diphtheria struck more down three days later, on the 11th. On Valentine's Day, some sections completed a brutal 21-mile hike in sleet and rain only to collapse in fields littered with human feces left by preceding collections of kriegies at dusk. By the time the groups began arriving on the banks of the Oder River on the 15th, approximately 750 boys who had set off from the camp outside of Gross-Tychow were absent from the rolls. While there is no question that a share of those who had been separated from the pack were collected up by the German military and transferred to hospitals and even fewer in number had endeavored to evade, many of these men, and more to come, would be unaccounted for by War's end, never to be seen or heard from again.

By the time the groups convened on the opposite bank of the Oder, and with the realization that they were now tramping on German soil, the marchers were sustaining themselves on "cigarette butts and coffee". Survivors remembered the German faux coffee as a disgusting "butter-grease" tea, its only saving attribute being its warmth and availability. Caches of Red Cross parcels had been shipped to sites along the path to accommodate the prisoners, but upon their arrival, the kriegies found the warehouses empty. Later, it was determined that the stores had been looted by *Wehrmacht* and *Volkssturm* units who then distributed the excess to the destitute locals. To offset the deficit, some kriegies, under the direction of the country boys, set snares and traps in hopes of catching small game, a few even managing to chase down a goose. Pairs of ravenous vagrants could be seen scurrying away from the column, headed for a nearby farm hoping to barter with the residents by exchanging watches, rings, chocolate bars, and soap for anything edible while their equally worn-out guards looked on. Unfortunately for all parties, most civilians lacked the ability, or the desire, to feed the emaciated enemy dregs that slowly tracked past their fields, nonetheless their own lot. As such, it was common for the prisoners to conduct forays into the countryside to "commandeer" any scant goods that they may come across. Lehere admitted that he was one of the many who survived on spoils retrieved from German farms.

More often than not, scavengers would rejoin their starving comrades on the road empty-handed and entirely defeated. On the rare occasion that they did return from a forage with spoils, it was with a frozen carrot, a handful of grain, moldy potatoes or a rotten onion and was doled out amongst a lucky few and happily devoured. Some men recalled eating "hog food," and at least one man attempted to consume a bundle of grass pulled from the side of the road when there was nothing else to be found. Finding himself famished but unable to swallow the fibers, he boiled them and then gulped down the bitter water. As they moved through

Rest stop, somewhere in Northern Germany, 1945, USAF Academy

the land, it became apparent to the fliers that the conflict had taxed virtually all of Europe in one form or another. War had brought a melancholy to every doorstep and ravaged the once-fertile soil of its riches, Germany more so than most.

Insufficient and inadequate nourishment aside, for the tens of thousands of airmen shuffling along the cow trails and "…worst damn roads in Jerryland", access to fresh water was virtually non-existent. Most of the walking was trotted over rural countryside as a strategy to sidestep any irritated citizenry, but occasionally long lines of Allied fliers could be seen snaking along the dirt lanes and down cobblestone streets of the random German hamlet or village. Passing through the center of these settlements, scores of prisoners would fall out and wait their turn to fill their cup or grab a handful of water from the community fountain. When a well was not to be had, the men took to eating snow and ice. At other times, in desperation, completely sapped of all energy and perpetually dehydrated, they swallowed down mouthfuls of stagnant water from small pools that had collected in depressions of the earth; the same recesses where other kriegies had previously trudged, slept, or relieved themselves.

Dysentery, pneumonia, diphtheria, typhus, trench foot, tuberculosis, and a plethora of other diseases had caused significant problems for the kriegies while confined within the camp's grounds but now free of the wire, the ailments became epidemic and ran rampant through the wasted masses of men. To ward off their constant intestinal afflictions, airmen consumed chunks of charcoal in hopes of remedying their cursed bowels. At first, those tormented by chronic diarrhea attempted to assuage the sickness by finding an improvised latrine, but eventually all succumbed to the gut-wrenching malady and could be found marching on in soiled and frequently blood-stained trousers. Whether they were stricken with "the trots" or not, most were concerned about falling behind to relieve themselves and being unable to muster the energy needed to catch up with the column. The majority of those who toppled from the ranks managed to pull themselves to the side of the road where they lay until one of their fellows noticed them and pulled them to their feet, allowing them to stumble on for a few more miles before repeating the agonizing process. It was an ordeal measured not in days or miles but by seconds, moments, footsteps, and inches.

While many men were revived by their comrades and continued on, others surrendered to exposure as there was little reprieve from the elements and sub-freezing temperatures. Frostbite ruined scores of prisoners, subtly paralyzing and destroying ears, fingers, toes, and feet. In the evenings, the men packed into commandeered farmhouses, stables, or storehouses one night only to be forced to try and find some sleep in a woodpile or an icy ditch alongside a barren meadow the next. It was "a tour of barns", reported one sore-footed kriegie in his journal. On the nights when a shelter was secured, fliers bunked in the stables alongside livestock only to wake the following morning half-frozen. Those unlucky farmers who were forced to play host did so grudgingly, and all efforts were taken to restrict the pest-encumbered boys from accessing their stores of straw and hay for bedding. After the prisoners departed, many perturbed planters would often discover that, despite their objections and endeavors, the filthy boarders had contaminated the hay with their parasitic hitchhikers. As if hurling their bombs upon the Fatherland was not insult enough, now these flying hoodlums were unleashing vermin.

Routinely, the kriegies broke out from beneath frost-covered blankets long before daybreak. Herded from the fields, barns, or cow sheds into line, the guards took a tally of the men and started their hike. On one intensely cold evening, Sgt. Gegenheimer made the mistake of removing his worn-out shoes before lying down in a farmer's field for the evening. Jim woke long before light the next morning and panicked as he found he was unable to put on his shoes as they had frozen solid during the night. For the next three hours, Jim worked his swollen, blistered, numb feet back into his boots. When the guards summoned the shivering band back to the road, the Gretna youngster was able to stomp out onto the lane in his ratty leather footwear before drawing the guard's attention. "When you were going along the road, if you collapsed or you couldn't go on any further, they would assign one guard, and they would get a cart maybe from the farm and God knows where they took you", recalled the gunner. Many similar scenes were recorded during "the March," some describing that the sound of a single rifle shot could be commonly heard after an exhausted walker was left behind. Gegenheimer would add, "I don't know how many people we may have lost that way, but it was not in your best interest to fall behind."

Those who endured the "Long Walk" passed by Schwinemunde on Usedom Island, then along trails between Anklam, Jarmen, Demmin, Malchow, Ludwigslust, and Tarnow. On one especially frigid day, a few groups came upon a strange facility deep in the forest, one closely resembling their former POW camp at Gross Tychow. As they sat shivering outside the confines of the wire where their escorts had halted them, many of the run-down kriegies became envious of the lodgings within. Rows upon rows of shut up barracks sprawled out before them. Smoke rose from every chimney and within each hut the occupants were presumed to be warmly huddled down beside roaring fireplaces as no prisoners could be observed roaming the camp's grounds. Unaware of it at the time, the airman would later be told that the site they saw that day was most likely one of the Nazi "death camps".

Back on the move, the men then backtracked to Usedom Bei Savenmunde before reversing course, once again, and heading west. Daily, the kriegies sidestepped around multitudes of German civilians fleeing west to avoid the Russians. The masses that the Stalag Luft IV boys had encountered were but a small portion of the total number of evacuees, refugees, and approximately 185,000 Allied prisoners that were hurried towards the German interior in the late winter of 1945. Later, the sum of these numbers was projected as being greater than 7 million persons, one of the largest mass migrations in human history.

Winter conditions still prevailed as March broke, and even more sick men were carved out of the ranks by disease, injury, fatigue, and despair. Just as Russian artillery had lit up the sky to the east of Stalag Luft IV in the days leading up to the evacuation of the camp,

new concussions now echoed from up ahead to the west as American and English cannon came into play, blasting away German resistance bit by bit. At various points along the roads, the men eyed the occasional foxhole or trench, dug by depleted *Wehrmacht* and *Waffen SS* detachments, and abandoned military trucks rested everywhere, starved of precious fuel. One day, the men found themselves lumbering along a road that ran adjacent to a tall, barbed-wire fence. As the prisoners passed by and gawked through the wire into the complex, guards barked at the group to keep their heads down and pushed the cluster onward, shoving them with the butts of their rifles as they went. A few among them were able to catch sight of what the Germans were trying to hide: a pair of V-2 rockets resting on their mobile platforms, ready and waiting to be deployed. Not only would Allied fighters buzz over the countryside virtually unopposed as the Luftwaffe had all but been knocked out of commission, the downed fliers regularly followed formations of heavies driving past overhead, making their daily rounds into the Reich, and breaking the monotony of the never-ending, senseless "March to Nowhere".

Late in March, bands began arriving at a pair of POW complexes outside of Fallingbostel called Stalag XIB and Stalag 357. Further augmented by the new arrivals from Stalag Luft IV, several factions from other internment camps were likewise being shifted to Fallingbostel, which was, itself, already teeming with thousands of Allied detainees. "Up until that time that was well over two months," recollected Sgt. Gegenheimer, "we didn't change clothes, we didn't bathe, we didn't shave, and then we didn't have Red Cross parcels". Although the earth-coated trotters finally had access to running water for showering and enjoyed a reprieve from the elements, very little food was to be found at the camp. Jim and his fellows became annoyed at the situation as being on the road had at least afforded them the opportunity to scavenge and forage.

Just two weeks after the *Green Hornets* arrival, English ground units secured Fallingbostel, liberating tens of thousands of captured Allied soldiers and fliers. However, not to be found among the ranks of the freed men were thousands of kriegies from Stalag Luft IV. Only a week prior, on the 6th of April and under the ring of heavy guns, the Germans had ordered the prisoners from Gross Tychow out of the camp and back onto the road where the march-and their detainment, resumed. While lagers C and D were paraded off towards Uelzen, the men of A and D lagers, the *Green Hornets'* gunners among them, moved haphazardly back to the east.

No more than 2,000 now remained, dispersed in multiple groups composed of destitute and despairing souls whose pockets were stocked with no more than fragments of bread, a portion of a Red Cross parcel, pinches of nicotine, and coffee. As scrawny prisoners, they had trudged along the roads of Western Poland and then slogged over trails in Northern Germany. Now, the boys had transformed into stumbling near-skeletons as they continued their arduous trek, crisscrossing what remained of the crumbling western territory of the Reich homeland.

On April 19th, the group was peppered by friendly fire from RAF Typhoon fighters who mistook the men for retreating German soldiers. Once the dust settled, the frazzled column took to their feet and hiked on, although their numbers were now lightened of sixty men- half wounded, half killed in the unfortunate accidental aerial ambush. Lehere, Riley, Ostrowski, and Gegenheimer and their dwindling bunch of ragged fellow survivors pushed on, crossing the Elbe River in the last days of April, only to be turned around and made to retrace their steps.

Just before noon on the 2nd of May, the sergeants were nearing the town of Gudow, Germany with their group when they were brought to a halt by their escorts. Only a handful of guards remained with the column now. After realizing the futility of their duties, scores had either slinked away from the formation when the opportunity presented itself, or had fallen out, they themselves being just as depleted as the prisoners. To the airmen's surprise, the few Germans who did remain passed out tins of canned sardines and then motioned for the ragtag band to continue ahead, unescorted. Unsure and skeptical of the edgy gang of rifle-wielding Germans, the fliers eased down the path heading west, slowly increasing the distance between themselves and their skittish guards until they disappeared from view. After a few minutes of high-stepping it down the lane, the mechanized clatter of armored vehicles was heard fast approaching.

Abruptly recovering from the jubilancy generated in their hasty stroll to freedom, the sergeants froze where they stood, certain that they had just doomed themselves by walking directly into the path of a force of some retreating *Wehrmacht* panzers. Just then, one of the group shouted, "Look what's coming up the road!" The scraggly, dust-covered, sunken-eyed conglomeration of English and American boys stood in shock as a British armored element roared down the lane towards them. The tankers, equally as confounded by the chance meeting, stared down upon the swarming, dirty pack of bearded men whose clothes hung in tatters and rags from their boney frames. Unable to delay their advance and tend to their sick, dog-tired, and most importantly, newly liberated allies, the blokes in the tanks "...gave us the 'hi' sign and said just head back that-away." The men headed off, trotting with a new-found energy towards Allied lines at Luneburg, 20 miles distant, where an advanced English base camp was located.

Failing to reach the camp by nightfall, Jim and his companions happened upon a derelict farm. As the sergeants were preparing to bed down in the barn for the night, the door swung open, and in stepped two men in uniform, the pair pausing in the flickering candlelight. To their disbelief, a couple of German infantry soldiers had unexpectedly stumbled upon the potentially valuable cache of Allied boys and now stood glaring at the gang of dumbfounded gunners. Without exchanging any words, the airmen eyeballed the Germans as they arranged themselves opposite their group, organized their gear, and then sunk down in the hay. Geg recognized that these soldiers meant no harm. "They were scared of us and we were scared of them," he remembered. Still eyeing their counterparts suspiciously, the Americans settled in and attempted to get a few hours of rest. It was their first night of freedom in over seven months, and they spent it sleeping peacefully beside the enemy. Upon waking, Gegenheimer watched the pair of Germans wander off into the countryside but not before removing their tunics and leaving behind their helmets, trappings, and rifles. "They were trying to get away", he recognized. "They commandeered some farm clothes 'cause the war was over for them too." Aware of their inevitable defeat and fearing retaliation by the Soviets, it was apparent that they, too, were seeking the safety of American or British lines.

Later that day, after living on the road and sleeping in fields, barns, and animal pens for a total of 86 days, Lou, George, Pete, and Jim reached Luneburg and unceremoniously walked into Allied frontlines. Awestruck soldiers directed the muddy collection to hastily constructed tents where Army personnel coated the fliers in delousing powder. Ushered off to the showers, the *Hornets'* gunners peeled off their faded, ragged uniforms and loitered under warm water that ran brown with the dirt and grime from hundreds of miles of marching. A shave with a new razor followed; quite a treat considering the combines had been sharing a single, dull blade while in the stockade. Once fresh-faced, they dressed in new uniforms, and meandered to the field kitchen, having followed the fragrant aromas of hot chow. To their annoyance, the cooks restricted them from scarfing down additional servings to prevent them from gorging. With their bellies fuller than they had been in months, the airmen waddled to their tents and fell into a deep slumber on cots trimmed with clean sheets and lumpy pillows.

For the next few days, the men recuperated, wrote letters to their families, and sought medical treatment for their injuries and ailments. They caught up on news of the progress of the War by skimming over news articles and magazines, but signs of the decline of their adversary, was visible firsthand, reported Gegenheimer. "At one point we saw the biggest conglomeration of troops-thousands of Germans had surrendered." Just days prior, some among these fragments of the last of Hitler's once-irresistible legions had gazed down upon this group of airmen with contempt as they scurried along the backroads of Northern Germany to elude the oncoming Allied tsunami. Now it was the American sergeants who stared back, but this time there was little animosity to be seen in the eyes of the victors.

As the gunners waited to be moved by truck to a collection camp for liberated prisoners situated at Le Havre, France, more men from Stalag Luft IV began arriving. The feeling of jubilation rose with the appearance of each new gaunt face, but Lou couldn't help but be shocked by the number of those missing from his lager. He pointed out that, "The reason this journey became a death march was that out of the 2000 men who began the march, we were down to about 300 at the end." Part of Lou Lehere's experience was summed up in Paul Cashdollar's book, *In Harm's Way: Stories of American Prisoners of War in Germany.*

> *We scratched lice, suffered from sickness and disease, and marched some more. We lived in filth, sleeping wherever we could find shelter, in a barn or a chicken coop, or anywhere. We were always subject to aerial strafing's while we were marching. As the Allied armies moved, they kept moving us until we had marched about 600 miles.*

On their third night at Luneburg, the *Green Hornets*, along with one British chum from Stalag Luft IV, slinked away from the camp, ironically the former POWs first breakout, and made their way to an adjacent airfield where the ragtag lot convinced an RAF aircrew for a lift. The "Tommies" stowed the Americans aboard their bomber and ferried the chuckling, exuberant boys to Belgium where they joined in the Victory in Europe celebrations on the 8th of May. A couple of jubilant, blurry, headache-filled days later, the sergeants secured another ride, this time flying from Brussels to one of the US airfields in England. In hopes of returning to the States by the most expeditious route, the newly-emancipated and conspicuously unaffiliated fliers tried to push their luck once more. As the unofficial representative and easy-going ringleader of the non-coms, Lehere made a respectable attempt to smooth-talk the operation staff at the airfield into moving the lot back to the US by airplane. AAF staff saw right through the ploy and denied the request. Now alerted to these four long-haired strangers who sported mixed uniforms, roamed the installation aimlessly, and guzzled bottles of Coca-Cola until they were nauseated only to fall asleep in the grass around the control tower, it was apparent that these characters were very much in the wrong place. Following a few puzzling phone calls between USAAF command staff, the administration officers had the gunners escorted to a transport plane. Amidst a flood of protests ripe with colorful language from the carefree bomber boys, the sergeants were loaded onto the aircraft and sent back to the other side of the Channel.

Lou, Pete, George, and Jim were shuttled to Camp Lucky Strike, one of the "cigarette camps" established by the US military to handle troop demobilization and, by year's end, nearly 75,000 former "Guests of the Reich". The men were run through a gauntlet of medical examinations, including blood and urine tests, x-rays, and, not surprisingly, more dreaded inoculations. Medical staff continued to monitor the GI's food intake, especially their access to the caches of doughnuts provided by the Red Cross and the unlimited supply of milkshakes that flowed freely at the mess hall. They were debriefed and interviewed by intelligence staff whose inquiries were primarily annoying, redundant, and, for many, reopened the mental and emotional trauma of some of the worst days of their lives.

At last, word came that the men would be trucked to Le Havre where the "Liberty Ships" that would take them west across the Atlantic, sat at dock. For the *Green Hornets* gunners: boys who upon volunteering had picked an airplane over a foxhole, their experience in the Air Corps had been one hell-of-a-jaunt.

22

THE JONES BOYS

9 June 1944
0905 hours
24,000 feet above San Giorgio di Nogaro, Italy

With the sun still hovering low in the east, Liberators of the 459th Bomb Group were being hammered by the Luftwaffe in the skies over northeastern Italy. It was from out of that blazing ball of fire that the Germans had pounced upon the B-24s, the ship that the fliers referred to as the "flying coffin" and, if their adversary had any say in it this day, a fitting moniker indeed. The violence had come quick, generating a frenzy of confusion amongst the US aircrews as the assailants cast shell and cannon fire into the shimmering ranks of the twin-tailed, four-motored beasts. Just as the formation of lumbering bombers began to come apart, jeopardizing the day's business in Munich, American P-51 fighter planes whined from out of the heavens and plunged into the whirling mess of Me 109s. Saddled in new Mustangs and sporting their iconic red tails, the American escort was provided by two squadrons from the 332nd Fighter Group. For the next hour, these black fighter pilots engaged their opposites in a fierce dogfight resulting in the Americans scoring multiple flaming victories and sending their leftovers scurrying away. That day, just as a shepherd tends to his flock, the Tuskegee airmen helped see the 15th Army Air Forces' bombers through to their target and home again. Even so, as a sacrifice, two of the Group's Liberators had been lost to the wolves; both giants and their mortal haul, shot out of the sky.

One of the B-24s that had been thrashed from the formation was seen spiraling down over the coastline of the Adriatic Sea. The bombardier of that aircraft, flying his inductive combat flight where he had been longing for the opportunity to drop his first bomb load, managed to free himself from the burning Liberator, landing under a full parachute in German-occupied Italy. The 2nd lieutenant was apprehended by Axis ground forces, moved by rail to Germany, interrogated and absorbed into the prisoner of war camp system. After being shifted around various facilities, the lieutenant arrived at Stalag XIIID, a camp at Nuremberg reserved for Allied Army and USAAF officers. The Germans had long utilized the area as parade and rally grounds for devout Nazis who flocked to the centrally located ancient Bavarian town by the tens of thousands. Immense neo-classical-inspired Reich's-party buildings had been erected southeast of the city, and vast plots of the adjacent countryside were cleared and improved to make way for an expanse of ceremony fields, training sites, and campgrounds; all dedicated to Hitler's vanity and megalomania.

After eight long months as a POW at Nuremberg, the lieutenant happened upon a new addition to the camp; a slim, dark-haired man who wore a warm, familiar smile. Bandages covered the man's left hand and as he moved through the compound, the bombardier picked up on the hint of a slight hobble in the stranger's gait. The two men stood in shock, then embraced as other kriegies gathered nearby, observing the emotional reunion as it unfolded, although only a few among them were aware of and appreciated the miraculous stroke of good fortune, the rare twist of fate playing out before them. By sheer luck, the men, two brothers named Larkin and Frank Jones, would spend the remainder of their confinement in German prisoner of war camps together, side by side.

Frank had been cut loose of the hospital in Meiningen in the middle of a frosty February after German staff had determined that his injuries had been treated sufficiently. Unlike his pilots, Jones' wounds had not qualified him for repatriation and instead, he was transferred to the Nuremberg camp to wait out the War. It was here at this "dirty, nasty place" where rats could be seen pawing down the walls of the huts that Larkin had watched the camp's numbers swell in late December as prisoners arrived from the bloody clashes in the Ardennes. Food was sparse for the prisoners, as it was for the general German population, and the cuisine consisted primarily of black bread and soup. In the morning, the prisoners sipped on what was assumed to be the German's interpretation of coffee, although all agreed that the burnt-charcoal flavored fluid was a poor attempt. When kindling became sparse, desperate men fought back the bitterness of that exceptionally chilly winter that had gripped all of Europe by pulling

boards from the barracks' walls to use as fuel. Eagerly, they welcomed the gradual progression toward Spring and the conflict's finale.

In January, strategic sites around the town of Nuremberg were bombed for two weeks straight. With the British striking at night and the Americans by day, virtually all of the city, the once-great beacon of National Socialism, was completely leveled. As such, it was inevitable that the area immediately adjacent to the

Frank Jones, Jones Family Collection

stalag-the officers were kept in an "*Offizierlager*" or "Oflag", was peppered more than once by fragments from Allied bombs. One fellow imprisoned with Larkin remembered that they "...could see our bombers release their bombs, which would arch down over us and land in the city of Nuremberg". As the German defense batteries protested by heaving their projectiles at the attackers, splintered metal from the detonated shells also showered down upon the camp and its luckless inhabitants. Not all visits by the USAAF were destructive, though, as the kriegies were often treated to the sight of a magnificent "8", sometimes a "9", manifesting in the sky above the camp. These blatant, bold gestures were the creation of skywriting 8th and 9th Air Force fighter jocks, equipped with smoke markers, whose lofty artwork was generated to produce a sign of solidarity for their grounded brothers below.

General George Patton's 14th Armored Division had driven hard through France in early 1945, and by late March, it had crossed the Rhine and steamrolled southeast into the Reich. The purpose of the offensive was to destroy the remnants of the German military, liberating POW camps in central and southern Germany along the way. Stalag XIIID- the reprehensible Nuremburg facility, was one such camp. As Patton's tankers rolled on ahead and with an Allied victory becoming more probable with every mile put behind them, rumors spread across the Stalag concerning the fate of the prisoners. Some men believed that they were to be hidden in the Alps and used as cover or ransom by Hitler as his troops prepared to hole themselves up in the mountains. One thing that was certain among the Allied POWs was Hitler and Goebbels' attitude towards "*terrorfliegers*" and "*luftgangsters*": none of whom, as another story explained, would be permitted to leave the camps alive. When Patton's tanks tracked up to the camp's gates on April 16th, aiming to free the masses, they found the site troublingly empty.

Only days before, on April 6th, Frank, Larkin, and the balance of the camp's population-nearly 9,000 in number, had been forced to leave the camp. Sensing that the arrival of the Americans was imminent, the prisoners were rushed onto the road and set off in the opposite direction at a hurried pace. As the exigency of the situation diminished with distance, the guards grew far more relaxed as if leaving the deplorable conditions and their mundane, unsavory camp duties of the Stalag behind exercised all remaining bitterness and animosity. The guards did warn the kriegies to be on the lookout for the SS and Gestapo agents as they would shoot any roving, unaccompanied prisoners. Even worse, gangs of menacing Hitler Youth patrolled the roads and were said to maliciously attack groups of POWs-even those under guard, beating and throttling captives at will and without repercussion. The idea of running into one of these unlawful adolescent squads was intimidating to the German guards and prisoners alike, but as long as the kriegies rejoined the camp each evening, they were given leeway to leave the column to rest, trade, and forage.

Like their brethren who had completed the winter of '45 "Death March" in Northern Germany, the Nuremberg kriegies slept in the open much of the time, completely exposed to winter conditions and rain. On the rare occasion, a church, barn, storage hut, or woodshed made their nights far more tolerable, as did the coming of Spring. They, too, had been mistaken for enemy troop formations and attacked by friendly fighter aircraft tasked with cleaning up the countryside of what was left of German resistance.

On rare occasion, bread-filled military trucks intercepted the column and unloaded *ersatzbrot*, and, though occurring infrequently, stacks of food parcels awaited the group at random points along the route. Besides augmenting their scant supply of rations and filling their bellies with just enough calories to fuel another leg of their journey, the parcels provided items to barter. At more than one village, inhabitants met the ragged line of soldiers and airmen with a cup of vegetable soup and set up impromptu bread stations. The generosity was much appreciated by the weary boys; even to those who believed the portions had been prepared less out of goodwill or charity and more out of the desire to soften the hatred of their enemy who was at present, their captives, but would soon be their conquerors. Whatever the intention of their civilian hosts, the Americans could find no malevolence in the Bavarian spectacle as they trekked along the Autobahn- the stunning panorama being a considerable shift from views from behind barbed wire.

About twenty-five miles outside Munich lay the small community of Moosburg. Frank's group came within sight of the twin towers of the town's cathedral late in the afternoon on the 17th of April, where, just beyond the village, an immense complex of nearly ninety fenced-in acres, called Stalag VIIA, was positioned. Unexpectedly, when the wearied, soil-covered multitude reached the massive camp, the prisoners were re-routed away from the compound. Rumors of their impending demise had circulated upon leaving Nuremberg and had all but died out during the march, but now, as the column was directed away from the Stalag along a discreet, secluded country road, the gossip, and with it, their apprehensions, only increased. Stories of the dreadful Dachau concentration camp had circulated through the ranks as the men had moved south but were considered by most to be little more than a morbid, albeit provocative, yarn. Now, with the "death camp" nearby, and as their German counterparts pushed them along the country back lanes, many airmen contemplated the possibilities.

After five or six miles of shuffling, the men were led to a stark brick structure, complete with what appeared to be a series of holding cells. After droves of fliers filed into the large chambers, each equipped with piping running along the ceiling and illuminated by a small, sealed window, the suspense of the situation lifted as water dribbled and then rained from the lines overhead. Their first proper soak in six months, the deluge washed away many of the men's anxieties-at least for the moment-along with weeks of dirt, soot, and filth that they had accumulated while on the long walk from Nuremberg. After their wash and a delousing, guards steered the group back to their new home at Stalag VIIA.

The camp, described as a "nightmare" by some of its unlucky guests, was originally designed to house 10,000 Allied POWs. By the time Frank and Larkin reached Moosburg, the compound was bulging far beyond capacity and was home to men from every nation of the Allied coalition. Only a fortunate few were able to secure a bed in the triple-decker wooden bunks, although fleas, lice, and bedbugs infested every gunnysack mattress. The majority curled up on the grimy floor below, spread out upon a table, or slept outside in one of the crowded tents. Every day the men were met with a pitiful helping of boiled potatoes or turnips, revolting watery soup, and dehydrated vegetables: more "green death" and, inescapably, the detestable black bread. Prevalent throughout all of the camps, dysentery and diarrhea plagued the captives but when combined with comorbidities like chronic dehydration and severe infections, the consequences were horrific and often fatal. The slit-trench latrines were always full, both of men afflicted with intestinal distress who had stood for hours in the never-ending queue and of volumes of putrid filth and stinking human waste. The sport of flee-flicking consumed much of the day as the men settled themselves on the ground around their huts and tents. Assuming the position, they proceeded to launch hundreds of these scoundrels from their clothes and straw mattresses during the day only to detect a small army of the buggers jumping across their boney chests and concaved stomachs by nightfall.

With the arrival of the new multitude of prisoners came gossip of approaching Allied troops and a good deal of nervousness for the prisoners as the thoughts of freedom or their potential execution tormented them. On April 28th, US infantry and armor were positioned only four miles from Moosburg and scrapped with remnants of panzer and infantry units. The town was strategically significant not only because of the prisoner camp, which Allied airplanes routinely buzzed, wagging their wings in a sign of recognition and support, all to the exuberant cheers of the kriegies, but it was also a vital road juncture and river crossing. The following morning a German proposal of armistice brought two senior American officers to the camp's main gate under a cease-fire agreement for a conference. The prisoners gawked at the two US commanders, one of whom glanced back at the haggard but optimistic faces staring at him from behind the wire. "You guys better find a hole. The war is about to start," he pronounced. At the meeting's conclusion, the American delegation confidently rejected the proposition, and the parties went their separate ways.

Soon after, small arms fire broke out in the woodlands encircling the Stalag. Errant rounds could be heard whizzing through the camp, prompting some to seek cover by diving into recessions in the earth. Others, thinking their liberation imminent, ducked and scrambled from their huts, now pockmarked with stray bullet holes, to the sinks where, with gritted teeth, they pulled a dull razor over their scruffy faces and raked in their matted hair. With the rattle of the fight escalating, hundreds of kriegies rushed to the perimeter fence-

Stalag VIIA newly-liberated POWs, 29 April 1945, USAF Academy

previously a clear invitation for the guards to dispatch the trespassers, but now just an annoyance to the distracted and edgy Germans. Gripping the wire between the rusty prongs and spurs, the airmen taunted their captors, advising that they should "...throw their guns down and come on in and be with us and safe..."

Following a swift and decisive battle, American troops took charge of the fields surrounding the Moosburg. A detachment of armored infantry made their way to the Stalag where the remaining guards swiftly conceded to the overwhelming US force. When a Sherman tank was driven, quite literally, through the Stalag's wire fences, a "...crazy bunch of ragged ass people" engulfed the tank and swarmed the liberators. A celebration ensued as a crescendo of roaring voices spread across the complex when the Nazi Swastika banner was pulled from the flagpole and up went "Old Glory", hoisted high above the camp. The sight of the Stars and Stripes fluttering in the breeze brought all-not just the Americans but tens of thousands of British, French, and others of various nationalities, to a proud position of teary-eyed attention. Later, General Patton himself made an appearance at the compound. Standing tall in his jeep, armed with his trademark six-shooter revolvers, and noticeably outraged by the condition of the masses cheering before him, the General vowed, "We will whip the bastards all the way to Berlin." For the next week, Frank, Larkin, and the remainder of Stalag VII's former prisoners were fed, deloused, registered, and medically evaluated before being evacuated to repatriation camps near Le Havre, France.

While the reuniting of the Jones brothers was far from an isolated coincidence during the war, the incident was no less incredible. Still, the event would have been even more astounding if a third Jones boy, Laurie, had not fallen sick just before D-day. Illness had prevented Laurie Jones from being deployed to England with his regiment to partake in the pursuits that followed the Allied invasion at Normandy. Instead, he was transferred from the unit and remained stateside, serving the war effort from across the ocean. He followed the progress of his former regiment, though, now attached to Patton's 14th Armored Division, from the time it began blasting its way out of southern France in October of 1944. After six months of hard fighting, Laurie's comrades were among the first soldiers to break into the enormous prisoner of war camp outside Moosburg, Germany, where over an estimated 100,000 Allied fliers and soldiers were liberated on April

Newspaper clipping of the Jones boys, Jones Collection

29th. Among the magnitude freed by his former unit were his brothers, Lt. Larkin Jones, and Flight Officer Frank Jones.

23
LIFE BEYOND WAR

From L to R: Irving Metzger, Frank Jones, George Ostrowski, James Gegenheimer

Not unlike many of his companions, Irving Metzger came home shaken by his encounters with war and captivity. From February 1945 until the summer of 1946: fifteen long, agonizing months, he received treatment for his wounds, first at Halloran Army Hospital, then at Walter Reed in Maryland, and finally at Valley Forge in Pennsylvania. Surgeons evaluated the lieutenant's damaged hands, which were absent all digits after being amputated at Obermassfeld and concluded that additional operations were necessary to aid in proper healing. As a result, a bone graft was taken from the 22-year-old's hip and transplanted onto a hand, fashioning what his son remembered as being similar to a "lobster claw". He returned to school, attended New York University, and earned a bachelor's degree in advertising.

While in recovery, Irving met Phyllis Ellis. The couple married and welcomed a daughter and one son and, as time passed, they were blessed with many grandchildren. Regardless of his dreadful ordeal beginning in 1944, Irving did find value in his time in the military. He took pride in being an Army pilot and cherished his friendship with Frank Jones, always trying to make a detour to his old navigator's home in Alabama when on family vacations south. Clearly motivated by his own battles, Irving was a passionate and dedicated advocate for the disabled. Phyllis preceded Irving in death, the old aviator himself passing at his home in Clearbrook, New Jersey, on January 23, 2013.

Frank Jones was struck with bouts of depression and anxiety after returning to the States in the summer of 1945. For a man to have gone through such a momentous ordeal, Frank was not known to hold any bitterness towards his crew, his captors, or a Higher Power; a testament to the man's outstanding character. The only thing he did loath, his family remembers, was pumpernickel bread as the black bake good evoked terrible memories of the unpalatable, grainy ersatz fare that was a staple in his diet as a POW. The ex-navigator returned to school but, now unable to properly manipulate the tools through the fine movements required of the trade, was unable to pursue a career in dentistry. Nevertheless, Frank did not sit idle long as he would graduate with a degree in Chemical Engineering, earned from Auburn, and he would go on to work for Monsanto for nearly thirty years. During that time, he and his wife, Miriam, moved around the South before settling in Montgomery.

Working for a time in management, Jones requested new duties after being delegated the unsavory responsibility of having to terminate an employee. He was all the warrior but also an incredibly empathetic man, always committed to his fellows. Frank and Miriam lived a charmed life and welcomed two children along the way, and their relationship is remembered as a model of love and devotion. Sadly, Miriam passed on in 1988 after a battle with cancer and her death hit the family hard, Frank most of all. He would later meet, fall in love with and marry Dorothy "Dot" Browder, "a great, strong Southern lady" who had two daughters of her own from a previous marriage. Besides being a devoted Christian and dedicated partner, she was instrumental in helping to care for Frank through his declining years and diminishing health.

Frank Jones died on November 18th, 2001. Dot would pass in 2015. Grandchildren remember the brave navigator displaying his scars like a badge of honor, a visual reminder of his sacrifices and service to the country. "I remember very clearly at his funeral, my dad being very upset that the mortician covered his hand with his jacket sleeve" recalls a grandson. "Dad reached in and rolled up the sleeve to show the hand as he felt that his dad would not have wanted it to seem as if he was hiding it."

For the remainder of his life, Lou Lehere would suffer a painful stomach disorder that he believed was due either to trauma sustained in the mid-air collision, a hypoxic event, or a combination of the two. Likewise, the deplorable conditions and persistent lack of adequate nourishment that existed in Stalag Luft IV, not to mention the "Death March" of '45, hadn't help the ailment either. Equally as problematic, the flight engineer was prone to recurrent vivid and disturbing dreams. Although his actions on September 11th were entirely reasonable, Lou feared that his crew, especially his pilot, believed that he had abandoned them. "I could have helped him out", he lamented just a few years before his death in 2001. Even though the decision continued to haunt him, Lou's guilt was entirely unfounded. In fact, all six of his surviving crewmembers would have nothing but endearing things to say about the sergeant who they knew to be a great man, a valued, dependable crewmate, and a wonderful friend.

Jane Lehere, like many of the wives of the men of the *Green Hornets* and those of countless other American soldiers, sailors, airmen, and marines, was influential in helping her traumatized serviceman adapt and shift back to civilian life. The handsome couple had three sons and would settle down on a fifty-acre farm in the rolling fields outside of West Sunbury, Pennsylvania where the combat veteran and former POW resumed his work at the American Rolling Mill Company. By the time he retired, he had given thirty-six years to the business. Lou was also an active member of the American Legion and found great satisfaction in supporting the local veteran community. Jane passed away in 1999 following fifty-five years of loving marriage. Louis would share only a few of his war experiences with his boys, unpretentiously wishing to leave much of his incredible odyssey in the past. Strangely enough, the 1911 US Army Remington pistol, issued to the gunner in the summer of '44, never found its way back to the US Army. On a side note, one of the gunner's sons holds in his possession a beautiful 1911 US Army Remington pistol, one, many might say, remarkably similar to the weapon issued to his father during the War.

On June 13th, 1945, Pete Riley finally set foot back on US soil. Still recovering from his time as a "kriegie", Army physicians

continued to monitor his health until October when he was discharged from the service and returned home to Philadelphia. As was the case with many veterans after the War, Pete was eager to resume the life he had before enlisting, although confinement in the lazaretts and stalags left a lasting impact on the man. "My dad was very worried about food insecurity" recalls one daughter, "not because his family didn't have enough food...[i]t was because of his time as a POW." In January 1946 Peter married Natalie Usher and the pair raised six kids who fondly reminisce on their father's love of golf, Hawaiian music, and unbridled passion for life. The

Natalie and Peter Riley, 1946, Espinoza Collection

Rileys lived well into their sixties, eventually relocating to the West Coast where they now rest in peace alongside each other under a marker that reads: "Given to us by God to teach us the meaning and strength of love", in Escondido, California.

After nearly a year apart, Jim Gegenheimer and Mary Lee quickly picked up where they had left off. While the heroic-yet-unassuming gunner ground through the misery of September '44, the months in captivity at Stalag Luft IV, and the four months on the road that followed, Mary Lee endured a war of her own. In the end, the happenings of 1944 to '45 only reinforced the couple's affection for one another, and on May 31, 1947, the beautiful pair wed. They would spend the next sixty-two years at each other's side, during which they raised four children and proudly enjoyed many grandchildren. Jim loved leading his sons on hunting and fishing adventures but, despite being a nature lover, exhibited a terrible fear of dogs-the angst resulting from the aggressive Alsatians and Dobermans that stalked the Stalag and circled his hut nightly in Poland in 1944. Loved and respected by his family, crewmates, and the Gretna community, he was also an adopted hero of the Green family. One of Jim's grandchildren, named in honor of the courageous airman, would follow the gunner's footsteps and serve with distinction in the United States Air Force.

As the Gegenheimers and Greens began settling into family life in the fall of 1945, Rose played middleman between the pilot and gunner as her husband dealt with his feelings of shame and embarrassment with the accident.

Hello Geg,

It was good to hear from you. And that photo of you-we go for that. I'm counting on it to even keep the collectors out. You should see you propped up on the desk, you and the rest of the crew and the B-17s! I'm sure our little ones will have wings somewhere. Speaking of little ones and I will[,] the little Green should be here about the last of the month. Can you imagine Merle dashing 'round for diapers? Geg, I sure wish it were possible for you to visit us. Any chance? Anytime will do. Why don't you hop something and come on up? Merle will take you buzzing in something. Geg, it would mean so much for him to see you and talk with you…

Regards,
Rose

A few months later, as the momentous year of 1945 was coming to an end, Jim opened another letter from the Greens. He pulled out a wrinkled, folded sheet of paper from the envelope and read:

Dear Geg,

This is my first attempt at writing with my right hand. It's a little rough but maybe you can make it out. Thanks for the picture, it is swell. I'll send you one of mine just as soon as they are ready. By the way I recommended both you and George for the DFC [Distinguished Flying Cross] for what you did when

*we had our collision. I am still in [the Army Air Forces] but
home for now.*

Barely discernable in the remaining paragraph of faintly
scratched cursive letters, Merle then abruptly ended the note with,
"This looks like hell doesn't it". Eyeing the scrawling, Jim flipped over
the wrinkled piece of paper and recognized more writing:

*Geg, after writing this Merle crumpled it up and threw it away
disgusted but I think its wonderful writing for his right hand.
I've been carrying it around all this time-Thought you might like
it. I'm pretty proud of this being his first writing.*

After struggling to hold the pencil in his wrecked right hand
and manipulate it to his satisfaction, Merle, frustrated, had rashly
crushed the paper into a ball and tossed it in the waste bin. Rose found
the letter, salvaged it, and secretly forwarded it to the delighted ball
turret gunner who genuinely appreciated his friend's attempt.

The meeting that Rose had requested for the two war buddies
failed to materialize for quite some years until, in 1952, Merle made the
venture south to visit Mary Lee and Jim in New Orleans. While the
visit was a delight and long overdue, Jim found it hard to look at his
friend's war injury. Little was mentioned about their trials in Germany,
but Merle did make one comment that stuck with the gunner. Unable
to look his friend in the eye, Merle confessed, "Maybe if I had turned
over controls to Metzger after the bomb run I might have seen the
other plane and we could have avoided the collision." Jim tried to
downplay his pilot's remorse and ease his worries, telling Green to
forget the idea and asserting that no one was to blame. Nothing more
was said about the crash between the two that evening, or ever again
in fact. Although the trio enjoyed their reunion, Gegenheimer found
himself unsettled by his friend's remark and couldn't help but sense
that something disturbing was lurking deep inside the man.

Jim was also not to be left unscathed by the events and
decisions of that day in September 1944. Plagued by his own self-
imposed transgressions, in the winter of 1945, he wrote Rose asking
for her advice regarding how to respond to the Hatfields, who had
been pressuring him for the specifics of their son's death. Jim found it
difficult to recall those last dreadful moments with his crewmate and

still felt regret and a sense of shame over his decision to push the incapacitated teenager out of the crippled aircraft. Rose offered the following:

> *About telling [the] Hatfields about Sid. I think you should. I've tried to get Merle to write them but Geg, whenever he hears their names he still cries about them. …Isn't this a strange Christmas? I know I never appreciated it before. Bet you do plenty of remembering that last one.*

Sadly, correspondence between the Greens and Gegenheimers would gradually become less frequent. Eventually, the annual Gegenheimer Christmas card returned to the family's Gretna home, unopened and stamped with "return to sender" postmarks. Unknown to Mary Lee and Jim, marriage issues had caused the Greens to separate, and their relocation and subsequent disappearance caused Jim decades of heartache. It wasn't until the 1990s when he received word of the deaths of his friends, their passing coming over ten years before. In a letter addressed to Merle's daughter and reestablishing a line of communication with his friend's family, Geg wrote:

> *I want you to know that your Father and Mother were wonderful people and my best friends and I have agonized for over 30 years because I could not locate them and continue our friendship. I can't help but think that your Father's horrible war experiences had to be the cause of your Mother and Father's post-war marital problems. I grieve because I just found out about their early deaths, but we all must take courage and believe that a just and forgiving God has taken them to Heaven and everlasting happiness. I can only close by telling you in all honesty that your Father and Mother were two of the finest people I ever met.*

Jim's wonderful Mary Lee, always loving and selfless, joined Rose and Merle in 2009. When Jim went to be with the Lord in December 2014, along with his two friends, Mary Lee was undoubtedly eagerly awaiting her flier's arrival.

George Ostrowski separated from the military in November 1945. Like every member of the crew, Ostrowski was awarded the Purple Heart for wounds he had sustained in combat but George, perhaps wanting to forget the turmoil of the past or feeling undeserving, ended up throwing his medal away. Although he had been injured while on a mission, what was not noted in his military record was the abuse and trauma that the sergeant had suffered during his time imprisoned at the interrogation center, while in Poland, and on the march across Germany. As a result, George would be prone to occasional "blackouts" and "convulsive seizures" for the rest of his life- a physiological souvenir doled out by the butts of German rifles during his time in the prison camp.

After he was discharged from the USAAF, George proposed to Helen Karpinski. The two wed, creating a loving union that lasted 56 years and produced two daughters. He enjoyed a successful career as an electrician, having built a reputation throughout his community for supplying exceptional, dependable service. Even the Milwaukee Sentinel couldn't help but describe him as "the sweetest guy in town". The paper had interviewed the former waist gunner about an instance when the Ostrowskis received a check for a service that George had

Green Hornets reunion

completed for a woman from the community. While the bill was $25, the check that she wrote was for the sum of $726; an extremely costly oversight that not only would have emptied the customer's account but one that elicited inquiry from Helen regarding George's "services". Ostrowski calmly explained the misunderstanding to his wife and gladly returned the check to the owner, politely noting that she had overpaid "only a little". The Mighty 8th veteran would pass away on the second of July 2001, at 79 years old.

Two months after being removed from the crew and sent to the 15th Air Force, Paul Klekot was flying with the 99th Bomb Group. He would serve with the unit until the end of the War, flying 27 sorties out of Italy as a togglier and aerial gunner. When he returned to the States, he settled with Valerie in Woonsocket and took up work at a local mill. In the 1950s, the couple left for Philadelphia but separated a few years later after having three children. Estranged from Valerie and the kids, Paul would wander south and spend the remainder of his days in the warmth of the Florida Keys. Valerie Klekot would pass on in 2009. As of the writing of this book, Paul's whereabouts and circumstances remain unknown.

Unquestionably a bittersweet gift, Sidney Hatfield's family gathered around the arrival of the gunner's personal effects late in '44 to sorrowfully comb through the items. Theodore gently set aside his son's New Testament, as well as a small camera that held a few frozen moments of the boy's great adventure. He also laid out a pair of air force gunner's flying wings that his son had proudly worn over his heart, along with a few books and a baseball mitt that the youngster had smuggled away in his gear bag before deploying to England. As if the gunner's death wasn't hard enough to bear, Sidney's body was still lost somewhere in Germany as the War entered its last months. In a letter to the Army, Theodore Hatfield wrote:

> *Sgt. Sidney I. Hatfield was just out of high school, was not married, was only 19 years of age when the army got him…I have received many of his personal belongings and if can be found want him returned after the war is over.*

Two and a half years would pass before the Hatfields would receive notification that Sid's body had, at last, been found. His skeletal remains were carefully lifted out of Russdorf cemetery soil on the night of January 8, 1948, under the supervision of a Russian disinterment team. Sgt. Hatfield was then relocated to the American Ardennes Cemetery in Neupre, Belgium. In mid-1949, at the family's request, the sergeant was exhumed once more and began his journey home to the US. Back on American soil, the tail gunner was escorted under military guard to Arlington National Cemetery, where he was buried on his birthday of June 22nd. He can be visited there today in section 34, site 4283.

It wouldn't be until the conclusion of the fighting in Germany that the search for the body of Jack Williams began. In conjunction with translated records from Dulag Luft and after reviewing additional German documents captured at War's end, the bombardier's remains were believed to be in the area of Gelnhausen, and in February 1946, Graves Registration units began looking into the report. A hunt for eyewitnesses followed, many of whom provided valuable clues, including a copy of a diary entry from a policeman who was at the scene of the crash and stood guard at the site in the following days. After being shown the graveyard, the team was drawn to an area where a weathered wooden cross stood, bearing the inscription "*hier ruht ein unbekannter amerikanischer soldat*". It was none other than Fritz Griessman who confirmed that the tomb was, in fact, the American flier pulled from the scorched B-17 bomber. The detail unearthed the airman, once again with the help of the locals, and transferred the skeletal remains to the Lorraine American Cemetery at St. Avold, France. There the body remained for two years until, at the request of Williams' mother, Carrie, the bombardier was re-interred in the American Ardennes Cemetery. 2nd Lt. Jack Williams is still there today, along with 5,321 other gallant Americans.

In 2009, at the age of 80, Gerhard Solzer passed away unexpectedly after a short illness. When the *Green Hornets* fell into Karl Koch's cornfield on the 11th of September 1944, Solzer was training to become a telecommunications technician; a role that he would dutifully carry out for, remarkably, the next 49 years. He and his loving wife, Olga, were blessed with three children and would remain in Lieblos, much-loved and admired by the community. A passionate footballer, Solzer's memorialized stint as goalie for the FC Victoria 1893 Lieblos, where he helped lead the team in a series of winning seasons, is still celebrated.

After graduation, Heinrich Goy worked as an industrial technician, promoting his way to the position of foreman for a large industrial company in Hanau am Main. Still going strong after celebrating his 93rd birthday in April 2022, Heinrich clearly remembers the events that he, as a schoolboy of 14, witnessed on the day that the *Green Hornets* arrived in the Kinzig Valley.

Six months after the fighting had ceased in Europe, authorities tracked down Oberstleutnant Aribert Bombach and Hauptmann Walter Pickhardt in Austria and arrested on reports of their "... organized reign of terror" at Stalag Luft IV. Both were brought before a War Crimes Committee but, astonishingly, the case was excused due to a lack of evidence. On the other hand, Hans Schmidt, the reprehensible guard known as "Big Stoop", would not escape justice. Following the liberation of the enormous POW camp outside of Moosberg in April of '45, eyewitnesses described seeing a group of ex-kriegies leaving the area where Schmidt's slaughtered body was later found. As it would seem, "Big Stoop's" deeds had apparently caught up to him as some of his tormented victims had relieved the ogre of his head and were observed carrying their prize off in a basket.

After returning to the States, Merle arranged an appointment with the Army liaison's office in Springfield and submitted an official deposition regarding the October 17th, 1944, incident involving his friend, Lloyd Carter, and the Luger brandishing "Gestapo Agent". The Army submitted Merle's testimony to the War Crimes Section of the Judge Advocate General's Office who welcomed the evidence, labeled it "secret", and added it to the stacks of similar reports that filled the docket of the Department's ongoing investigations. In July 1945, Lloyd mailed a thank you note to Merle and notified him that he had finally returned to the States and was dedicated to fattening himself up after his confinement at Meiningen and then Moosburg, where he was liberated on April 29th. Wasting no time, Carter married his love, Katherine Jones, immediately upon returning home to Oklahoma. Lloyd Carter died in 2001 at the age of 80, the bullet fragments from the Nazi slug still embedded in his face.

Two years after the end of the conflict, Karl Stoll, the man who had placed the bullet into the face of Lloyd Carter as he scrambled up the riverbank near Griesheim, Germany, would be summoned before a court at Dachau to answer for his actions. The adamant local Nazi labor leader professed that he was suffering from a traumatic brain injury at the time and that his mental angsts were the catalyst that caused the shooting of the unarmed, surrendered American pilot. However, due to the testimony of two German witnesses present on the day of the crime, Stoll was sentenced to ten years imprisonment. With the Americans wanting to heal war wounds between the two nations, Stoll would serve just over a year-and-a-half

Escorted under a military honor guard, the common burial

casket containing what were believed to be the remains of Charles Duda, Noman Tipton, Richard Bishop, Thomas Mazurkiewicz, Joseph Cunneen, and Edward Moore was interred in the Zachary Taylor National Cemetery in Kentucky on January 16th, 1950. The bodies of the balance of the crew: Thomas Kulak, John Caro, and Walter Howard, had been individually returned to the States beginning in 1947 and were laid to rest in their hometown cemeteries. Although records show that the crew's remains had been buried by German civilians in the days after the mid-air collision and finally recovered by a US Graves Registration unit at War's end, numerous irregularities exist within both German and American reports concerning the nine fliers and their recovery. Further research by the author, in collaboration with local historian Olaf Becher of Pegau, Germany who has conducted interviews with eyewitnesses present to the crash of *Daring Doris* outside of Audigast, Germany on the 11th of September 1944, reveals the possibility of an alternative fate of the some of the crew. Investigations into the event are ongoing.

After partaking in the post-war "Nickle Mission" drops and shuttling much-needed supplies to a ruined Germany, the 94th Bombardment Group remained at Station #468 until December 1945 when the unit was transferred back to the States and deactivated. During nearly three years of active operations in Europe, the Group launched 325 missions. One hundred fifty-six aircrews, a total of 1,453 men, had been lost in 68,153 hours of combat flight. The Group's "heavies" burnt over eight-and-a-half million gallons of gasoline during a period of operation that cost the 94th 2.6 million rounds of ammunition and 19,151 tons of bombs. After their departure, the RAF reassumed charge of the field until it was converted to a civil airport for light aircraft in 1948. It is still in active use to this day.

Three-quarters of a century past, East Anglian soil and fauna continue to slowly but steadily reclaim those 5,000 acres that lie between Bury St. Edmunds and the village of Rougham. Nonetheless, the hidden history still resurfaces from time to time, churned up by the machines of farmers or stumbled upon by history buffs and nature lovers exploring the peaceful countryside. "Chairleg", now absent the radio chatter and busied staff, can still be seen squatting over the airfield. Converted in the 1990s by the Rougham Tower Association, the construction stands as one of the best-preserved examples of USAAF WWII infrastructure in England. Most notably, it endures as a reminder of the sacrifices of the men and women of the USAAF, of the 94th Bomb Group, and of their English hosts who, together, weathered the storm of the Second World War and fought and gave their lives in the pursuit of freedom for untold millions and generations to come.

The "Lucky Bastards" of the 94th left behind many acquaintances and adopted families by the time the unit vacated the airfield at the end of 1945. Clifford Hall was one such friend, but it was not to be the last that he would see the Americans. Seven decades later, Cliff continues to advocate for his comrades in the 94th. His contributions and efforts were instrumental in the dedication of numerous memorials that can still be found around Rougham and "Bury". Even to this day, Hall continues to devote himself to protecting the memory of the Group and his extended family from "across the pond". He has authored two remarkable books, The Pictorial History of the Men and Aircraft of the 94th Bombardment Group (H) 1942-1945, and Memories of Rougham Airfield and the 94th Bombardment Group (H), each containing a wonderful collection of pictures and personal accounts that preserve the history of the unit. In 1975 the 94th Bomb Group Memorial Association was formed "...with the retention of wartime friendships and the recording of history as the prime goal." Over the years, the 94th BGMA organized several reunions and helped coordinate a few ventures back to East Anglia, where the former airmen paid a visit to that beloved "wide spot in the road".

Fred Koval arrived at Rougham in the fall of '43 and, amazingly, survived twenty-five grueling quests with the 94th BG. After completing a second combat tour and applying for a third, the USAAF banned him from further business in the ETO and sent him to the Pacific just as the conflict in the Far East was wrapping up. He would find himself back in Western Europe in the late '40s when he took part in the "Berlin Airlift". It wasn't until 1963 that then Lt. Colonel Koval retired from the US Air Force, but perhaps Fred's most triumphant undertaking was his 63 year-long "never-ending waltz" with his beloved Ann. The couple's romance would produce eight children. The Kovals relocated to Biloxi, Mississippi where, many years later, in the aftermath of Hurricane Katrina, much of the family's treasured possessions, including many of Fred's war ribbons, were lost. The old war hero passed on in 2016 at 94 years young.

Returning to his hometown of Bellingham, Washington after weathering his tour, Basil Pullar picked up work as a logger where he and his brother had labored before answering the call-to-arms. Pullar settled into civilian life and married Kathryn Hunt. The couple welcomed a son and lived out their days in the Pacific Northwest where Basil enjoyed fishing in the cool waters of Chuckanut Creek. In 1993, at 75 years old, Basil Pullar passed on. Two years later, Kathryn followed her husband and was buried alongside him in an unmarked grave in a community cemetery.

On the 6th of October 1944, Merritt Fausnaugh was killed during a strike on an industrial target. Passing over Berlin, his *Sassy Suzy* had been ripped apart moments after the bomb run, losing its vertical stabilizer and suffering an explosion in the nose compartment that annihilated his navigator and co-pilot in the process. Mortally wounded himself, Merritt somehow found the superhuman strength to hold the ship steady long enough for the crew-those who remained, to flee the dying Fortress before it careened into German farmland. When official word finally reached his heartbroken family, Merritt's brother was heard to remark, "I'm going to go over there and personally kick Hitler's ass". He enlisted the following day and was sent off to training but to the family's relief, the War ended before his deployment. Remembered as "the best of us" by his loved ones, Merritt was returned to the US and buried amongst family in Sparta, Indiana. Among the pilot's personal items and keepsakes left behind in his bunk at Rougham after his last fateful mission was a picture of his infant son, a boy he would never meet, born only six weeks before his premature death.

"He was the greatest man ever!" remembers a grandson of the bold American aviator, Robert Hall. The lieutenant returned home from the greatest, most destructive conflict in human history finished with fighting and dying and war. Upon completing his tour with the 94th, he had distributed 97.5 tons of explosives over thirty-five combat launches on German targets. As an acknowledgment for his bravery and sacrifice, he had been awarded a Flying Cross and multiple Air Medals: befitting honors for a young man who had perfected his craft and departed the Air Force as a model pilot. Even so, Robert was fully confident that it was not of his own doing, but that it was only by the hand of God that brought him home each mission. After completing his last assignment on March 9th, 1945, Hall resolved himself to never again fly in combat- a vow that he still upheld when the Air Force came calling for experienced officers during the Korean War. Instead, Robert relocated to Dallas from Kansas City, Missouri with his wife, Terry, and enjoyed a long life working for Drexel Heritage Furniture. The pair raised two kids, one son and a daughter. Robert Hall would take to heavenly skies on the 8th of August 2002.

The day before the 94th's own General Castle was killed on Christmas Eve, 1944, Antolin Algorri, a navigator in the 332nd Bomb Squadron, completed his thirty-fifth and final mission with the 8th Air Force. "Praise the Lord and drop the bombs," he scribbled in his wartime diary after his last flight featuring a heated scrap between the 94th and the legendary Luftwaffe. Algorri reentered service in 1948, electing to take a cut in rank to, once again, serve his country. His dedication and sacrifice would endure beyond the Second World War as he flew B-29s in Korea. He completed 56 missions before the end of the conflict and then served on the crew of a B-52 bomber during Vietnam, racking up another 16 flights over hostile territory. After being under enemy fire for countless hours during his career, Al would walk away from the service with only a minor flak wound-one he received while high above Merseburg, Germany in July of '44, along with the rank of Lt. Colonel. One nephew, Ernie Algorri, fondly remembers his uncle Antolin, who passed away in 1997 as "...a devout catholic, and a quiet, humble man of wisdom and compassion who was the embodiment of loyalty, duty, and integrity." When war broke in Europe and the Pacific, he, along with his four brothers: all Spanish immigrants, enlisted in the US Armed Forces. Ernie would establish the Ernest Algorri Sr. Memorial Scholarship at Loyola Law School for veterans in honor of his father and four uncles.

Morton Kimmel, a 332nd bombardier, returned home to Pennsylvania after carrying out thirty-five charges over Europe. Finally home, the lieutenant renewed his focus on his education, using the GI bill to attend college. In 2016, Kimmel was one of the surviving veterans tracked down after filmmakers remastered William Wyler's footage from "*The Memphis Belle: A Story of a Flying Fortress*" with the aims of producing a documentary. Kimmel's fascinating interview can be seen throughout this exceptional film, titled "*The Cold Blue*". After sitting for her first viewing of the documentary, Kimmel's wife, Edith, joked, "you're a star!" "Oh yeah, I'm a star", replied the modest airman, downplaying the valiant deeds he had performed as "a kid", nearly eight decades before. Those who are lucky enough may just find themselves admiring Mr. Kimmel's collection of cotter pins; one for each of the missions he survived, beginning after his arrival in the days following D-Day until December 1944. Certainly, the 94th's armament personnel are still awaiting the return of those misplaced fuse pins.

On March 24, 2021, at 97 years old, Morton Kimmel passed away peacefully while in the company of his loved ones. Despite all the unfortunate events he had witnessed during his combat tour, Kimmel was known for always being delighted to talk about his time in the "Mighty Eighth". In a conversation with the author in November 2020, Kimmel remarked:

Morton Kimmel, Voight Collection

I always said that this is an experience that I was fortunate, lucky enough to get through, and I did not want my son or grandson to play any part of it in anything like it when they were of age.

At the conclusion of the interview, one of multiple, wonderful opportunities that this writer was blessed to have had with Mr. Kimmel, the humble warrior was sure to add, "I often said when I was asked 'would you do it again?' …and I honestly said…'not for a million dollars!'"

24

ALL THE EVIL AND ALL THE GOOD YOU DO

All the evil and all the good you do, you do to yourself.
-Rose Marie Green

18 July 1945
Judge Advocate General Office
Springfield, Illinois

Q[uestioner]. How did you come to be captured?

M[erle Green]. We were involved in a midair collision with another crippled bomber, two engines knocked out and on fire. I gave the order to bail out but found that two boys' chutes were knocked clear of the ship. Then I crash landed.

Q. What happened then?

M. We were captured within about 2 minutes after hitting the ground.

Q. How many German soldiers took part in the capture?

M. Quite a number.

Q. What was your physical condition?

M. Pretty bad. Our hands were frozen. The radio operator got a deep gash in the head.

Q. Name anyone else who was injured.

M. There were five of us. One boy was killed, Lieutenant Jack O. Williams. Second Lieutenant Irving Metzger had both hands frozen; Flight Officer Frank Jones had a hand frozen and a broken leg. I had frozen hands and internal injury.

Q. Where were you taken immediately after you were captured?

A. To a local jail in a small town, then got transported to Frankfurt.

Q. What was done about the injuries of you and the members of your crew?

M. Nothing. We asked for medical attention. Our landing kits containing medical supplies was taken away from us.

Q. Whom did you ask?

M. Seemingly the officer-in-charge. What his rank was I don't know.

Q. Was he the first one you asked for medical attention?

M. Yes, Sir

Q. What did he say?

M. He said we would receive medical attention at Frankfurt.

Q. At that time, what was the apparent condition of your hands?

M. Black and stiff, and I was spitting up blood from internal injury.

Q. Did you show your hands to the German noncommissioned officer?

M. Yes, Sir.

Q. Could he see you spitting blood?

M. Yes, Sir.

Q. Where did you go after that?

M. We were taken by truck on to Frankfurt, Germany.

Q. Describe what occurred there.

M. As soon as we arrived, we were taken before the interrogating officer.

Q. Could you identify him?

M. Yes, Sir. I could.

Q. Do you know his name?

M. No, Sir.

Q. What was his rank?

M. I couldn't say, but he was a commissioned officer.

Q. Do you know his branch of service?

M. No Sir. Except that he was connected with the interrogation branch.

Q. Can you give a description of him?

M. About medium stature. Black hair. Fair complexion. Not sure about the eyes. That's about all I can remember.

Q. What was his height?

M. Approximately 5' 10".

Q. Slender or stout? What was his weight?

M. He was slender. Weighed about 150 pounds.

Q. Did you notice anything of distinguishing nature about him, such as a scar, peculiarity of speech, manner, etcetera?

M. No Sir. He could speak English very well.

Q. What did you say about your injuries to him?

M. I asked for medical attention for myself and crew.

Q. What was his reply?

M. That we would get it later.

Q. Did you display your hands to him?

A. Yes, Sir.

Q. Were you still spitting up blood?

M. Yes, Sir

Q. Were their injuries of the other men apparent?

M. Yes, Sir. I might say here that the radio operator was told by the Germans that if he didn't divulge certain information that no medical attention would be given to him or to the other members of the crew.

Q. Where did you go then?

M. To Moosburg, Germany.

Q. What occurred then?

M. Still didn't receive any medical attention from the Germans. I don't know about the other men. They were sent on to Obermassfeld. That is, the other two officers were. Later on, I came in contact with the noncommissioned officer.

Q. What did you do by way of asking for medical attention?

M. Asked the guard. Supposedly, the commanding guard that was there.

Q. Up to that time you had not received medical attention for yourself or for your group?

M. That's right. Then the two officers were sent to a hospital, but I wasn't.

Q. When did you first receive medical attention as a result of your request for it?

M. Well, on September 12th, the hands were opened, drained, and wrapped-that was the day after the capture.

Q. Who did that?

M. A German. An aidman, perhaps. I don't think he was a doctor. He had no supplies other than bandages. He was not in uniform. He was in civilian clothes.

Q. You said he opened your hands?

M. Yes, Sir. The back of them and let the water out of them.

Q. Then he bandaged them?

M. Yes, Sir.

Q. What did he do for the rest of the group?

M. Opened the back of hands of the other two boys, Metzger, and Jones.

Q. Did you ever receive any medical treatment for your condition from the Germans other than the treatment given by the aid men that day after your capture?

M. No, Sir.

Q. What was the ultimate result of those injuries in your own case?

M. Loss of fingers on my right hand.

Despite presenting at Dulag Luft with severe injuries comparable to his co-pilot and navigator, Merle had been transferred in the days following the crash not to a hospital for proper treatment but instead was condemned to a permanent prison camp. It had taken four long, agonizing days for the rail convoy, overloaded with scores of Allied prisoners, to traverse the 230-plus miles of *Reichsbahn* between Frankfurt and Moosberg, Germany. The delay owed, in part, to the destructive deeds of English and US bomber boys, like himself, who had smashed the rail stations and marshaling yards that dotted the dwindling network of rail lines running south. The circuitous commute was not only made miserable because of the extent of Merle's untreated injuries but also by the neglect of the accompanying detachment of German guards. The train halted and shifted randomly along the route and seldom were the carriage car doors slid open for the bedraggled, filth-spattered occupants to exit and rush to the side of the embankments to void their bowels. Neither did the captors provide enough water for the men, which did nothing but madden the riders and exacerbate the conditions of those, including the lieutenant, who was already in waning health. Six days out from the crash, Merle's ailments had only worsened, requiring the feeble pilot, then in a much-weakened state, to sweat out the tortuous trip, wrapped in a blanket and propped up between his fellow passengers and the wood-slatted boxcar wall.

Arriving at Stalag VIIA, *kriegsgefangenen #52800* was separated from the herd and shown to the camp's lazerett, which despite its label, proved little more than an aid hut with beds. Although it was apparent that the lazarett was ill-equipped and wholly unable to manage conditions far less severe than the lieutenant's trauma, an "English aid man" entrusted to the station did his best to ease Merle's misery. The medic removed the foul bandages that covered the officer's waxy, stiff hands and replaced them with repurposed gauze. As days filled with protests and appeals turned from one seemingly hopeless week to another, Merle's wound care extended no further than infrequent dressing changes and the occasional soak in warm water.

As could be expected, the lieutenant's condition deteriorated. The sores on his hand continued to fester and the skin that remained turned ashen and began to slough off. His fingers, originally blanched white from the freezing and then reddened from swelling and infection, had now become black. The flesh at the tips of each digit had receded, lending the ghoulish appearance of what looked like charred finger bones protruding through decaying flesh, reinforcing the impression as if death was slowly taking hold of him, literally one finger at a time. Far more concerning, however, Merle was overcome by a fever, and, at times, he lingered near delirium. Between short periods of turbulent slumber, where fantastically vivid images of the sickening hellishness from the doomed mission ran rampant through his dreams and jolted him from his sleep, Merle awoke only to agonize, day after day, over his ruined mitts. Recognizing that the prisoner's health was fast fading, German staff at Stalag VIIA decided to rid themselves of what they thought was more than likely an unsalvageable case and relinquished custody of the American to authorities at the specialty center at Reserve Lazarett. By the time Green reached the hospital at Obermassfeld where, at long last, he received his first access to actual medical care, three weeks had passed since he had been injured on the fateful quest to Bohlen.

In late February 1945, following a week of examinations and interviews in New York after returning home on the *Gripsholm*, Merle was transferred to what was then the Army's largest convalescent center at Wakeman General Hospital in Indiana. There, for the next six months, physicians studied the 24-year-old's wounds. The frostbite damage to his ears and nose had healed surprisingly well but the Army doctors were bothered with the condition of his badly mauled right hand. The injury and surgical incisions continued to become reinfected and caused him persistent pain. Ulcers covered the scarred "clubbed mass" of finger stumps, and the back of his hand had become plagued with excruciating sores. In response to the severe bone

Merle talks with his nurse at while at Wakeman, Schwanke Collection

destruction and overall poor healing of the wound, damage only exacerbated by complications of gangrene while in the hands of the enemy, a skin graft surgery was performed on September 21st, more than one year after the injury had occurred. The state of his wound was still so serious that surgeons were required to perform an additional operation the following month. Merle would seek further care for the injury, treatment for the accompanying arthritis, and a solution for the nagging pain, for the next 22 years.

Newly promoted to 1st lieutenant, the relocation to Wakeman allowed Merle easy access to family in Illinois when granted leave, as well as "every weekend and then some", as his delighted wife wrote to a friend. Merle had always been well-liked in circles around "the Plains" and his reappearance sparked much curiosity among his relieved extended family and proud acquaintances. When asked about his trials overseas, Merle would politely respond, "I don't want to talk about it" or "That's all in the past. I just want to move on", and quickly change the conversation. In the few instances that Rose was successful in getting him to open up to her about his time in England and Germany, Merle would quickly become visibly distraught, clearly overwhelmed with guilt, and openly express regret that he had survived when his friends had not.

Despite the reminders, Merle proudly displayed photographs of his crew in the den of their home. One of the images on his desk had been taken during the team's training in Florida before being sent overseas. In it, he, and his team: ten smiling faces, stood alongside an old, war weary training Flying Fortress in between flights. The photographer had captured a perfect moment, a snapshot of idealistic, patriotic American youth preparing for war. Back then, they were unspoiled-still far removed from the tests to come in the skies over Germany, from the difficulties that they all would soon face and that all would be shaped by, and from which a few would not return. All too often, Rose would find her husband at his desk, sobbing as he sat in front of the photograph of he and "the boys". Heartbreaking as the experience had been, Merle was sure to express to Rose that through the entire ordeal she had always been there with him; that he had endured the drudgery of the prison camps by envisioning their future together, how she had been there with him on the flight deck of his shattered *Green Hornets* that September day, and how, despite the pain, doubt and fear, it was the premonition of her voice that had inspired him to battle on.

Close-mouthed as Merle was, Bob Green was one who managed to work a few details out of his older brother and, expectedly, the accounts were unsettling. Among them were stories of being tossed away in "a dungeon" where a mess of "fat rats" kept him company in his cell; that was until he was pulled into the interrogator's office, pressed for details, and reprimanded physically for his noncompliance. "Because of his rank…," relays Bob's wife, Dorothy Green, in a 2021 interview with the author, "they thought he knew something, but Merle was not ever going to give anything up. They tried to crucify him."

On July 18, 1945, Merle sat before the local Judge Advocate General liaison officer in Springfield. With the assistance of a stenographer, Lt. Green gave a testimony that would be submitted to the US War Crimes Office concerning the lack of medical treatment for he and his crew while in the hands of the enemy. Jaded by the damage done to his person but incensed by the disfigurement of his crewmates as a result of the disregard of their German captors, Merle not only felt obligated to advocate for his men, but ultimately responsible for their injuries. This sentiment, along with his own scarring, he carried with him for the remainder of his days.

Jack and Merle

The disfigurement of her husband proved to be not one bit of a distraction for Mrs. Green who gleefully wrote to their good pal, Jim Gegenheimer, in December 1945 to inform him of the birth of their first son. "He's really homely but we're gonna keep him," she wrote facetiously. "I think Merle sort of goes for him. You'd think he'd gotten his P38." As for the newcomer's name, Rose consulted Jim:

> *Don't you think Mrs. Williams would like Merle's naming the baby after Jack? He wanted to name it Jackie James but Geg, I've been counting on having some part of its name. Anyway he probably figures on a whole crew so he can name them after all of you. Wish you were around to be godfather.*

In April of 1946, Merle's affiliation with the military ended as the 1st lieutenant received an honorable discharged from the USAAF after a medical board deemed him permanently disabled due to his injury. Merle quickly went about continuing to distance himself from his warrior persona, fully committed to put his experience in combat and confinement behind him. Initially, Merle and Rose settled into a house in Springfield but swiftly relocated to the family's farm outside Pleasant Plains. For a time, the move looked to be a good choice, especially to Otto who had taken ill and, with the addition of Bob and his wife, Dorothy, welcomed the help. Things picked up from where they had left off before Merle enlisted; the milking business was prospering, the family was expanding, and even Hattie and Rose's subtle feud was seen to resume. It was just like old times.

Merle's Stearman, 1946

When one askes "Plains" locals and acquaintances what they remember about the pilot after the War, the reply is usually the same: "Oh, he was a character", one friend remembered with a chuckle. "He used to buzz the farmers!" Another mirroring the sentiment, recalling Green's shenanigans, recollects, "We knew it was Merle because of the do-dads he'd do." Even with only one good hand, the aerialist, whose abilities by that time had been honed by years of pre-war flying and hundreds of hours of professional military training, was far more talented than most. One day the pilot decided to get into some mischief by buzzing his sister, Zenobia's, husband while he was operating his tractor. Merle dipped his white Stearman low over the field, opened the throttle, and zipped past the startled planter at breakneck speed, only feet away. Regaining his bearings and accepting the playful challenge, the farmer grabbed a wrench, climbed atop his seat, and stood waiting for the flier to circle back around. This time when Merle whizzed by it was he who was surprised by the sight of his playful brother-in-law who, again only paces away, feigned tossing the tool into his flight path and thus putting an end to the day's skylarking. Another story tells of how Merle, toying with the idea of utilizing his G.I. Bill for college, hopped in his plane with a cousin and made an impromptu visit to Harvard, situated along the border between Wisconsin and Illinois where copies of their academic records were being stored. Just before lifting off, Green phoned ahead, ultimately making contact with a town councilman to let him know of his impromptu plans to drop in. The representative was thrilled with the prospect of the stopover as airplanes still

Merle with nephew, Mendenhall Collection

captured the attention of many of his constituents in the tiny rural community and having a veteran combat-tested Army aviator from the now-famous 8th Air Force behind the stick only made the visit that much more captivating. The man's only concern, he coyly advised the flier over the line, was, ironically, the town's lack of any runway; apparently a trivial detail for the pilot as, after a quick moment of silence, Merle simply told the man to expect him directly and hung up the receiver. The chairman spent the next hour scampering around the countryside until he "found the level field outside Harvard and flagged the boys down."

Minus the fingers on his aching right hand, Merle returned to many of the same pursuits he had enjoyed before enlisting. He filled his time hunting and fishing, zipped around town on a motorcycle, and coached basketball for his old high school. He developed an interest

A wreck during a race in Iowa. Merle can be seen mid-tumble in the #3 racer (center).

in auto racing and, steering with the nubs of his hand, found that the sport provided him a pleasant, and exhilarating, distraction. Merle stored his midget racer in the family barn where, when not competing at the "Little Springfield Speedway", he would boost his nephew up into the driver's seat, fit his helmet onto the boy's head and let the kid's imagination run wild. "I never lost a race," kidded the youngster many years later. Reminiscing on those cherished times with his uncle he added, "He was my hero."

Although racing awarded the adrenaline-addicted pilot more injuries from high-speed rollovers and run-ins with track walls than actual trophies, it didn't discourage further attempts. In fact, having survived the numerous accidents, collisions, and crashes that he did, Merle seemed only to become more reckless. He was seriously injured in a race in Nashville and had a close call with another vessel while speeding his boat across Lake Springfield, the same body of water where, not long before, he had been hospitalized after the engine of his friend's boat blew up, singeing all aboard. Merle had always been a thrill-seeker, but it was apparent to many close to him that something had changed within the man. "His grin, that smirk, was gone. His mind was always busy. He just couldn't get over it [the past]," says Dorothy Green. Understandably, rumors began to spread that Green's excessively cavalier attitude was built from a desire to find freedom from the guilt he had developed after his experiences in the War. Many worried that what Merle was seeking was only achievable in death.

Wrestling the Boeings through streams of heavy contrails and prop wash for nearly three hours on the 11th of September 1944 had fatigued even the most veteran of the Group's pilots that day. By the time the 94th BG released their bombs on Bohlen's hydrogenation plant- the mission's halfway point, the aviators were thoroughly rundown. A harsh, accurate, tracking maelstrom of anti-aircraft fire, coupled with an aggressive enemy fighter force, only added to the stress created by the evasive action taken to dodge the friendly bomber formation while on the bomb run. Although effective, the maneuver created confusion among the organization and had upset all unit integrity. At "bombs away," records show that the altitude of "B" flight had shifted two hundred to five hundred feet in elevation, depending on the aircraft. Moreover, aside from the vertical displacement, a substantial amount of lateral disorganization within the Flight can also be suspected. "Chuck" Duda and his team had been assigned the number five slot in the lead element while Lt. Green flew in the number three spot of the low-positioned, third element. Per Group operating procedures, this assignment positioned *Daring Doris* approximately fifty feet above and seven hundred and fifty feet ahead and to the right of Green's Boeing. Furthermore, in this configuration, at least three other B-17s from the Group were slotted into positions between the two ships.

Roughly one minute after bomb release at 1244 hours, the Group performed an approximate 90 to 140-degree heading change off the target. Instead of following the same flight path and delaying their turn, the trailing twelve "strung out" Fortresses of "B" Flight "wheeled" south, in essence cutting the corner, in an attempt to catch up to the lead B-17s and close the gaps in their jumbled formation.

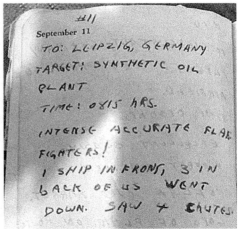

Morton Kimmel's 11 September combat Diary entry, Voight Collection

The consequence saw most of the scrambled bombers completing the heading change as individual aircraft; far from the projected, synchronized maneuver of maintaining formation position as pilots guided on their wingman. As a result, the haphazard turn caused many of the bombers to converge in the exact same airspace at the exact same time. It was during this move, without warning, that the *Hornets* collided with Duda's *Daring Doris*. "All of a sudden, they were above us," recalled Louis Lehere, who, in a discussion with author Paul Cashdollar, described the seconds before the *Green Hornets* impacted Duda's ship.

The War Department's investigation into the mid-air collision had concluded that a series of unfortunate and unavoidable events contributed to the accident. Although the USAAF had officially cleared Merle of any wrongdoing in mid-1945, mission records and 94th BG histories document the event much differently. Lt. Green's aircraft "slid over and hit A/C #153 [*Daring Doris*], breaking the latter in two near the ball turret." Likewise, when the 94th's intelligence unit described the loss of Lt. Duda's crew in the finalized 11 September 1944 mission report, it was recognized that "this A/C [Lt. Duda's] was hit by #653[*Green Hornets*] in the target area immediately after bombs away." In actuality, the collision may have been the consequence of different circumstances.

While being treated at Halloran Hospital and Camp Atterbury, Lt. Green had submitted statements advising investigators that his bomber did collide with *Daring Doris*; a collision that subsequently impacted so violently that the force of the crash ripped off the pilot's and co-pilot's flight gloves, in addition to propelling, or jarring the other crewmembers into unconsciousness. Merle elaborated on the event, stating that the crash occurred only after Lt. Duda's B-17 had been struck by anti-aircraft fire, causing "Chuck's" Fortress to swerve into his flight path. In Lt. Green's Army personnel file, additional documents indicate that the *Green Hornets*, "collided in mid-air with another ship in the squadron which had been hit." Furthermore, his promotional record noted that his injuries were "incurred as a result of a mid-air collision with a derelict bomber during a combat mission". Sitting before Army Intelligence officers to testify on a non-related matter, Green was recorded in saying, under oath, that prior to his capture, he and his crew "…were involved in a mid-air collision with another crippled bomber." With the War concluded, the benefit of hindsight and the dissipation of the "fog of war" had allowed the War Department to judge the incident more accurately but to Merle, the

Green Family Vacation to Florida

verdict of his peers held far more sway. To the *Hornets'* pilot, the incident was a stain on his reputation.

Merle was not the only crewmember whose account would lend credence to the "errant bomber" narrative. A friend of Metzgers remembered hearing that on Irv's "first mission over Germany his plane gets hit", implying that ship 653 was, instead, struck. Merle's waist gunner, George Ostrowski, would also confirm that as the Group was being riddled by exploding German anti-aircraft fire during the turn to the rally point, he had witnessed *Daring Doris* being hit by a shell and then was bounced out of position by the concussion of another flak burst. Following the detonation, Duda's Boeing, he explained, appeared to lose control, and swerved into the path of his B-17.

Although there was substantial evidence to adequately refute the Group's adopted cause of the collision, Merle would never bring himself to correct the assertion; a move that would have helped to set the historical record straight but more importantly to the aviator, remedy his tarnished legacy. Whatever the cause, the accident and subsequent loss of life were tragic and unfortunate. While the exact sequence of how the two bombers collided may never be known, what is certain is that that the surviving *Green Hornets* considered themselves fortunate to have had the "Chief" at the controls on that mission to Bohlen. Merle, however, didn't see it that way at all. To Jim Gegenheimer, Rose writes about her spouse, "Somehow he thinks he should have been the one not to come back...".

Despite her best efforts, Rose was at a loss about how to fix her tormented and emotionally retreating partner. She discovered he had been nursing his anxiety with alcohol, and he was prone to mood swings ranging from debilitating depression to a seething temper. Merle became even more isolated and was found to be absent from their home for days at a time. Rose, ever possessing unconditional love for her husband, found strength through her Faith and, while growing more frustrated, remained devoted and patient.

The Merle Green of 1942 would have thought his deliverance from the catastrophes that would befall him two years later was only possible but by the grace of God. Now, instead of feeling

Thomas and Merle

blessed by overwhelmingly good fortune and embraced by a Higher Power, he felt he was being punished; consigned to suffer the sickening guilt and destined to forever carry the awful burden. Friends and family began to realize that the upbeat, personable young man had gone off to war only to return forever transformed by the experience. Perhaps he just required some time to come to terms with his encounters before he could transition back to civilian life, they had thought, but as time went on, Merle's demons only became more pronounced.

Beginning in the late 1940s and well into the 1950s, America experienced a skyrocketing, record-high divorce rate. Regrettably, the Greens were not immune to these statistics, and the couple separated in 1946. Amidst this difficult period, Merle received a message from Air Force authorities notifying him that he was to receive the Distinguished Flying Cross, the highest award for remarkable aerial achievement, for his actions on September 11th. When word got out, "the Plains" community began organizing plans to celebrate the occasion with a public award ceremony, followed by a parade in the airman's honor. The festivities were ultimately abandoned as Green, still burdened with the weight of the collision, declined the invitation. After some persuasion, the pilot agreed to a small, private meeting with delegates. The commendation reads as follows:

> *For extraordinary achievement while participating in aerial flight on 11 September 1944. While serving as a Pilot of a B-17 type aircraft during an aerial assault over Bohlen, Germany, Lieutenant Green's aircraft was seriously damaged in an accidental mid-air collision and several of his crewmen were injured. After losing power in three engines, and with the lives of his crewmen depending on his skill and leadership, Lieutenant Green maneuvered the crippled plane to a successful crash landing. Lieutenant Green's unusual Flying technique and courageous devotion to duty reflect great credit upon himself and the Army Air Forces.*

In Merle's eyes, the commendation was unnecessary, more embarrassing than anything. As he saw it, eleven men, nine of his comrades on the Duda crew and two of his "boys" were dead because of his actions, and the Army wanted to give him a medal. To his annoyance, the fanfare would continue when Merle, one of nine local veterans from the now-famous 8th Air Force, was invited as a guest of honor to attend the Springfield premiere of the acclaimed film, *12 o'clock High*.

By early 1949, things began to look up for the Greens as the

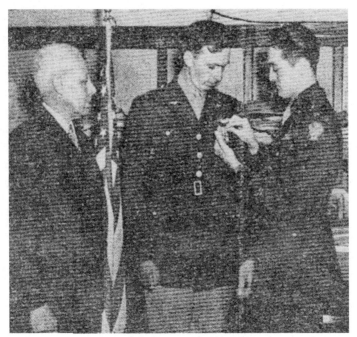

Merle being awarded his DFC

pair reconciled and welcomed their second son, Thomas, in December. Their household expanded over the next decade, and by the mid '60s, the couple was busy raising six children; Jack, Tom, Tim, Rick, Rebecca Jude, and Matt. Concerned only with winning and holding their father's attention, the youngsters took little notice of his distorted hand. As one son notes, "It didn't slow him down at all. He raced cars, went shooting, drove speed boats, and rode a motorcycle." Though Merle would never speak to the kids about his time in Europe, the specters of the past had a way of manifesting themselves in the Green house.

Many times during the night, the children, tucked in their beds, could hear the whimpers and sobs of their father as he was besieged by a torrent of night terrors. The cries, like a wounded animal, could be heard but, inevitably, a soft, calming sound would resonate from the other room. It was the voice of their mother and, like the premonition on the *Green Hornet's* flight deck decades before, Rose was heard guiding her husband through the ordeal. Memories of their mother easing Merle through the horrors of war that returned to haunt him would leave a lasting impression on the children.

Other times in the Green household are remembered as being

The Green Kids (L to R): Jack, Rebecca Jude, Rick, Tom, Tim

far more lighthearted. When an envelope from the "White House" arrived in the mail addressed to her father, Rebecca Jude assumed the letter originated from the tavern down the road: an establishment that bore the same name. The envelope had not been sent from the bar but had actually been mailed to their father from the office of the President of the United States and held a certificate "...awarded by a grateful nation in recognition of devoted and selfless consecration to the service of our country...".

As they grew older, the kids heard stories from their mother, hushed tales discussed at opportune times when the patriarch was out of earshot or away from the house. The stories told of how their father was "shot down" over Germany, how the enemy had taken him prisoner and that he had undergone some abuse at the hands of his captors. This, they assumed, contributed

Rebecca Jude and Matt Green

to the noticeable "quietness about him", as one son described. While Rose steered the children along a path of Faith, Merle was much more the disciplinarian, with any deviations promptly addressed. When

Green/Denny family gathering. Rose and Merle (Kneeling on left).

trouble found the Green boys, chastising members of the community would scold the youngsters with "Do you know who your father is?", which was usually followed by a phone call home, leaving the boy to sit and sweat out the arrival of "the Lieutenant". Sadly, as the years went by and Merle became absent for more extended periods, the connection between the flier and Rose and the kids would deteriorate as the man grew increasingly distant, both physically and emotionally. Eventually, the relationship became virtually non-existent.

Dislocated from his family, as well as his parents and siblings, most of the final two decades of the maverick's life are left to speculation, mystery, and rumor. A Bill of Sale shows Merle partnering with Cullen

Cullen Goss (seated) and Merle 1946

Goss, an old Army buddy, and becoming co-owner of the "Guntersville Speedway" in Albertville, Alabama. For the next few years, Merle bounces between the racetrack and Illinois, reuniting with his perturbed but devoted wife every so often. He owns a bar in downtown Springfield for a time and becomes sales manager at a local car dealership. Reports of friends with mafia allegiances hailing from "the Windy City" to the north run abound, and during this time Merle is involved in a terrible, yet mysterious, accident while driving his car. Somehow surviving the wreck, Merle walks out of the hospital but only after months in intensive care and with new scars to show for it. To this day, the circumstances surrounding the wreck remain shadowy, but the cause is suspected to be less than an accident.

In his wayward travels, Merle pursues a short-lived employment opportunity in Denver. He appears at the doorstep of the

Merle Green

Lehere's in Pennsylvania and the Jones' in Alabama, and then lives in Detroit for a time. He surfaces in California and revisits Florida before anchoring in Chicago where he gains works as an air traffic controller. Unable to tolerate the stressors of the job, Merle quits soon after. Based out of O'Hare, Merle flies tours to Las Vegas and word has it that some of his patronages are mafia clientele. Merle had already earned his private pilot's license and was more than qualified to fly the company's new DC-7. Even without considering his flight experience beginning as a teenager, Green possessed coveted

military flying skills needed to manage the new, sleek airliner and, not surprisingly, felt right at home in the large, four-engine aircraft. Eventually, he relocates to Vegas and invests in a hotel and casino property, although the venture fails to pay out.

In the last weeks of 1975, Zenobia, accompanied by her daughter-in-law, visited Merle in the hospital ward at Nellis Air Force Base. She had heard that her brother was sick as he was battling liver failure and decided to make the trip to help with his arrangements and reconnect with her beloved brother one last time. Just weeks later, on the 15th of January 1976, Merle launched off on his "last flight West".

When Rose received word of her husband's death, she promptly began making arrangements and had his body returned to Springfield. Upon seeing their father, the boys couldn't help but notice how the influence of stress, loss, anger, and grief had aged the man far beyond his 54 years and that his penchant for recklessness had taken a toll. "He looked well beyond 80 years old", remembered one son. His body carried a roadmap of scars, some from car wrecks, some from plane crashes, and some, a result of the subsequent medical procedures that he had endured as a consequence. But there were also other noticeable wounds; physical mementos that he had acquired in the skies and camps of Germany in 1944 and 1945; ones that he carried with him, along with a surplus of psychological wounds, for the rest of his days.

Rose Marie Green

Six rambunctious Green kids kept Rose active, and, like the burden that she endured during the War, she took on the venture with determination, love, and poise. Having never filed for divorce, she held committed to her marriage vows for the remainder of her life. Her Faith and devotion to God took precedence over all things, and she continued to frequent Sacred Heart Catholic Church almost daily. Still radiant well into her later years, Rose Marie was known to be contentious but also remarkably kind-hearted. One son points out, "She could curse you out and ask you what type of pie you'd like in the same sentence." Not to confuse her tact and sympathy with weakness, Rose was well known for being a formidable adversary, especially to any who dared challenge or provoke her brood. This included the local police department, her mother-in-law, errant Catholics, city court judges, and, regularly, her former beau. Even the neighborhood riffraff was not given a pass.

During one visit to the neighborhood market, Rebecca Jude was standing in the checkout line with her mother when two young men, armed with a small pistol, strode into the store. The pair first went about lightening the cash registers and then moved on to the frightened patrons. When one of the muggers stepped up to see what he could lift off Rose, Mrs. Green spun into action. Coming face to face with the thief, Rose proceeded to administer such a berating upon the erroneous thug that, despite gripping the gun, seemed to rapidly deflate before assuming the appearance of a scolded puppy. Unwilling to be relieved of any of her possessions and bored of the youngsters' nonsense, Rose collected up her groceries and ushered her stunned daughter away. Moving on, Rebecca Jude braced herself for an inevitable shot-in-the-back as her mother continued to direct a torrent of insults at the puzzled hooligans. As the two high-tailed it away from the store, Rose, now safely out of sight, was noticeably shaken. In spite of this, she swiftly regained her composure, strolled across the street, entered a store, calmly wrenched the receiver out of a surprised employee's hand mid-conversation, and coolly phoned the police. That was Rose: bold, fiery, and unwavering, even in the face of adversity and through challenging times. An intense, passionate, strong, and complex woman of good courage, Rose Marie Green braved the obstacles with grace to the end, battling breast cancer in her final year of life. She passed away on her birthday, July 18th, 1983. In 2021, a great-granddaughter entered the world and was named in her memory.

Two of the most extraordinary of souls, exemplars of the best of America's potential and spirit, forever among the finest of their great generation: Rose Marie and Merle Dean Green are buried in Camp Butler National Cemetery in Springfield, Illinois. Their memorial marker stands among rows upon rows of similar white marble stone slabs that designate the final resting place of thousands of some of the finest American patriots. Woodlands safeguard the thirty-nine undulating, beautifully manicured emerald acres, helping to preserve the tranquility and hallowed grounds within. All about the site, squirrels bound between the markers and rabbits scurry through the fields as family and well-wishers can be seen paying visit to the gravesites of loved ones gone, but never forgotten. Emanating from the lush canopies overhead comes whistling melodies of songbirds, peaceful refrains that serenade guests during their visit; an enduring soundtrack for the revered departed. One among the most plentiful variety of avian crooners found winging around cemetery grounds, sharing its spirited song for any who would listen, is none other than the common blackbird.

Justin R. Burke

ACKNOWLEDGMENTS

First and Foremost: To my beautiful wife, Carlina, who survived over three years of my research and writing. Thank you for your boundless encouragement and support-this project would not have been possible had it not been for you. To my mother, Rebecca Krikorian: We are all so fortunate for your efforts to preserve the family's amazing history. I cannot thank you enough for helping me time and time again. Also, to Tim, Matt, and Tom Green: I have genuinely enjoyed listening to all of your stories. Thank you for sharing your resources and memories. Uncle Jack and Rick-You are not forgotten. To Joshua Green and Mitch Green; thank you for your support and for sharing your keepsakes. Jeanne and Roger Burke-You have been so instrumental in helping with so many details of this project and for supporting me. Thank you. To my brothers: Daniel, Michael and Cody-I hope you enjoy this story. To Will, James, and Jack; I can't thank you enough for being so patient. YOU are my heroes.

Thank you to the Beverly Mendenhall, Barbara and Alan Mendenhall and the Mendenhall Family, the Hughs Family-what amazing people you are. Thank you especially to Kim and Don Schwanke; I owe you one heck of a tank of gas! Much thanks to Denise and Marty Green and to Dorothy Green for sharing all of your stories! To Bob, Zenobia and Chester, Hattie and Otto and the Denny family; I hope you feel this does the story some degree of justice.

To the Gegenheimers: James, David, Paul, Jamie, Claudia. Thank you for allowing me such incredible, personal insights into your family and "Geg's" life. It is an honor to know you all. Much appreciation to David Jones and the Jones family, Sue Haag, Charles Maahs and the Ostrowski family, Marty Metzger, Rita Schwartz, Heather Berger, Sheryl Riley, Sue Ann Espinosa, Don Hatfield, Pam and Larry Lehere, and Valerie Klekot. To Jonathan Hoy, I was so fortunate to be able to connect with you. Thank you for your encouragement, and interpretation services throughout this process. Much thanks to Charles Buehler, Jeff Buehler, and Larry Colangelo for introducing me to the Duda family, and to Cheryl Tipton and to Tom and Susan Gagnon. While the events that drew our families together are unfortunate, I am sure that the men are pleased that you honor their sacrifices and keep their memory alive. They are all heroes.

Eckard Sauer: Ich kann Ihnen nicht sagen, wie unglaublich hilfreich Ihre Arbeit für mich war. Vielen Dank. An Heinrich Goy, Gerhard Solzer und die Familie Solzer und die Gemeinde Lieblos: Vielen Dank, dass Sie den Amerikanern geholfen haben, die an diesem Tag im September 1944 bei Ihnen vorbeigeschaut haben. Olaf Becher- Vielen Dank für Ihre Recherche und Ihr Engagement. Ihre Arbeit und Freundschaft wird sehr geschätzt. Stephan Schilling, Gunter Kahnt, Lothar Kahnt, Hilmar Herling, Rainer Wagner - vielen Dank.

To Roger Watts: Your willingness to assist me has been a such a blessing. To the 94th Facebook bomb group community: Thank you all for sharing your stories and for your encouragement. Chris Argent: you are missed. To Wendy and Graham Sage, Cliff Hall, the Rougham Tower Association and volunteers and the Bury St. Edmunds community: Your dedication to the men and their legacy is incredible. To Ronnie Voight: thank you for your help and for allowing me to connect with your father, the 94th's "movie star", Morton Kimmel. Mr. Kimmel you are a great American, a true hero, and missed by many of us. Merritt Fausnaugh, Gregg Feagans: thank you for sharing such amazing information with me.

Many thanks to: Dr. Vivian Rogers-Price, Heather Thies, and the National Museum of the Mighty Eighth. Debra Kujawa and the 8th AFHS, the USAF Academy, the Pima Air and Space Museum and the Commemorative Air Force Museum of Mesa, Az and the passionate, dedicated volunteers, mechanics and flight crews who keep our great history alive. Thanks to Jim West at Freeman Airfield Museum and Jordan Deters of Greenville Army Airfield. Steve Snyder: I appreciate your guidance and advice. Your book has been an inspiration. Thank you to the following as well: Vickie Gould, Ernie Algorri, Paul Oppenheim, Paul Cashdollar, Marc Koval, Scott Anderson, Christie and Jill Hughes, D'Anna Boot and the Ralph Taylor family, Kurt Clemens, Sally Dixon, Mark Supina, Zach Brown and the Moulton Family, the Muehler Family, Erik Forsgren, Cheryl

Scott Turnbull, Autumn Hendrickson, Jeremy Pitts, Ian Simpson, Cheryl Taylor, Nancy and Bob Hall, Ed Burton, Sue Fox Moyer, Louis Machovec, Chris Hall, Trey Hall, Barb Haller, Marc Benson, Colin Preston, Timothy and Harold Motz, Joanne Kledaras, Cathie Cely, Kevin Pearson, Brad Schwartz, John A. Clark, Michelle Mays, Lee Andrews, Tiffany Green, Jennie Clements, Terri LeVeque LeMasters, Job Congers, Kevin Michaels and the Texas Raiders, Sylvia Struck, Manfred Kopp, the State Journal-Register, Curtis Mann, the Lincoln Library, the Gretna Historical Society, the Prairie Skies Public Library District, Marcia Sommer Masten and the Pleasant Plains Veterans Memorial Association, Evelyn Brandt, Mary Radtke and the Mt. Pulaski Township Historical Museum.

Please forgive me if I have failed to mention those of you whom I have had the pleasure of researching and corresponding with. Without you all, there would be no Of Good Courage. You are greatly appreciated.

ABOUT THE AUTHOR

Justin Burke was born in Springfield, Illinois and grew up in Phoenix, Arizona. Attending Northern Arizona University, Burke graduated with a degree in Paramedicine, with coursework in archaeology. A firefighter by day, Justin is also the author of, "An Unknown American Soldier Rests Here," an article published in the September 2021 issue of the 8th Air Force Historical Society. He is a member of the Commemorative Air Force Museum in Mesa, Az and has a passion for historical preservation, and international travel. Justin and his wife, Carlina, have three children.

Further information www.facebook.com/ofgoodcouragebook

SOURCES

BOOKS/PUBLICATIONS/ARTICLES

Algorri, A. (1944). 35 Missions-Antolin Notes. Ernie Algorri Collection.

Allison, R. (2014). Operation Thunderclap and the Black March: Two World War II Stories from the Unstoppable 91st Bomb Group. Casemate Publishers.

Arthur, W.H. (n.d.). A Pilot's Diary: William H. Arthur. Mission 20. 91st Bomb Group. http://www.91stbombgroup.com/mary_ruth/Chapter_6.htm

Ashcroft, B. (2005). We Wanted Wings: A History of the Aviation Cadet Program. HQ AETC Office of History and Research. https://media.defense.gov/2015/Sep/11/2001329827/-1/-1/0/AFD-150911-028.pdf

Avriett, C.E. (2018). Coffin Corner Boys: One Bomber, Ten Men, and Their Harrowing Escape from Nazi-Occupied France. Regnery History.

Balestrieri, S. (2018, January 29). "The Mighty Eighth" Was Born on This Day 1942. SOFREP. https://sofrep.com/specialoperations/eighth-air-force-mighty-eighth-born-day-1942/#:~:text=One%20German%20infantry%20soldier%20joked%20during%20the%20Normandy,sights%20on%20German%20fuel%20production%20and%20transportation%20networks.

Beech, M. (2017). B-17 Brennan's Circus: The Plane Who Wouldn't Die. Michael Beech.

Best, G.A. (2010). Belle of the Brawl: Letters Home from a B-17 Bombardier. Inkwater Press.

Blanchard, R. (2019, February 12). Sobering Stats: 15,000 U.S. Airmen Killed in Training in WWII. https://www.realclearhistory.com/articles/2019/02/12/staggering_statistics_15000_us_airmen_killed_in_training_in_ww_ii_412.html

Bloxham, G.P. (n.d.). "Ice Cold Katie": The Story of Aircraft No. 43-38183; Her Crew; 35 Missions in Europe 24 June 1944 to 4 November 1944-Based on the Diary of bombardier George P. Bloxham, Jr. AO-769090

Caplan, L. (Formerly Major, MC, ASN 0-41343). (1947, December 31). Perpetuation of Testimony of Dr. Leslie Caplan: In the matter of the mistreatment of American prisoners of war at Stalag Luft #4 from November 1944 to May 1945.

Cashdollar, P.K. (2006, March 29). In Harm's Way, Stories of American Prisoners of War in Germany. Moonglow Publishing.

Clark Jr., P. (1970, January 01). Leading Lady Preface. Retrieved November 19, 2020, from http://kilo39.blogspot.com/2013/03/leading-lady-preface.html

Collins, E.V. (2016). Flak over Target: WWII Experiences of Thomas H. Collins. Flak over Target: WWII Experiences of Thomas H. Collins.

Collins, G. (2012). 14. Flak Division. Axis History. Retrieved from https://www.axishistory.com/list-all-categories/151-germany-luftwaffe/luftwaffe-ground-units/5652-14-flak-division.

Daily Illinois State Journal. (1927, February 15). Public Sale. p.15.

Daily Illinois State Journal. (1947, August 23). 227-AcreHigh Class, Black Level Improved Farm at Auction. Pg. 11

Dolim, A.L. (2001). Yesterday's Dragons: The B17 flying fortress over Europe during WWII: a navigator from Hawaii recalls his 51 missions over enemy territory. Communication Concepts.

Dorfmeier, D. (2016). C-Lager: Stalag Luft IV & the 86-Day Hunger March. David\Dorfmeier; First edition.

Frank, M.E.V. (1990). The Forgotten POW: Second Lieutenant Reba Z. Whittle, AN. Defense Technical Information Center.

Fletcher, Z.B. (2020, November 7). How Goebbles Convinced German Civilians to Murder Allied Airmen: A sinister plot by Nazi propagandist Joseph Goebbels turned civilians into brutal murderers targeting Allied airmen who parachuted into Germany. https://www.historynet.com/goebbels-airmen/?f

Gabay, J. (1944, February 10). Diary of a Tail Gunner. 17. BRUNSWICK, GERMANY. The History Place. https://www.historyplace.com/specials/personal/gunner-diary2.htm

Ganzel, B. (n.d.). Aerial Crop Dusting. Wessels Living History Farm. https://livinghistoryfarm.org/farminginthe40s/pests_04.html

Groom, W. (2015, September). The Aviators: Eddie Rickenbacker, Jimmy Doolittle, Charles Lindbergh, and the Epic Age of Flight. National Geographic.

Hall, C. (2019). Memoirs of Rougham Airfield and the 94th Bombardment Group (H). Clifford Hall.

Hall, C. (2011, December 1). Pictorial History of the Men and Aircraft of the 94th Bombardment Group (H) 1942-1945. Clifford Hall.

Hall, K. T. (2018). Luftgangster over Germany: The Lynching of American Airmen in the Shadow of the Air War. Historical Social Research

Hansen, J. (2016). Walking Home from Germany. CreateSpace Publishing.

Harvey, I. (2015, February 7). Germany's Bombing of Britain. War History Online. https://www.warhistoryonline.com/war-articles/germanys-luftwaffe-bombing-britain.html?edg-c=1

Hickman, K. (2020, January 20). History of the Boeing B-17 Flying Fortress American Heavy Bomber Used Throughout WWII. ThoughtCo. https://www.thoughtco.com/boeing-b-17-flying-fortress-2361503

Kuest, L. (1942). My Life in the Service: The Diary of Leroy W. Kuest. Remington-Morse Publishing. Retrieved from file:///C:/Users/jusbu/Downloads/LEROY%20KUEST%20WAR%20DIARY%2042-45.pdf

Lawrence Jr., P. (n.d.). Paul Lawrence P. Jr. Memorial. https://museum.dmna.ny.gov/application/files/1915/9464/5763/Paul_Lawrence_P_Jr_Memoir.pdf

Makos, A. (2014). A Higher Call: An Incredible True Story of Combat and Chivalry in the War-Torn Skies of World War II. Dutton Caliber.

McManus, J.C. (2016). Deadly Sky: The American Combat Airman in World War II. Dutton Caliber.

Miller, D.L. (2006). Masters of the Air: America's Bomber Boys who Fought the Air War Against Nazi Germany. Simon and Shuster.

"Missing Air Crew Reports," digital images, Fold3. (https://www.fold3.com/browse/hVZf1Up9jQDhigsBdypK-4eEj). (Accessed February 2, 2019), Missing Air Crew Report 8840, p8, 10, 12, 14, Publication Number

M1380. Roll number 03201-03300. Report number 8840.

Mission # 206 Field Order #414, 8 September 1944, 94th "A" and "B" Groups. From RG: 18, World War II Combat Operations Reports National Archives Identifier: 2871022 Entry Number NM67A Creator" War Department. Army Air Forces. 6/20/1941-9/26/1947 Box 512 @ 190: 58/8/5 Item # REP0006C. National Archives at College Park, College Park, MD.

Mission # 206 Field Order #414, 9 September 1944, 94th "A" and "B" Groups. From RG: 18, World War II Combat Operations Reports National Archives Identifier: 2871022 Entry Number NM67A Creator" War Department. Army Air Forces. 6/20/1941-9/26/1947 Box 512 @ 190: 58/8/5 Item # REP0006C. National Archives at College Park, College Park, MD.

Mission # 208 Field Order #414, 10 September 1944, 94th "A" and "B" Groups. From RG: 18, World War II Combat Operations Reports National Archives Identifier: 2871022 Entry Number NM67A Creator" War Department. Army Air Forces. 6/20/1941-9/26/1947 Box 512 @ 190: 58/8/5 Item # REP0006C. National Archives at College Park, College Park, MD.

Mission # 209 Field Order #414, 11 September 1944, 94th "A" and "B" Groups. From RG: 18, World War II Combat Operations Reports National Archives Identifier: 2871022 Entry Number NM67A Creator" War Department. Army Air Forces. 6/20/1941-9/26/1947 Box 512 @ 190: 58/8/5 Item # REP0006C. National Archives at College Park, College Park, MD.

Murray, W. (1983). Crew Losses Eighth Air Force (Heavy Bombers). [Illustration]. Strategy for Defeat, The Luftwaffe 1933-1945. p. 176. University Press of the Pacific. https://www.ibiblio.org/hyperwar/AAF/AAF-Luftwaffe/

The New York Times. (1945, February 23). 10 OF Returned Wounded Heroes Receive Medals During Brief Ceremony at Halloran Hospital. The New York Times. p.12.

The New York Times. (1945, February 21). Gripsholm Due Today. The New York Times. p.9.

National Museum of the USAF. (1944, September). 12 Sept. 1944 Bomb Plot. https://447bg.smugmug.com/MICROFILM/SEPTEMBER-1944/i-j3DgDDR. Motz Family Collection.

National Museum of the USAF. (1944, September). 623 11 September 1944. https://www.americanairmuseum.com/media/25922. Motz Family Collection.

Nichol, J. Rennell, T. (2003). The Last Escape: The Untold Story of Allied Prisoners of War in Germany 1944-1945. Penguin UK.

94th Bomb Group: Mission Report September 11, 1944, From RG: 18, World War II Combat Operations Reports National Archives Identifier: 2871022 Entry Number NM67A Creator" War Department. Army Air Forces. 6/20/1941-9/26/1947 Box 512 @ 190: 58/8/5 Item # REP0006C. National Archives at College Park, College Park, MD.

Onkst, D. H. (n.d). Barnstormers. U.S. Centennial of Flight Commission. https://www.centennialofflight.net/essay/Explorers_Record_Setters_and_Daredevils/barnstormers/EX12.htm

Pleasant Plains Township High School. (1937). 1937 Plainsman. [Yearbook]. Prairie Skies Public Library District.

Record for Jack O. Williams, O-718039; Individual Deceased Personnel File, [Electronic Record], [Retrieved from RES912201612, transfer# W092-70A0001A, box 9910], National Archives and Records Administration, St. Louis, Mo.

Record for Sidney I. Hatfield, 35773987; Individual Deceased Personnel File, [Electronic Record], National Archives and Records Administration, St. Louis, Mo.

Richardson, W. (2012). Aluminum Castles: WWII from a Gunner's View. Cantemos.

Sacred Heart Academy. (1941). Sacred Heart Academy Yearbook. [Yearbook]. Green

Family Collection

Salem, C.R. (2014). Ever the Patriot: Recollections of Vincent J. Riccio, World War II Veteran and POW. Createspace.

Sauer, E. (2013). Absturz im Kinzigtal: Die Luftfahrt im hessischen Kinzigtal von 1895 bis 1950. Books on Demand; 1st Edition. Auflage, Grundau.

Shea, G.H. (n.d.). Treasure Island Fair: Golden Gate International. Expositionhttps://www.foundsf.org/index.php?title=Treasure_Island_Fair:_Golden_Gate_International_Exposition

Slater, H.E. (1980). Lingering Contrails of the Big Square A. 94th Bomb Group (H). Slater; Limited First Edition.

Smithsonian National Air and Space Museum. (n.d.). LtCol William F. Cely. https://airandspace.si.edu/support/wall-of-honor/ltcol-william-f-cely

Snyder, S. (2015). Shot Down: The True Story of pilot Howard Snyder and the Crew of the B-17 Susan Ruth. Sea Breeze Publishing.

Stapfer, H. (1988). Strangers in a Strange Land. Squadron/Signal Publications, inc.

Stringer, L. (1911). History of Logan County. Pioneer Pub. Co.

Time. (1949, June 6). GERMANY: Into Plowshares. https://content.time.com/time/subscriber/article/0,33009,801903,00.html

Toliver, R.F. (1997, December 1). The Interrogator: The Story of Hanns Joachim Scharff master interrogator of the Luftwaffe. Schiffer Military History.

U.S. Air Force Academy. (2022, April). Papers of Lt Gen Albert Patton Clark, Clark Special Collections, SMS 329, United States Air Force Academy

US Army. (1942, September 7). US Army Enlistment Record. US Armed Forces. Green Family Collection.

US Army. (n.d.). The Requirements, Classification, Training and Duties of Air Force Personnel Nashville Army Air Center (AAFCC). [Pamphlet]. https://web.ccsu.edu/vhp/Rodin_Jack/The_Requirements,_Classification,_Training_and_Duties_of_Air_Force_Personnel_pamphlet.pdf

U.S. Army Air Forces. (1942, June). Preflight 44-A. The Aviation Cadet Social Fund Maxwell Field. https://aafcollection.info/items/list.php?item=000574

War Crimes Case 12-2441. [Retrieved from Ref:00Dt0GzAV._500t0mu6Iw]. [Affidavit]. National Archives and Records Administration, St. Louis, Mo.

Wanless, Frances. (n.d.). Interview and Memoir, O-W187, Container: Tape; Container: et al. UIS Archives/Special Collections.

Weapons and Warfare. (n.d.). Attacking a B-17 formation from the German side. https://weaponsandwarfare.com/2020/12/23/attacking-a-b-17-formation-from-the-german-side/

Western Union Company. (1942, September 18). [Telegram]. Green Family Collection.

Wooley, R.B. (2017). Roy E. Trask B-17 Bomber Crew, Lookout Mountain, Tennesse. http://www.306bg.us/history/crew_histories/Trask,%20Roy%20E/Roy%20E%20Trask%20Crew-10.pdf

Young, (n.d.). Letter from Young to 'whomever it may concern'. [Letter of Recommendation]. Green Family Collection.

INTERVIEWS

Algorri, Ernest. (2019, July). Personal Communication [Email Correspondence].

Berger, Heather. (2022, February 3). Personal Communication [Email Correspondence].

Buehler, Charles. (2019, August 7). Personal Communication [Email Correspondence].

Colangelo, Larry. (2021). Personal Communication [Email Correspondence].

Espinoza, Sue Ann. (2022, April). Personal Communication. [Email Correspondence].

Fausnaugh, Merritt. & Feagans, Greg. (2021, October 6). Personal Communication [Phone

Interview] [Email Correspondence].

Gegenheimer, David. (2019). Personal Communication. [Phone Interview] [Email Correspondence].

Gegenheimer, James. (2019, April 29). Personal Communication. [Phone Interview] [Email Correspondence].

Green, Dorothy. (2021, December). Personal Communication [Phone Interview].

Green, Thomas. (2020). Personal Communication [Phone Interview].

Hall, Ryan. (2021). Personal Communication. [Email Correspondence].

Hoy, Johnathan, (2019). Personal Communication [Email Correspondence].

Jones, David. (2020). Personal Communication. [Email Correspondence].

Kimmel, Morton. (2020, November 9). Personal Communication [Email Correspondence].

Koval, Marc. (2019, May 1). Personal Communication. [Email Correspondence].

Mendenhall, Alan & Barbara. (2022, January). [Interview]. Springfield, Illinois.

Metzger, Marty. (2019, March 30). Personal Communication [Email Correspondence].

Riley, Sheryl. (2022, January). Personal Communication [Email Correspondence].

Sauer, Eckard. (2019). Personal Communication [Email Correspondence].

Schilling, Stephan Rolf. (2021). Personal Communication [Email Correspondence].

Schwanke, Kimberly. (2021, December). [Email Correspondence] [Zoom Conference].

Voight, Ronnie. (2020). Personal Communication [Email Correspondence].

Watts, Roger. (2019). Personal Communication [Email Correspondence].

WEBSITES

Air Force Historical Research Agency. http://www.afhra.af.mil/
Airwar Over Europe. https://www.luftkrieg-ueber-europa.de/
American Air Museum in Britain. https://www.americanairmuseum.com/
American Heritage Museum. https://www.americanheritagemuseum.org/
Ancestry.com. http://home.ancestry.com
Army Air Forces Collection. http://www.aafcollection.info/
Boeing. http://www.boeing .com
Camp King Oberursel. http://www.campkingoberursel.de/
Eighth Air Force Historical Society. http://www.8thafhs.org
European Theaters of Operations Farmers' Almanac. https://www.farmersalmanac.com/
Find A Grave. http://www.findagrave.com
Fold3. http://www.fold3.com/
Fraternal Order of Eagles. https://www.foe.com/About-The-Eagles/
Greenville Fliers. https://www.greenvilleflyers.com/
Holocaust Encyclopedia. https://encyclopedia.ushmm.org/
Illinois GenWeb Project. https://logan.illinoisgenweb.org/
Logan County Genealogy and Historical Society. https://www.logancoil-genhist.org/LogCoSpots/LoganCo/SYNOPSISx%5b42187%5d.pdf
Marshall Stelzriede's Wartime Story: The Experiences of a B-17 Navigator During World

War II. http://www.stelzriede.com/
Mount Pulaski Township Historical Society.
    https://www.mountpulaskitownshiphistoricalsociety.com/
National Archives and Records Administration. http://www.archives.gov/
National Museum of the Mighty Eighth Air Force. https://www.mightyeighth.org/
National World War II Museum. http://www.nationalww2museum.org/
Pleasant Plains Veterans Memorial Association. https://www.facebook.com/Pleasant-
    Plains-Veterans-Memorial-Association-132218286824765/
Sangamon County History. http://sangamoncountyhisotry.org/
Smithsonian National Air and Space Museum. https://airandspace.si.edu/
S/SGT James E Theiss. http://www.powjamestheiss.com
Stammlager Luft VI and IV. http://www.stalagluft4.org/
U.S. Air Force Academy. http://www.usafa.af.mil/
Witness to War. http://www.witnesstowar.org
World War II 306th Bomb Group (H). https://www.306bg.us/
384th Bombardment Group (Heavy). https://384thbombgroup.com/
392nd Bomb Group. https://www.b24.net/index.html

PHOTOGRAPHS (Not including Green Family Collection)

CHAPTER 1

Photographer Unk. (n.d.). Hattie, Merle, and Otto. [Photograph]. Ivan Falconer Collection.
Photographer Unk. (n.d.). Kin Photo. [Photograph]. Schwanke Family Collection.
Photographer Unk. (n.d.). Ennis, Merle, and Zenobia. [Photograph]. Schwanke Family
    Collection.
Photographer Unk. (1910). Wright Brothers 1910 Bi-Plane-Train Race. Mount Pulaski
    Township Historical Society Collection.
Photographer Unk. (1926, April 10). Charles Lindbergh Airmail Practice Flight at
    Springfield. Sangamon Valley Collection, Lincoln Library.
Photographer Unk. (1927, August 15). Charles Lindbergh's Ryan NX-211airplane.
    [Photograph]. Sangamon Valley Collection, Lincoln Library
Photographer Unk. (1934, October 21). Amelia Earhart visits Municipal Airport.
    [Photograph]. Sangamon Valley Collection, Lincoln Library
Photographer Unk. (n.d.). Young Merle Portrait. [Photograph]. Schwanke Family Collection.
Pleasant Plains Township High School. (1937). 1937 Plainsman. [Yearbook]. p. 27. Prairie
    Skies Public Library District.
Ibid. p. 23

CHAPTER 2

Photographer Unk. (1942-1943). A captured Fw 190A-4. [Photograph]. National Museum of
    the U.S. Air Force. Image Gallery. Accessed April 10, 2022.
Photographer Unk. (1942-1943). Messerschmitt Bf 109E of the German Luftwaffe.
    [Photograph]. National Museum of the U.S. Air Force. Image Gallery. Accessed
    April 10, 2022.
Aceto, Guy. (1940). Shadows of the Blitz in Today's London. HistoryNet. NARA. Retrieved
    from https://www.historynet.com/shadows-of-the-blitz-in-todays-london/Fold3
    smoking b-17
USAF. (n.d.). B-17 under Luftwaffe Attack. NARA.
Fold3. (1944, September 21). A Boeing B-17 "Flying Fortress" Of The 324Th Bomb
    Squadron, 91St Bomb Group Comes In For A Landing. [Photograph]. NARA.
    Ref. No. 342-FH-3A06112-79284AC. 342, FH. Retrieved from
    https://www.fold3.com/image/32444123

CHAPTER 3

Photographer Unk. (n.d.). Merle Green Graduation Photograph. [Photograph]. Schwanke
    Family Collection

Photographer Unk. (n.d.). Merle and Otto Green Family Gathering. [Photograph]. Green
    Family Collection

CHAPTER 4

Green, M.D. (1943, March 13). Letter from Merle to Hattie. [Letter]. Schwanke Family
    Collection

Photographer Unk. (1941). Lodwick School of Aeronautics Airplanes on the Flight Line.
    [Photograph]. Albert Lodwick Photo Collection. Lakeland Public Library.

Photographer Unk. (1941). Lodwick School of Aeronautics RAF Cadets on the Flight Line.
    [Photograph].

Albert Lodwick Photo Collection. Lakeland Public Library.

Burke, J. (2022). Merle D. Green Flight Record and Log Book Cover. [Photograph].
    Author's Collection

Green, M. (1943, July 18). Letter from Merle to Hattie. [Letter]. Schwanke Family Collection

US Air Force. (1943). BT-13 Valiant. [Photograph].
    https://es.m.wikipedia.org/wiki/Archivo:BT-13_Valiant.jpg

US Air Force. (1943). Beechcraft AT-10 Wichita. [Photograph].
    https://www.wikiwand.com/en/Beechcraft_AT-10_Wichita

Photographer Unk. (1943, January 30). Merle D. Green Wins Commission. Daily Illinois
    State Journal. Green Family Collection.

Fold3. (n.d.). Boeing B-17 Flying Fortress with bomb-bay door open. [Photograph]. NARA.
    Ref. No. 342-FH-3A19842-53030AC. 342, FH. Retrieved from
    https://www.fold3.com/image/ 39018998

CHAPTER 5

Photographer Unk. (n.d.). Louis and Jane Lehere. [Photograph]. Lehere Family Collection.

Photographer Unk. (n.d.). Sgt. Peter A. Riley. [Photograph].]. S. Espinoza Collection

Photographer Unk. (n.d.) James Gegenheimer Aerial Gunner Training. [Photograph].
    Gegenheimer Family Collection.

Photographer Unk. (1944). Jack Williams Headshot. [Photograph]. J. Hoy Collection.

Photographer Unk. (1944) Flight Officer Frank Jones. [Photograph]. D. Jones Collection.

Photographer Unk. (1947) Irving Metzger NYU Class Photograph. [Photograph]. M.
    Metzger Collection.

CHAPTER 6

Photographer Unk. (1944). 2nd Lt. Jack Williams. [Photograph]. J. Hoy Collection.

CHAPTER 7

United Kingdom Government. (n.d.). Rougham Airfield. [Photograph]. Royal Ordnance
    Survey. British Government.

National Archives and Record Administration. (1943, September 6). "Flying Fortresses" On
    A Practice Mission Over Molesworth. [Photograph]. National Archives at College
    Park. Grp. 342. ID. 204842848

Fold3. (1943, June 24). A Boeing B-17 "Flying Fortress" Of The 324Th Bomb Squadron,
    91St Bomb Group Comes In For A Landing. [Photograph]. NARA. Ref. No. 342-
    FH-3A06112-79284AC. 342, FH. Retrieved from
    https://www.fold3.com/image/32444123

Fold3. (1943, December 14). FLAK OVER MUNSTER. [Photograph]. NARA. Ref. No.
    342-FH-3A19509-26719AC. 342, FH. Retrieved from

https://www.fold3.com/image/39013036

Photographer Unk. (1945). Lt. Basil Pullar Crew. [Photograph]. Anderson Family Collection

Fold3. (1943, December 14). Battle damaged Boeing B-17. [Photograph]. NARA. Ref. No. 342-FH-3A05558-A27137AC. 342, FH. Retrieved from https://www.fold3.com/image/29022818

CHAPTER 8

Photographer Unk. (n.d.). Merritt Fausnaugh Cadet Photograph. [Photograph]. Fausnaugh Remembrance.

Fold3. (1944, March 6). Boeing B-17 Flying Fortresses Of The 452Nd Bomb Group. NARA. Ref. No. 342-FH-3A20850-54775AC. 342, FH. Retrieved from https://www.fold3.com/image/39018998

Fold3. (1944, March 6). Supplies being dropped by parachute from Boeing B-17 Flying Fortresses. NARA. Ref. No. 342-FH-3A18072-54292AC. 342, FH. Retrieved from https://www.fold3.com/image/39018998

US Air Force. (1945). Me-262 Being Shot Down. [Photograph]. Impact Magazine. Volume 3, Number 1, page 40

Photographer Unk. (1944). Lt. Antolin Algorri. [Photograph]. E. Algorri Collection.

CHAPTER 9

Photographer Unk. (n.d.). Robert Hall Crew Photo. [Photograph]. R. Hall Collection.

Photographer Unk. (n.d.). Heavenly Comrade. [Photograph]. R. Hall Collection.

Photographer Unk. (1944). 11 September, 1944 Mission Plot Map. [Photograph]. Motz Family Collection. National Museum of the United States Air Force.

Fold3. (1943, May 19). In a Rare Accident. [Photograph]. NARA. Ref. No. 342-FH-3A20850-54775AC. 342, FH. Retrieved from https://www.fold3.com/image/50798152

Photographer Unk. (1944). Lt. Charles "Chuck" Duda. [Photograph]. Buehler/Colangelo Collection.

Fold3. (1944, February 5). A Formation Of Boeing B-17S Drop Their Explosive Loads. [Photograph]. NARA. Ref. No 342-FH-3A15827-59090AC. 342, FH. Retrieved from https://www.fold3.com/image/ 161320924

CHAPTER 10

US Air Force. (n.d.). Consolidated Vultee B-24 Liberator USAF. [Photograph]. https://commons.wikimedia.org/wiki/File:Consolidated_Vultee_B-24_Liberator_USAF.JPG

Kay, David. (n.d.). Nose gun and bombardier turret on WWII-era B-17 Flying Fortress. [Digital Image]. https://www.shutterstock.com/image-photo/nose-gun-bombardier-turret-on-wwiiera-36237391

Fold3. (1944, February 5). Boeing B-17 Flying Fortresses Of The 91St Bomb Group. [Photograph]. NARA. Ref. No 342-FH-3A18404-61031AC. 342, FH. Retrieved from https://www.fold3.com/image/49500966

Fold3. (1943, May 19). Nazi Fighter Plane Attacking A Boeing B-17 "Flying Fortress". [Photograph]. NARA. Ref. No 342-FH-3A15971-62641AC. 342, FH. Retrieved from https://www.fold3.com/image/38859447

CHAPTER 11

US Air Force. (n.d.). Norden M-1 Bombsight. [Photograph]. https://www.wikiwand.com/en/Bombsight

National Archives and Record Administration. (1944, September 11). [Map]. 11 September, 1944 Navigational Mission Map. Mission # 209 Field Order #414, 11 September, 1944, 94th "A" and "B" Groups. From RG: 18, World War II Combat Operations Reports National Archives Identifier: 2871022 Entry Number NM67A Creator"

War Department. Army Air Forces. 6/20/1941-9/26/1947 Box 512 @ 190: 58/8/5 Item # REP0006C. p.34. National Archives at College Park, College Park, MD.

Fold3. (1944, February 5). Boeing B-17 "Flying Fortresses" of the 8th Air force take off. [Photograph]. NARA. Ref. No 342-FH-3A05856-26363AC. 342, FH. Retrieved from https://www.fold3.com/image/ 29023581.

National Archives and Record Administration. (1944, September 11). [Photograph]. 94th Bomb Group. Mission # 209 Formation Chart, 11 September, 1944, 94th "A" and "B" Groups. From RG: 18, World War II Combat Operations Reports National Archives Identifier: 2871022 Entry Number NM67A Creator" War Department. Army Air Forces. 6/20/1941-9/26/1947 Box 512 @ 190: 58/8/5 Item # REP0006C. National Archives at College Park, College Park, MD.

Voigt, R. (2021, February 12). 11 September 1944 Cotter Pin. [Photograph]. R. Voigt Collection.

CHAPTER 12

National Archives and Record Administration. (1944, February 24). Down the Road to Brunswick. [Photograph]. 342-FH-3A19828-27546AC. National Archives at College Park. ARC. 204898738.

Fold3. (1943, November 5). These Waist Gunners Are At Their Posts Ready For Action. [Photograph]. NARA. Ref. No. 342-FH-3A15869-69384AC. 342, FH. Retrieved from https://www.fold3.com/image/38859326

Fold3. (1943, May 19). Tail Gunner Of The Boeing B-17 "Flying Fortress" Hell's Angels. 303Rd Bomb Group. [Photograph]. NARA. Ref. 342-FH-3A12612-A61854AC. 342, FH. Retrieved from https://www.fold3.com/image/48255116

Fold3. (1943, May 19). Capt. W.E. Sticklen, Bombardier, At His Position In A Boeing B-17 "Flying Fortress". [Photograph]. NARA. Ref. 342-FH-3A12112-69338AC. 342, FH. Retrieved from https://www.fold3.com/image/48254038

Fold3. (1945). Germany - Vertical True High-Level. [Photograph]. NARA. Ref. 342-FH-3A19435-B57629AC. 342, FH. Retrieved from https://www.fold3.com/image/39016353

Maya, Alvaro. (n.d.). World War II Flying Fortress B-17 with blue sky and clouds in the background. [Digitized Image]. https://www.shutterstock.com/image-photo/world-war-ii-flying-fortress-b17-1714781845.

CHAPTER 13

Houlihan, J. (2022). B-17 Cockpit View. [Photograph]. Retrieved from March Field Air Museum Facebook page.

Fold3. (1943, May 19). A Boeing B-17 Flying Fortress of the U.S. 8th Air Force, bomb bay gaping. [Photograph]. NARA. Ref. No 342-FH-3A19759-56622AC. 342, FH. Retrieved from https://www.fold3.com/image/39014622.

Photographer Unk. (1944). Jack Williams European Theater. [Photograph]. J. Hoy Collection.

Photographer Unk. (1943). Irving Metzger Cadet Photograph. [Photograph]. M. Metzger Collection.

CHAPTER 15

Fold3. (n.d.). B-17 returning from Trondheim. [Photograph]. NARA. Ref. No 342-FH-3A26525-26069AC. 342, FH. Retrieved from https://www.fold3.com/image/ 47649274

CHAPTER 16

Photographer Unk. (1945). Goy, Horr, Thienhaus in US dingy. Heinrich Goy Collection.

Hasselroth, Hessen, Germany.
Photographer Unk. (1954). Gerhard Solzer im Jahre 1954. [Photograph]. Geschichtsverein
Gründau.
Sauer, Eckard. (n.d.). Green Hornets Bordaxt-Lieblos. [Photograph]. Eckard Sauer,
Grundau.
US Air Force. (12 September, 1944). US 7GR/3279 12 SEPT. 44 Aerial Reconnaissance
Photograph. [Photograph]. Eckard Sauer, Grundau.
Photographer Unk. (n.d.). Gerhard Solzer. [Photograph]. Geschichtsverein Gründau.
Photographer Unk. (n.d.). Friedrich Griessman. [Photograph]. Geschichtsverein Gründau.

CHAPTER 17

Photographer Unk. (n.d.). View from Dulag Luft guard tower. [Photograph]. Camp King
Archive Collection. Oberursel, Germany.
US Air Force Academy. (n.d.). Dulag Luft. [Photograph]. SMS 329, Papers of Lt Gen Albert
Patton Clark, Clark Special Collections, United States Air Force Academy.
Photographer Unk. (n.d.). Dulag Luft. [Photograph]. Camp King Archive Collection.
Oberursel, Germany.
Photographer Unk. (n.d.). 'The Cooler'. [Photograph]. Camp King Archive Collection.
Oberursel, Germany.

CHAPTER 18

Fold3. (1945, May 2 Utter Destruction Is the Result Of Allied Air Attacks On Frankfurt.
[Photograph]. NARA. Ref. No 342-FH-3A21308-66063AC. 342, FH. Retrieved
from https://www.fold3.com/image/50813742
US Air Force Academy. (n.d.). Typical Living Room 10-14 Men. [Photograph]. SMS 329,
Papers of Lt Gen Albert Patton Clark, Clark Special Collections, United States Air
Force Academy.

CHAPTER 19

Illinois State Journal. (1945, February 16). 2 Local Men, Held By Nazis, To Return Home on
Gripsholm. [Article]. Wakeman-US Army. Illinois State Journal Archives.
Springfield, Illinois. Green Family Collection.

CHAPTER 20

Fold3. (1944, January 4). Vapor Trails Stream Behind A Formation Of Boeing B-17 Flying
Fortresses Of The 91St Bomb Group. [Photograph]. NARA. Ref. 342-FH-
3A19872-61058AC. 342, FH. Retrieved from
https://www.fold3.com/image/39020516
Fold3. (1944, July 24). A pillar of smoke reaches the height of these Boeing B-17 Flying
Fortresses. [Photograph]. NARA. Ref. No 342-FH-3A26924-52909AC. 342, FH.
Retrieved from https://www.fold3.com/image/47657661

CHAPTER 21

US Air Force Academy. (n.d.). On the March. [Photograph]. SMS 329, Papers of Lt Gen
Albert Patton Clark, Clark Special Collections, United States Air Force Academy.
US Air Force Academy. (n.d.). Rest Stop on March. [Photograph]. SMS 329, Papers of Lt
Gen Albert Patton Clark, Clark Special Collections, United States Air Force
Academy.

CHAPTER 22

Photographer Unk. (n.d.) Frank Jones. [Photograph]. D. Jones Collection.
US Air Force Academy. (1945, April 29). There is a Tank Under This Pile of Humanity.
[Photograph]. SMS 329, Papers of Lt Gen Albert Patton Clark, Clark Special
Collections, United States Air Force Academy.
Photographer Unk. (1945, June 24). Brothers Met in Nazi Prison. [Article]. D. Jones

Collection.

CHAPTER 23

Photographer Unk. (1946). Natalie and Peter 1946. [Photograph]. S. Espinoza Collection.
Photographer Unk. (n.d.). Morton Kimmel the Cold Blue. [Photograph]. R. Voigt
    Collection.

CHAPTER 24

Illinois State Journal. (1945, May 5). "It was like this". [Photograph]. Wakeman-US Army.
    Illinois State Journal Archives. Springfield, Illinois. Schwanke Family Collection.
Photographer Unk. (n.d.). Merle and Alan. [Photograph]. A. & B. Mendenhall Family
    Collection.
Voigt, R. (2021, February 12). Morton Kimmel Journal Entry 11 September 1944.
    [Photograph]. R. Voigt Collection.

Printed in Great Britain
by Amazon

38436640R00198